W9-BEA-214

Research programmes in economics usually emerge from the intersection between a new analytical approach and a real economic problem. In the last few years, such a programme has emerged in international monetary economics, which is underpinned by a theoretical framework grounded in stochastic calculus and the increasing prominence in the real world of the international monetary arrangements under which national monetary authorities attempt to keep exchange rates within bands or 'target zones'. This new programme of research also covers switches in exchange rate regimes.

This volume from the Centre for Economic Policy Research and the National Bureau of Economic Research includes contributions – as authors or discussants – from most of the active participants in the development of this new field, and will serve as a useful introduction and basic text for this new research programme.

It opens with an account of the basic economic model of a currency band developed by Paul Krugman, which is followed by two papers that extend this approach. Other chapters study the regime switches entailed in Britain's return to the gold standard in 1925 and the preannounced entry of a floating currency into a band such as the EMS. Essays on sustainability and realignment consider the possible outcomes of speculative attacks on such bands, and the volume ends with a paper on econometric testing of models of this type.

Exchange rate targets and currency bands

Centre for Economic Policy Research

The Centre for Economic Policy Research is a network of some 125 Research Fellows, based primarily in European universities. The Centre coordinates its Fellows' research activities and communicates their results to the public and private sectors. CEPR is an entrepreneur, developing research initiatives with the producers, consumers and sponsors of research. Established in 1983, CEPR is already a European economics research organization with uniquely wide-ranging scope and activities.

CEPR is a registered educational charity. Grants from the Leverhulme Trust, the Esmée Fairbairn Charitable Trust, the Baring Foundation, the Bank of England and Citibank provide institutional finance. The ESRC supports the Centre's dissemination programme and, with the Nuffield Foundation, its programme of research workshops. None of these organizations gives prior review to the Centre's publications nor necessarily endorses the views expressed therein.

The Centre is pluralist and non-partisan, bringing economic research to bear on the analysis of medium- and long-run policy questions. CEPR research may include views on policy, but the Executive Committee of the Centre does not give prior review to its publications and the Centre takes no institutional policy positions. The opinions expressed in this volume are those of the authors and not those of the Centre for Economic Policy Research.

Since this volume is a record of conference proceedings, it has been exempted from the rules governing critical review of manuscripts by the Board of Directors of the National Bureau (resolution adopted 8 June 1948, as revised 21 November 1949 and 20 April 1968).

1 March 1991

Exchange rate targets and currency bands

Edited by

PAUL KRUGMAN

and

MARCUS MILLER

Cambridge University Press

Cambridge New York Port Chester
Melbourne Sydney

Published by the Press Syndicate of the University of Cambridge
The Pitt Building, Trumpington Street, Cambridge CB2 1RP
40 West 20th Street, New York, NY 10011–4211, USA
10 Stamford Road, Oakleigh, Melbourne 3166, Australia

First published 1992

Printed in Great Britain by Redwood Press Limited, Melksham, Wiltshire

A catalogue record for this book is available from the British Library

Library of Congress cataloguing in publication data applied for

ISBN 0 521 41533 0 hardback

CE

Contents

Figures

Tables

Preface

This volume contains most of the papers presented at the conference on Exchange Rate Targets and Currency Bands organized jointly by the Centre for Economic Policy Research and the National Bureau of Economic Research and held at the University of Warwick on 9–11 July 1990. Several additional papers have also been included to convey a more complete picture of how research in this fast-growing field has developed.

We would like to express our appreciation to authors and discussants for their readiness to help in the preparation of this volume, and to all the conference participants for their lively contributions, including the panel discussion, organized by Jeffrey Shafer (OECD), where economists from Central Banks gave their own perspective on this research. Summaries of the presentations and discussions have been published in the CEPR *Bulletin*, No. 40, August 1990, and in the NBER *Reporter*, Fall 1990.

We are pleased to thank Geoffrey Carliner of NBER and Stephen Yeo of CEPR for their encouragement and support in convening the conference and proceeding with the publication. Funding for CEPR was provided by the Ford and Alfred P. Sloan Foundations as part of their support for the Centre's International Macroeconomics programme. Support from the NBER was provided by the Starr Foundation. The setting for the Conference itself was the annual Summer Economics Research Workshop held at the University of Warwick, funded in large part by the UK Economic and Social Research Council, whose support was also most welcome.

Our thanks go to Ann Shearlock of CEPR and Mandy Broom of the University of Warwick for the smooth running of the conference, and to Laura Papi for acting as rapporteur. David Guthrie and Sarah Wellburn guided the volume to press as efficiently and rapidly as possible; and we were pleased to work once again with John Black of the University of Exeter as Production Editor. Together they kept editors, authors and discussants to a tight production schedule so as to get the material in this lively, policy-relevant research area to a wider audience with the minimum delay.

Two of the additional papers, included after the conference, have appeared in print elsewhere, namely the shorter technical papers by Froot and Obstfeld and by Ichikawa, Miller and Sutherland. We are grateful to the publishers of *Econometrica* and *Economics Letters* respectively for permission to include them here.

The previous occasion on which CEPR and NBER joined forces to produce a selection of research papers in International Macroeconomics was in 1985 with the publication of *International Economic Policy Coordination*, edited by Willem Buiter and Richard Marston. The focus then was on the welfare gains from cooperation; now it is the positive economics of exchange rate stabilization. But the objective is the same: to give prompt circulation to ideas which promise to throw fresh light on major issues of international economic policy.

Paul Krugman
Marcus Miller March 1991

Conference participants

Renzo Avesani *Università di Trento*
Leonardo Bartolini *Princeton University, CEPR and NBER*
Giuseppe Bertola *Princeton University*
Jane Black *University of Exeter*
Willem Buiter *Yale University, CEPR and NBER*
Andrew Carverhill *University of Warwick*
Mervyn Coles *University of Essex*
Martin Cripps *University of Warwick*
John Driffill *Queen Mary and Westfield College, London, and CEPR*
Bernard Dumas *University of Pennsylvania and NBER*
Kenneth Froot *MIT and NBER*
Peter Garber *Brown University and NBER*
Vittorio Grilli *Yale University, CEPR and NBER*
Brian Henry *Bank of England*
Masaki Ichikawa *University of Warwick and Economic Planning Agency, Japan*
Andrew Hughes Hallett *University of Strathclyde and CEPR*
Nobuhiro Kiyotaki *LSE and NBER*
Martin Klein *Universität Bonn*
Paul Krugman *MIT, CEPR and NBER*
Olli-Pekka Lehmussaari *Bank of Finland*
Ben Lockwood *Birkbeck College, London*
Christopher Melliss *HM Treasury*
Philippe Michel *Université de Paris I*
Marcus Miller *University of Warwick and CEPR*
Philippe Moutot *Banque de France*
Gabriela Mundaca *Bank of Norway*
Maurice Obstfeld *University of California, Berkeley, CEPR and NBER*
Francesco Papadia *Banca d'Italia*
Laura Papi *University of Warwick*

William Perraudin *International Monetary Fund*
Paolo Pesenti *Yale University*
Emmanuel Pikoulakis *University of Hull*
Neil Rankin *University of Warwick and CEPR*
Hossein Samiei *Fitzwilliam College, Cambridge*
Jeffrey Shafer *OECD*
Gregor Smith *Queen's University, Ontario*
Michael Spencer *Queen's University, Ontario*
Alan Sutherland *University of Warwick*
Antti Suvanto *Bank of Finland*
Lars Svensson *Institute for International Economic Studies, Stockholm, CEPR and NBER*
Ian Tonks *University of Exeter*
David Webb *LSE*
Paul Weller *Cornell University and CEPR*
Michael Wickens *University of Southampton and CEPR*
Athina Zervoyianni *University of Hull*
Frédéric Zumer *Université de Paris*

1 Editors' Introduction

PAUL KRUGMAN and MARCUS MILLER

A research program in economics usually emerges out of the intersection between a new analytical approach and a real economic problem to which that approach seems relevant. In the last few years such a program has emerged in international monetary economics. Underlying the research is a modelling style that relies on stochastic calculus; the real-world motivation is the increasing prominence of international monetary arrangements under which monetary authorities attempt to keep exchange rates within bands or target zones.

This new research program goes under a variety of names. Some refer to it as the literature on 'target zones', which remains its principal focus; others, emphasizing the techniques involved, refer to 'regulated Brownian motion' or, more generally, to 'stochastic process switching'. The most popular name at MIT is one devised by Rudi Dornbusch, who carefully mangled the name of a concept that plays a key role in many of the models to come up with the term 'smooth pastry'!

Whatever one calls it, the field has grown rapidly, far outpacing the ability of normal channels of publication to keep up. Much credit for the enterprise should go to the policy advocates of target zones, notably Williamson (1983), who have long argued for research into their functioning. At the technical level, the pioneering work by Flood and Garber (1983), who used stochastic process switching techniques to study anticipated changes in exchange regimes, also helped to prepare the ground. The particular intersection between issue and method that defines the field emerged, however, during intensive discussion of a crude version of 'Target Zones and Exchange Rate Dynamics' (1988), presented by Paul Krugman at an NBER conference on the European Monetary System in December 1987.

Though that paper had still not been published two and a half years later, the literature that derived from that discussion had already grown to several dozen papers. Stimulated by this, and by the evident interest shown at the 'smooth pasting sessions' organised at the NBER Summer Institutes in 1988 and 1989, we felt that it would be useful to get some of the main researchers in the field together, to swap ideas and to codify the state of the art. With the support of CEPR and NBER, a two-day conference was held at the University of Warwick in July 1990. This volume is the result.

1 Modelling currency bands

In the first part of the volume, Paul Krugman outlines the canonical model (in essence what was presented at the NBER in 1987) and indicates the key features of the approach adopted. It involves expressing the exchange rate as a deterministic, stationary function of economic fundamentals which evolve according to a stochastic process. In this monetary model, where the stochastic fundamental is the velocity of money (labelled v) which follows a random walk, the solution takes a simple exponential form, whose parameters are tied down by a tangency condition closely related to the 'smooth pasting' condition of options theory. Various extensions and modifications of this approach are included in this volume; four others are suggested.

2 Currency bands: extending the model

Perhaps the most obvious weakness of the basic model is the very stringent and essentially arbitrary restrictions it places on the behaviour of the fundamental determinants of the exchange rate. Implicitly, the model assumes that nature does not make jumps: that the money supply changes only through intervention at the edges of the band, and that intervention when it takes place is always infinitesimal. The model also assumes that stochastic fundamentals (represented by the shift term v) follow a pure random walk with neither drift nor mean-reversion, a technically convenient assumption with no economic justification.

Flood and Garber address the issue of large interventions: such large interventions lead to more complicated dynamics than small, but the authors provide an extremely elegant derivation of the tangency condition as a limiting result as interventions get smaller. (They also point out that thinking about large interventions builds a bridge between the target zone analysis and the older literature on speculative attack – a bridge that is built in a somewhat different way in the chapter by Krugman and Rotemberg also included in this volume.) In his comments Paul Weller shows how these ideas can be applied to monetary interventions for stabilizing real exchange rates in a model with sticky prices. Large or discrete interventions are associated with 'realignment rules'; and the tangency solution emerging in the limit corresponds to John Williamson's target zone proposal for indexed currency bands with marginal monetary accommodation.

The assumption that fundamentals simply follow a random walk has made all of us uncomfortable. Adding a trend term is not very hard, as is shown in passing in the chapter by Froot and Obstfeld. In many economic contexts, however, a minimum satisfactory model seems to require some mean-reversion in fundamentals. Delgado and Dumas show that for a constant coefficient of mean-reversion a tabulated solution is available. So the apparent intractability of this case may have been exaggerated – unless one is allergic to the confluent hypergeometric function! They show that the basic smooth pasting story holds up; indeed they emphasize that there is a sense in which target zones become more important the narrower the band. In a well-defined sense, the exchange rate becomes less and less related to the fundamentals the smaller the target zone. In commenting on the results, Bartolini notes that adding mean-reversion does not help to reconcile the canonical model with data on forward premia for EMS currencies. To do that, he argues that one must drop the assumption that the band was fully credible.

3 Regime shifts: returning to the gold standard and joining the EMS

The simplest target zone model treats the zone as a permanent regime. But many of the episodes to which one might want to apply the new methodology involve shifts of regime: joining the Exchange Rate Mechanism of the European Monetary System for instance; or – the classic case studied earlier by Flood and Garber – Britain's return to the gold standard in the 1920s, in which there was an announced intention to move from a floating rate to a fixed rate when the pound had returned to its pre-war parity with the US dollar.

Froot and Obstfeld interpret this to mean that Britain would only return to gold 'when the fundamentals were right', and they note that for 'irreversible' regime shifts of this sort the exchange rate is no longer tangent at the boundary. But they show that the same exponential solution used to characterise the behaviour of the rate inside a currency band still applies – with a different boundary condition. Their paper provides an explicit solution for Flood and Garber's model of sterling's float; and it emphasises the essential unity of approach between the study of credible target zones on the one hand and 'stochastic process switches' on the other (see also Froot and Obstfeld, 1989). The authors go on to place this particular example in the context of a more general framework for analysing regime changes triggered by an asset price. They show that the policy defined by the statement 'fix the exchange rate when it reaches a given level' leads to multiple equilibria: only if the statement is coupled with precise conditions about the nature of the pegging policy does the outcome become determinate.

In contrast to Froot and Obstfeld's treatment where the value of the fundamental which triggers the switch is fixed but the timing is endogenous, Ichikawa, Miller and Sutherland examine the case where the date of the regime shift is fixed for sure whatever the level of the fundamentals. Such a time-dependent joining condition is found to lead to a non-stationary solution, where the exchange rate depends explicitly on time as well as fundamentals. This is illustrated for a preannounced currency band where the exchange rate converges upon the stationary 'smooth pasting' solution as the date of entry draws nearer.

In their paper on regime shifts, Miller and Sutherland argue that time-dependent elements played an important role in Britain's return to gold; and that Keynes's 'speculative anticipations' can only be understood in these terms. In addition, they relax another assumption of the canonical model – that of perfect price flexibility. To capture what they regard as the key feature of Britain's return to gold, namely the conflict between the prompt appreciation expected for sterling and the sluggishness of prices in response to this, they adopt instead a stochastic version of the classic Dornbusch model where prices are slow to adjust. The use of the flex-price monetary model is, however, defended by Greg Smith, who cites evidence of large price movements in the early 1920s in support. He also suggests ways of testing non-stationary solutions against the data.

4 Limited reserves and sustainability

In both the theoretical analysis of fixed exchange rates and their operation in practice, there is a problem of sustainability: the monetary authorities may not have the reserves necessary to defend a parity indefinitely. And when a parity is known or suspected to be unsustainable, there will be speculative attacks by investors attempting to anticipate the collapse of the fixed rate regime. The same issues arise for target zones, and are the subject of three of this volume's chapters.

The chapter by Krugman and Rotemberg builds a direct link between the speculative attack literature and the new target zone models, showing that with small modifications the basic model gives rise to speculative attacks when reserves fall below a critical level. The smooth pasting solution emerges as a limiting result when reserves are sufficiently large. They then use this framework to produce a simple model of speculative attacks under a gold standard, which they argue can be regarded as a boundary between two one-sided target zones. In his discussion, Bernard Dumas points out that Krugman and Rotemberg consider only a special case from a much wider universe of possible international reserve regimes.

Buiter and Grilli pursue a more ambitious goal, using the methodology of the target zone literature to produce a comprehensive analysis of a paradox that arises when one tries to analyse speculative attacks in the face of uncertainty. One version of this paradox was noted in the context of a gold standard by Krugman and Rotemberg (1989); Buiter and Grilli show that the paradox extends much more widely, and suggest that it may be necessary to introduce additional agents into the model in order to guarantee that any equilibrium exists. Obstfeld argues, however, that the non-existence of equilibrium is the direct result of inconsistent policy rules, so the resolution ultimately lies in the adoption of more sensible rules and not the introduction of additional market agents.

Finally, Bertola and Caballero examine the case of an exchange rate regime in which occasional realignments are undertaken to avoid exhaustion of reserves. They show that over the long run the average relationship between fundamentals and the exchange rate reverts to a 45-degree line – that is, target zones affect only the local, not the global relationship. As Svensson points out in discussion, however, this striking result – that target zones do not matter in the long run – depends on the assumption that they do not affect the process governing stochastic fundamentals in the model.

5 Estimation and testing

Empirical work in this field has been expanding rapidly and the volume concludes with a paper on hypothesis testing. Smith and Spencer offer a notable demonstration of the advantages for empirical workers of the agnosticism that the new approach allows about the nature of the underlying fundamentals. In contrast to the conventional empirical exchange rate model, which attempts to fit a structural relationship between a list of presumed fundamentals and the exchange rate – and which almost invariably comes to grief, producing negative signs on money, etc – Smith and Spencer presume that the fundamentals are unobservable and set out to extract them from the behaviour of the exchange rate. (We might note in this context that other researchers have exploited the possibilities of agnosticism to focus not on the determinants of exchange rates but on the behaviour of related variables; Svensson, 1990, provides an example.) Hossein Samiei welcomes the exercise of testing the predictions of the targets zones literature by using the method of simulated moments; but he puts in a plea for identifying the underlying determinants as well.

6 Conclusions

The striking thing is the speed with which the target zone field has grown, from a rough and confused draft presented in late 1987, to a worldwide program of research by mid-1990. Insights and results have spread rapidly around the world via workshops, conferences, and working papers. We hope that this volume will serve as a useful introduction and basic text for this remarkable enterprise.

REFERENCES

Flood, R. and P. Garber (1983), 'A model of stochastic process switching', *Econometrica* **51**, 537–51.

Froot, K. and M. Obstfeld (1989), 'Exchange rate dynamics under stochastic regime shifts: A Unified Approach', mimeo (IMF).

Krugman, P. (1988), 'Target zones and exchange rate dynamics', NBER Working Paper No. 2481, January.

Krugman, P. and J. Rotemberg (1989), 'Target zones with limited reserves', mimeo.

Svensson, L. E. O. (1990), 'The term structure of interest rate differentials in a target zone: theory and Swedish data', Seminar Paper No. 466, Institute for International Economics, Stockholm.

Williamson, J. (1983), *The Exchange Rate System*, Washington: Institute for International Economics.

PART I
MODELLING CURRENCY BANDS

2 Exchange rates in a currency band: a sketch of the new approach

PAUL KRUGMAN

1 Introduction

Those who can, do; those who cannot, carefully define their terms. Rather than trying to offer some definition of what 'smooth pastry' is about, I will present a basic model that has already become more or less canonical. Once we have this model under our belts, it will be easier to define the characteristics of the new approach.

Consider, then, a stripped down monetary model of the exchange rate.[1] We suppose that at any point in time the logarithm of some country's exchange rate is a linear function of the log of its money supply, a shift term, and the expected rate of change in the exchange rate:

$$s = m + v + \gamma E[ds]/dt \qquad (1)$$

where the shift factor v is a general purpose term encompassing changes in real output, money demand, and anything else other than the money supply and expected depreciation that could affect the exchange rate.

We will treat m as a policy variable; indeed, the behaviour of m will define an exchange rate regime. The shift term v, however, will be assumed to be subject to random shocks. In this simplest model, v has no forseeable dynamics, simply following a random walk: so

$$dv = \sigma\, dz \qquad (2)$$

where σ is a constant and dz is the increment of a standard Wiener process.

It is hard to imagine a simpler model than this one. Yet it is sufficiently flexible to allow us to represent a number of different exchange regimes, and to derive some results that were surprising when first presented.

First consider freely floating exchange rates. In this case we simply think of the monetary authority as leaving m unchanged, and allowing s to go wherever it goes. Given the absence of any predictable trend in v, it seems

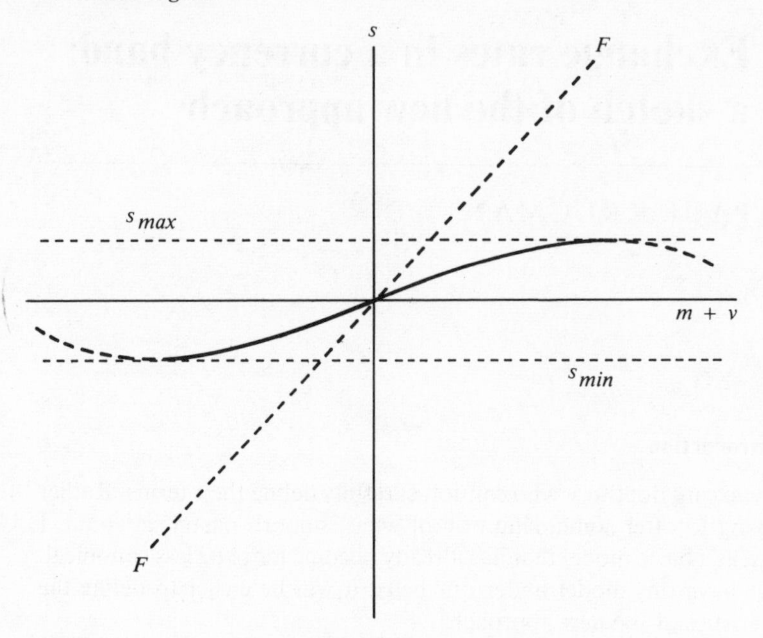

Figure 2.1 The exchange rate in a currency band

natural to suppose that under pure floating $E[ds]/dt$ will be zero, and thus that the exchange rate will simply equal $m + v$. In Figure 2.1, which plots s against $m + v$, the exchange rate would slide up and down the 45-degree line FF.

Under a fixed exchange rate, by contrast, the monetary authority would alter m to offset any change in v. Again $E[ds]/dt$ would be zero, so in Figure 2.1 we would stay at some particular point on FF.

Under a stylized target zone system the monetary authority would stand ready to buy foreign exchange at some minimum price s_{min}, and to sell it at a maximum price s_{max}, thus keeping s within a band.[2]

It might seem reasonable to suppose that the target zone would function like a cross between a fixed rate and a floating rate: that the exchange rate would slide up and down the 45-degree line as long as it would lie within the band, but be constrained from wandering outside the band. If investors have rational expectations, however, this supposition would be wrong.

To see why, imagine for a moment that the supposition were true, and ask what would happen if s were very close to the maximum value s_{max}. Then a fall in v would lead to an equal fall in s; but a rise in v would be offset by a fall in m, and thus would not lead to a rise in s. But this means that near the top of the band s would on average be expected to fall, i.e., there would be an expected appreciation. Such an expected fall in s would itself tend to drag s down; so near the top of the band the relationship between $m + v$ and s would lie below the 45-degree line. Similarly, near the bottom of the band the relationship would lie above FF. Intuitively, it becomes obvious that if investors know that the central bank is committed to defence of a target zone, the equilibrium relationship between $m + v$ and s within the band is not a 45-degree line but something like the S-shaped curve illustrated in Figure 2.1.

Notice that the relationship is dragged off the 45-degree line even when the exchange rate is not close to the edge of the band. The reason is the curvature of the S, which interacts with the randomness of v to give rise to expected appreciation or depreciation through Jensen's inequality. That is, even though v has no trend, $E[ds]/dt$ is negative in the concave upper half of the S and positive in the convex lower half.

To derive an explicit representation of the S-curve, we turn to stochastic calculus. It is by now familiar that the general solution to the model (1) and (2) with m held constant is

$$s = m + v + Ae^{a(m+v)} + Be^{-a(m+v)} \tag{3}$$

By Ito's lemma we find that

$$E[ds]/dt = \frac{a^2\sigma^2}{2}[Ae^{a(m+v)} + Be^{-a(m+v)}] \tag{4}$$

which implies that

$$a = \sqrt{\frac{2}{\gamma\sigma^2}} \tag{5}$$

The first two terms in (3) evidently represent a sort of fundamental exchange rate, the rate that would prevail if no future change was expected. Under a freely floating rate, $m + v$ can range without limit. If we impose the reasonable condition that the exchange rate cannot diverge arbitrarily far from its fundamental value, then under a free float we must have $A = B = 0$, implying the equation

$$s = m + v \tag{6}$$

Under a target zone, the possible range of variation of $m + v$ is bounded. We can simplify by choosing units so that $s_{min} = -s_{max}$. We may then suppose that the relationship is symmetric around zero, so that $B = -A$ giving the exchange rate equation

$$s = m + v + A[e^{a(m+v)} - e^{-a(m+v)}] \tag{7}$$

For A negative, this defines a family of S-shaped curves.

But which S-curve is the right one? The answer, which can be derived in several different ways, is that it is the particular curve that is *tangent* to the edges of the band. Perhaps the easiest way to motivate this result is to notice that if the curve were to hit the edge of the band at an angle, there would be a kink in the relationship between $m + v$ and x; such a kink would, by Ito's lemma, imply an infinite rate of expected appreciation or depreciation – in effect, a one-way option. So arbitrage rules out any curve except one that is tangent. (Several alternative derivations are offered in the papers in this volume.)

This tangency condition bears a close relationship to the concept known in option-pricing theory as 'high order contact' or 'smooth pasting'; hence Rudi Dornbusch's name for the field. By coincidence, monetary modellers stumbled into the use of smooth pasting at the same time that Dixit (1989) and Dumas (1988) introduced the concept into the study of other dynamic issues in international economics; while there has been little explicit interaction between the two lines of research, there is little question that there has been a strong reinforcement effect.

Two interesting points should be noted about this simplest model of a target zone. First, the model clearly shows that the knowledge that the monetary authority intends to defend a zone should stabilize exchange rates inside the zone, even if no active intervention is currently in progress. This may be seen from the fact that the S-curve is flatter than the 45-degree line, so that variations in $m + v$ are less than proportionately reflected in the exchange rate.

Second, the model implicitly predicts that the forward premium on foreign exchange will be negative when s is high, positive when it is low, i.e., that interest differentials will point toward the middle of the band. This essentially reflects the point that when s is high, it has more room to go down than up, and conversely.

This minimalist model illustrates the main characteristics of the new approach. Let us review them.

2 Characteristics of the new approach

Four characteristic features of the new approach are explicit or implicit in the model just described.

First, this is an approach in which uncertainty plays a key role. The essential determinant of the exchange rate is not the best forecast of what may happen to money demand and supply, but the distribution of possible changes in money demand and the implied monetary responses. There is no way to get the essence of the results in some certainty-equivalent framework.

Second, the method of analysis avoids treating time explicitly, looking instead at an equilibrium relationship between fundamentals and exchange rates. It turns out that the statement and derivation of this equilibrium is ideally suited to the elegant methods of stochastic calculus. Candour requires that we acknowledge that this is not an unimportant part of the field's appeal to theorists: it provides a prominent and policy-relevant nail at which they can swing one of their favourite hammers.

Third, nonlinearity plays an essential role in the model. Many monetary models assume linearity or rely on local linear approximations. Here we start with a linear model, but in the solution curvature plays a key role, and must not be linearised away.

Finally, although the basic model presented above assumes a purely monetary process of exchange rate determination, in general the approach allows one to be somewhat agnostic about the actual determinants of the exchange rate. That is, the 'fundamental' could be anything: fiscal policy, real shocks, whatever. Again, candour requires that we admit that this agnosticism explains some of the field's appeal to empirical workers: since attempts of researchers to identify fundamental explanatory factors for exchange rates have been notably unsuccessful, it is a relief for them to work on a subject that sidesteps the whole question.

3 Where do we go from here?

The target zone literature has expanded so rapidly that one hesitates to offer any suggestions for further work – indeed, anything one might suggest is probably already being worked on somewhere in the world! Nonetheless, a survey of the field to date suggests four main directions I would like to see explored.

First and always, we need empirical work. The target zone approach has suggested a useful style of empirical work, in which a number of variables may be related to the position within an explicit or implicit band. Considerable work has already been done along these lines. We still lack, however, a secure set of stylized facts to inform our theory. Even the EMS data has not been fully examined, and there are many other examples one would like to look at. It would be helpful to reexamine how the gold standard really worked, the experience of 'capped' floating during the 1920s, the dollar-dollar rate of Canada against the US in the 1950s, and so on.

Second, the insights of the new approach need to be integrated with more acceptable underlying economic models. One of the ironies of the target zone literature is that it has given a new lease of life to the simple monetary exchange rate model, which had been all but abandoned on empirical grounds, and which most of those working in the new area had long criticized. The new turn to simple monetarism took place not because the monetary model looks any more plausible, but because it is the easiest one in which to express the basic target zone approach. Miller and Weller (1990) have taken the first steps toward getting back to models we can (almost) believe in; the rest of us need to remember that ease of modelling is not, alas, always truth.

Third, a difficult issue, is the need to reconcile the new approach with the growing evidence that financial markets are *not* efficient. Again, there is an irony here: many of the target zone modellers have in other work taken to heart extensive evidence against rational expectations, or at least against the joint hypothesis of rational expectations and stable risk premia, in asset markets in general and foreign exchange markets in particular. Yet the target zone models assume rational expectations. This is more than a technical problem: there is a major tension in all analysis of financial market prices between the clean analytics of efficient markets theory and the growing evidence that EMT is an inadequate empirical description.

Finally, the target zone literature has given us a wonderfully lucid account of how a currency band might work, but it has shed little light on why such an exchange regime might be desirable. That is, we have positive economics but little welfare analysis. This is, of course, a general failing of international monetary economics. These are, however, times of dramatic international financial reform: Europe appears to be on the road toward a common currency, and schemes to limit exchange rate variation have new respectability around the world. Target zones are a halfway house between fixed and floating rates. Do they combine the best of both worlds or the worst?

NOTES

1 This is essentially the model presented at the NBER in 1987. A more thorough treatment is given in Krugman (1991).

2 Actual target zone systems, like the EMS, are of course more complex. Most intervention in the EMS is sterilized, most of it takes place inside the band instead of at the edges, and there are occasional realignments. Some of these real-world issues are taken up by papers in this volume.

REFERENCES

Dixit, A. (1989), 'Hysteresis, import penetration, and exchange-rate pass-through', *Quarterly Journal of Economics*, **104**, 205–28.

Dumas, B. (1988), 'Pricing physical assets internationally', NBER Working Paper No. 2569.

Krugman, P. (1991), 'Target zones and exchange rate dynamics', *Quarterly Journal of Economics*, forthcoming.

Miller, M. and P. Weller (1990), 'Exchange rate bands with price inertia', CEPR Discussion Paper No. 421 (forthcoming in the *Economic Journal*).

PART II
CURRENCY BANDS: EXTENDING THE MODEL

3 The linkage between speculative attack and target zone models of exchange rates: some extended results

ROBERT P. FLOOD and PETER M. GARBER

1 Introduction

Agents in the public or private sectors often follow one systematic set of actions when their environment lies within some prescribed boundaries and switch to another set when the boundaries are reached. Their recognition of the presence of the boundaries ties the two sets of actions together and determines the prices of assets whose payoffs are keyed to the actions. In a stochastic setting, several authors have recently investigated such an environment with a set of tools that readily generate closed-form solutions for exchange rates controlled in a target zone.[1]

In this paper, we will generalize the target zone exchange rate model formalized by Krugman (1988, 1989) and extended by Froot and Obstfeld (1989).[2] The main contribution of these pages consists of linking the recent developments in the theory of target zones to the mirror-image theory of speculative attacks on asset price fixing regimes.[3] We also use aspects of this linkage to provide an intuitive interpretation of the 'smooth pasting' condition, generally invoked as a boundary condition in this literature. We will study a system in which the exchange rate zones are either permanent or temporary.[4]

We aim to unify these two literatures by showing that the solution concepts in both are identical. Indeed, we can show that in the target zone context 'speculative attacks' on reserves must generally occur as a result of a policy to defend the zone.[5] Thus, Krugman's recent (1987, 1988) work is actually a step toward coming full circle on his (1979) contribution on balance-of-payments crises.

We present our results in the four remaining sections. In Section 2, we present the exchange rate target zone problem in a standard exchange rate model. The target zone literature developed thus far has considered only the case of infinitesimal interventions. We extend the analysis to situations in which the policy authority may use discrete interventions. This extension provides the link between the earlier literature on discrete attacks on foreign exchange reserves and clarifies the latitude available to a policy authority while maintaining the target zone. In Section 3, we examine the interest rate implications of adopting a target zone in this model. Finally, in Section 4, we extend the possibility of discrete interventions to Krugman's (1989) recent work on collapsing target zones.

2 A model of target zones

The target zone is a nonlinear compromise between fixed exchange rates and freely flexible exchange rates. In an exchange rate target zone, a country or group of countries sets explicit margins within which exchange rates will be allowed to fluctuate. While the exchange rate is within those boundaries, policy can be directed toward other goals. When the boundary is reached, the policy maker focuses resources on maintaining the boundaries. The target zone does not preclude foreign exchange interventions inside the boundaries. Indeed, the target zone studied by Krugman simply does not specify government behaviour inside the target zone boundaries. This is the point of the target zone: while the exchange rate is inside the band, policy can be directed as desired toward goals other than fixing the exchange rate.

Krugman (1988) was able to characterize the behaviour of the exchange rate within a target zone when exchange rate fundamentals are driven by regulated Brownian motion. In Krugman's case, the unregulated fundamentals follow nondrifting Brownian motion. The intervention which regulates the process is triggered by the edges of the target zone, which are symmetric about zero. Froot and Obstfeld (1989) extended Krugman's results to the case of fundamentals driven by Brownian motion with constant drift and of non-symmetric zones.[6]

To study the behaviour of the exchange rate inside a band, Krugman and Froot and Obstfeld use a standard law of motion for a flexible price exchange model.

$$x(t) = k(t) + aE[dx(t)]/dt \qquad a > 0 \tag{1}$$

$x(t)$ is the logarithm of the exchange rate, a can be interpreted as the Cagan interest rate semi-elasticity, and the expectation operator is conditioned on current information. Only information about the forcing variable $k(t)$ is relevant. In a standard monetary approach model, $k(t)$ is a linear combination of the logarithms of foreign and domestic money supplies, real incomes, money demand disturbances and real exchange rate movements.

$k(t)$ can be controlled by intervention of the monetary authorities. Specifically, the authorities can control $k(t)$ to ensure that

$$x^u > x > x^l \tag{2}$$

where x^u and x^l are the upper and lower bounds of the exchange rate target zone, respectively. For example, the authorities could intervene with a monetary contraction to prevent the exchange rate from exceeding x^u. Krugman and Froot and Obstfeld assume that the authorities interfere with the motion of k only when x reaches the boundaries of the target zone.[7] When the exchange rate is inside the target zone boundaries, k follows a random walk with drift that is independent of the exchange rate:[8]

$$dk = \eta\, dt + \sigma\, dz \tag{3}$$

where η and σ are constants and z is a standard Wiener process.

2.1 *A derivation of the functional form of the exchange rate solution*

We now follow Krugman and Froot and Obstfeld to develop explicitly the functional form of the exchange rate solution, $x = g(k)$. If $g(k)$ is the solution $E[dx]/dt$ can be derived by applying the Ito differential

$$dx = g'(k)\, dk + \tfrac{1}{2}g''(k)(dk)^2 \tag{4}$$

Taking the expectation of each side of equation (4), conditional on current information:

$$E[dx]/dt = g'(k)\eta + \tfrac{1}{2}g''(k)\sigma^2 \tag{5}$$

Substituting from equation (5) into equation (1), we derive

$$x = g(k) = k + a[g'(k)\eta + \tfrac{1}{2}g''(k)\sigma^2] \tag{6}$$

The general solution to (6) is

$$x = g(k) = k + a\eta + A\exp[\lambda_1 k] + B\exp[\lambda_2 k] \tag{7}$$

where $\lambda_1 = -[(\eta^2 + 2\sigma^2/a)^{1/2} + \eta]/\sigma^2$ and $\lambda_2 = [(\eta^2 + 2\sigma^2/a)^{1/2} - \eta]/\sigma^2$. The constant terms A and B are to be determined by the boundary conditions given by the upper and lower bounds on the exchange rate target zone.

To solve for A and B in equation (7), researchers have imposed the 'smooth pasting condition', a requirement that $g'(k^u) = 0$ when $x^u = g(k^u)$ for some high level k^u of k at which intervention occurs. Similarly, $g'(k^l) = 0$ when $x^l = g(k^l)$ for some low value of k. These conditions provide sufficient boundary information to determine A, B, k^u and k^l; and we plot the form of the solution in Figure 3.1.

In using these conditions, Krugman implicitly and Froot and Obstfeld explicitly assume that such interventions are infinitesimal; they associate the attainment of x^u with the simultaneous attainment of k^u. In the generalization to discrete interventions, the events of hitting the zone limit and having an intervention will not coincide.

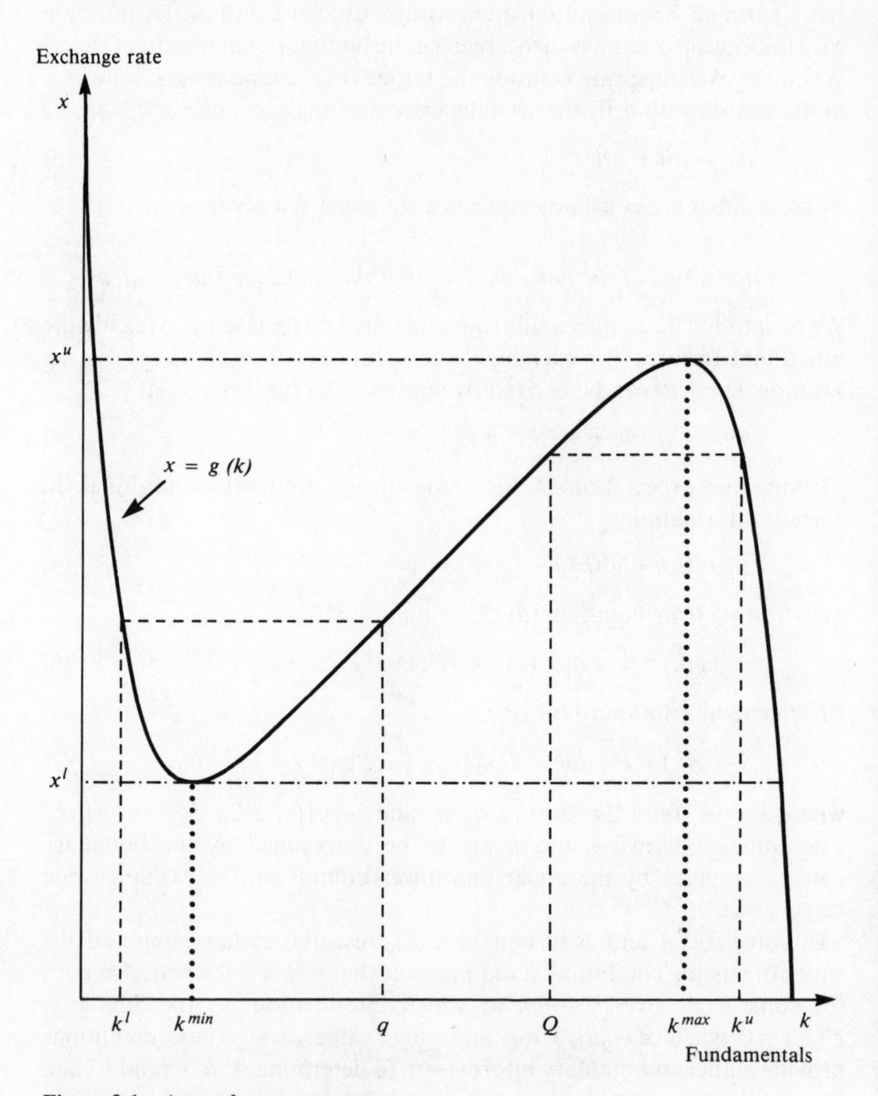

Figure 3.1 An exchange rate target zone

2.2 An exchange rate solution with discrete intervention

Nevertheless, the functional form is invariant to the size of the intervention, since the intervention size will affect neither A nor B for a given target zone. Once the upper and lower bounds of the zone are defined, A and B are set. We have drawn Figure 3.1, however, with extensions for values of k beyond the point at which the function reaches its maximum and minimum levels.

Consider a situation in which the Brownian motion process k is controlled with discrete interventions. When it is between the bounds k^u and k^l in Figure 3.1, k follows the Brownian motion process of equation (3). When k hits the upper bound k^u, a monetary intervention throws k discontinuously back to the interior point Q, where $k^u - Q$ measures the magnitude of the contraction. At Q, the k process resumes the random motion given in (3). If k hits the lower bound k^l, a discrete monetary expansion throws it back to the point q.[9] These discontinuous shifts in k can be interpreted as interventions that occur to maintain the exchange rate x within its prescribed bounds.

The pair (k^u, Q) is constrained only by a requirement that the exchange rate be continuous at the time of the intervention. Hence, for the function g associated with a given zone, any pair (k^u, Q) such that $g(k^u) = g(Q)$ defines an intervention capable of maintaining the upper bound on the zone. A similar condition constrains the pair (k^l, q).[10 11]

What is the intuition behind the continuity of the exchange rate in the presence of discrete foreseen interventions? This is a natural requirement familiar from the speculative attack literature. If there were an exchange rate discontinuity in response to an anticipated intervention, i.e. if $g(k^u)$ did not equal $g(Q)$, there would be a foreseeable profit at an infinite rate. Speculators would act to remove this opportunity.

Recall that in the speculative attack literature by Krugman (1979) or Flood and Garber (1984a, b), domestic credit is usually rigged with upward drift. An attack on a fixed exchange rate system is timed to prevent a discontinuity in exchange rates. In the context of equation (1), exchange rate continuity in the face of an expected attack on the fixed exchange rate regime requires the exchange rate to be the same in the instant just before and the instant just after the attack. The expected rate of change of the exchange rate would jump discontinuously from zero to a positive number, driving down money demand and accommodating the sudden loss of reserves at the moment of the attack.

The logic for a discrete intervention in a target zone is identical. When the distance from k to k^u is infinitesimally small, there will be a shift from k^u to Q with probability one. Now evaluate equation (1) at k^u and at Q, respectively, and subtract the two results. Since the exchange rate is the same at the two k values, the result is $k^u - Q = -\alpha\{E[dx(k^u)]/dt - E[dx(Q)]/dt\}$. The discontinuous shift in k (i.e. the reduction in foreign reserves or bondholdings of the policy authority) exactly offsets the discontinuous shift in expectations.

In this target zone problem, the shift in the expected depreciation adjusts to the arbitrary magnitude of the intervention. In the speculative attack literature, the magnitude of the intervention adjusts to the specified shift in expected depreciation rates rigged into the problem. Otherwise, the problems are identical.

Indeed, there is even a run on reserves in the target zone model. When k reaches a high enough level, speculators will approach the policy authority to convert domestic currency for reserves, thereby forcing an intervention of the prescribed magnitude. This 'run' serves to preserve the target zone, however.

Because of the many possible quadruples (k^u, Q, q, k^l) consistent with a given zone, simply announcing a specific target zone is not a fully specified policy. A particular target zone can be supported by an infinity of intervention strategies. This incompleteness is not an indictment of the target zone policy, which was designed as part of a broader policy. Indeed, the incompleteness allows policy to be directed toward other goals with only occasional attention to the maintenance of the target zone.

2.3 *The smooth pasting condition*

To see that the smooth pasting condition is valid in the cases studied by Krugman and Froot and Obstfeld, again consider Figure 3.1. Define k^{max} and k^{min} as the solutions of $g'(k) = 0$. Note that $k^u > k^{max} > Q$ and $k^l < k^{min} < q$. Now let k^u and Q converge toward each other, always assuring that $g(k^u) = g(Q)$. Also, let k^l and q similarly converge. Q and k^u will then converge to k^{max} and q and k^l will converge to k^{min}. Therefore, for infinitesimal interventions, $g'(k^u) = g'(k^l) = 0$, the smooth pasting condition. Whatever the intervention policy may be, the smooth pasting condition is applicable for determining the values of A and B in solving for the exchange rate function g. Nevertheless, the assumption that the target zone boundary points are attained simultaneously with the k boundary points is true only in the case of infinitesimal intervention.

3 The volatility of exchange rates and interest rates

Krugman (1988) showed that the target zone will stabilize the exchange rate. This result occurs because the function $g(k)$ is everywhere less responsive than the functional relation between x and k in a pure floating regime. Yet, the possibility of achieving some exchange rate stability without actually having to intervene has the disturbing appearance of a free lunch. Where does the volatility go?

To address this question, let us assume that the domestic interest rate i equals the constant foreign interest rate plus the expected rate of depreciation. Since the foreign interest rate is constant, the only volatility in the domestic interest rate stems from movements in $E[dx]$. Then

$$V(i(k), t) = a^{-2} V(g(k) - k, t) \tag{8}$$

where $V(y, t)$ is the variance of the variable y over an interval of length t.

For both fixed and floating exchange rates $V(i(k), t) = 0$ in the constant drift cases that we have considered. Since $g(k) - k$ is not constant for the target zone, however, $V(i(k), t) > 0$ in the target zone. Thus the exchange rate becomes less volatile at the expense of raising interest rate volatility.

4 A collapsing target zone with discrete intervention

Krugman (1989) split the variable k into two components, m and v, where m is the logarithm of the money supply and v is an exogeneous variable encompassing other factors that drive the exchange rate. The money supply $m = ln(D + R)$, where D is the level of domestic credit and R is foreign exchange reserves. The variable m and its components remain constant until an intervention occurs, taking the form of a change in R. If R falls to zero, no further intervention will occur. We assume that v is a Brownian motion process with no drift, i.e. $dv = \sigma dz$.

If x rises toward its maximum level x^u because v rises, an intervention involving a sale of reserves and a decline in the money supply will occur. This decline might be infinitesimal, aimed at offsetting infinitesimal increases in v. Alternatively, the decline in the money supply may be discrete and large. Conversely, if x tended to its minimum value x^l because v was falling, the intervention would entail an increase in the money supply through a purchase of reserves.

Figure 3.2 depicts the exchange rate solution, drawn on the basis of a discrete intervention policy. For a given money supply, the curve labelled 1 represents the exchange rate as a function of v, where v is permitted to reach an upper bound v^u before an intervention aimed at maintaining the zone occurs. Thus, as v rises, the exchange rate rises and then falls before the intervention occurs, as we saw earlier. The intervention in this case involves reducing reserves and the money supply discretely. Since this is a credible policy, the intervention comes as no surprise; and there is no

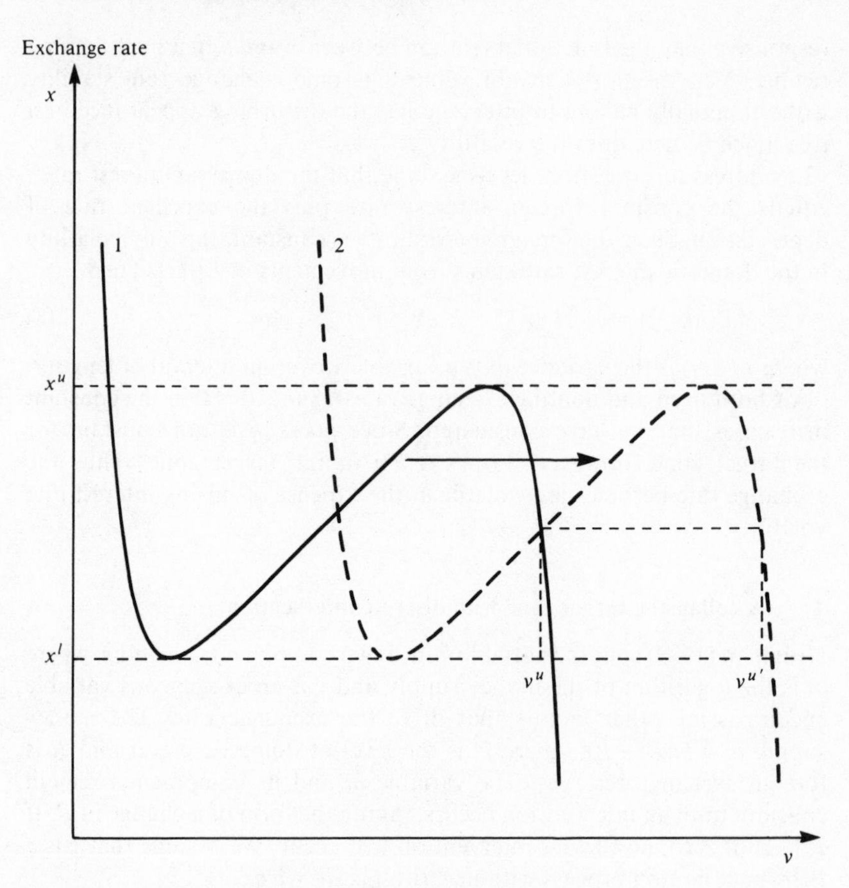

Figure 3.2 Discrete intervention with declining reserves

jump in the exchange rate with the intervention. Since v is exogeneous, it does not change from v^u as a result of the intervention, however. The monetary contraction has the effect of shifting the exchange rate function from the curve labelled 1 rightward to the curve labelled 2. The shift occurs by an amount which maintains exchange rate continuity when the new solution is evaluated at v^u; v then evolves freely from this starting point v^u. If it moves up to $v^{u'}$, another contractionary intervention occurs, and the process repeats.[12]

4.1 The collapse of a target zone

Any lower bound on reserves, however, will be approached at some time. For example, in Figure 3.3, suppose that when v reaches $v^{u'}$, reserves have

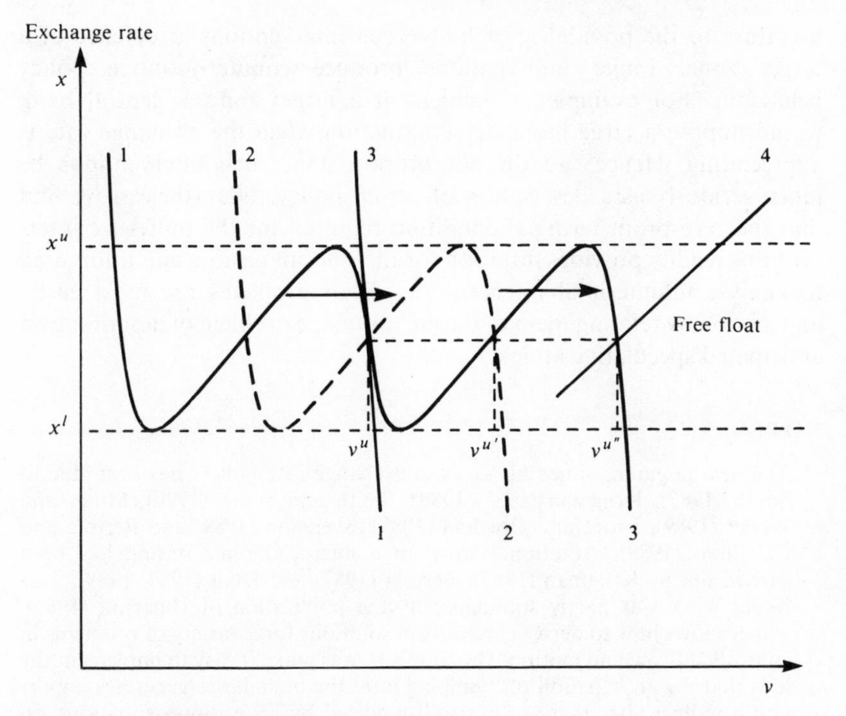

Figure 3.3 Collapse with discrete intervention

declined to a level such that one more intervention of the usual size will push reserves exactly to zero, after which the authorities will expend no further reserves to maintain the zone. The intervention policy is then credible for one last time, so the exchange rate will move along the new target zone solution path indicated by curve 3. If v continues to rise to $v^{u''}$, the intervention will occur as promised, but thereafter further interventions are no longer credible. The exchange rate solution will then follow curve 4, the usual linear function of the fundamentals. Note that exchange rate continuity will be maintained at $v^{u''}$.

5 Conclusions

Public and private sector agents often adopt one set of actions when some indicator is within certain bounds and switch to another set of actions when the bounds are reached. Examples of such action patterns are widespread in policymaking circles and seem to describe an important part of the policymaking process not captured by linear rules.

The purpose of the present paper was primarily technical: to extend the literature to the possibility of finite-sized interventions in defence of a target zone. Finite interventions produce counter-intuitive policy behaviour. For example, to implement a target zone, a central bank would impose a large monetary contraction when the exchange rate is appreciating. Hence, we do not propose that such interventions be taken seriously as a description of actual policy. Nevertheless, we find that the zero-profit terminal condition required for the finite-size interventions readily provides intuition for the smooth pasting condition used to analyse infinitesimal interventions. Both problems are most easily understood by relating them to the mirror image problem of describing an anticipated speculative attack.

NOTES

1 The new research, aimed at issues in exchange rate policy, has been due to Smith (1987), Krugman (1987, 1988), Smith and Smith (1990), Miller and Weller (1989), Froot and Obstfeld (1989), Svensson (1989) and Bertola and Caballero (1989). Additional work in a microeconomic setting has been carried out by Krugman (1987), Bertola (1987) and Dixit (1987, 1988). This recent work was partly stimulated by the publication of Harrison (1985), which shows how to derive closed-form solutions for a variety of problems in controlled Brownian motion. Harrison's results make it easy to implement the idea that the anticipation of 'bumping into' the boundaries generates important non-linearities that are not well modeled by linear approximations. In previous work, we have studied economic behaviour in similar situations, but we found it difficult to produce closed-form solutions. In Flood and Garber (1980, 1983b), we studied the impact of a random future endogenous triggering of monetary reform on the current price level in the German hyperinflation. In Flood and Garber (1983a) we considered the determination of the current floating exchange rate when the regime would switch to a fixed rate system at an endogenously determined, random time.

2 The Krugman target zone is in spirit a simplified version of the target zone blueprint offered by Williamson and Miller (1987).

3 For some literature on speculative attacks, see Salant and Henderson (1978), Krugman (1979), Salant (1983), Flood and Garber (1984a, b), and Obstfeld (1984, 1986).

4 The target zone models can be integrated with models of speculative attacks either of the buying or selling varieties, if a limit is placed on the amount of reserves or bonds that the authorities are willing to buy or sell to defend the zone. Krugman (1989) has developed this result for the case of a selling attack.

5 Because of the upper and lower bounds in a target zone, these may be either buying or selling attacks as in Grilli (1986).

6 Froot and Obstfeld (1989) have also extended these results to the case of a different forcing process, the Ornstein-Uhlenbeck process, and to the case of absorbing barriers. The absorbing barriers case was studied by Flood and Garber (1983a) with closed form solutions first derived by Smith (1987).

7 Both x and k are functions of time, but we will usually suppress the time-dependence notation in the following presentation.

8 Krugman assumes a zero drift parameter. Froot and Obstfeld argue that the policy specification in Krugman is incomplete since both discrete jumps in k and infinitesimal interventions are compatible with a given target zone. They base their discussion on a similar point made in Obstfeld and Stockman's (1985) discussion of an indeterminacy in Flood and Garber (1983a). Nevertheless, they consider only the case of infinitesimal intervention. It turns out that this case implies intervention only at the boundaries of the target zone.

9 When $k^u = Q$ and $k^l = q$ and these values are the critical values of the function g, we have the case of Froot and Obstfeld: asymmetric reflecting barriers with infinitesimal interventions. When, in addition, $\eta = 0$ and $k^u = -k^l$, we have the symmetric special case of Krugman.

10 Of course, the pairs are constrained to provide exchange rate realizations within the zone. Also, Q must exceed k^l and k^u must exceed q.

11 The continuity condition requires that $g(k^u) = g(Q)$ and $g(k^l) = g(q)$. These two conditions are also sufficient to determine A and B in equation (5) as functions of the policy quadruple (k^u, Q, q, k^l). The pair (A, B) associated with a specific target zone can then be generated by an infinite number of combinations of value for the inner and outer bounds on k.

12 Alternatively, the intervention might be infinitesimal, as in Krugman. Such an intervention can be depicted in Figure 3.1 by setting v^u equal to v^{max}, the argument at which the exchange rate function represented by curve 1 is flat. Repeated infinitesimal interventions then slide the solution curve continuously rightward in the zone.

REFERENCES

Bertola, G. (1987), 'Irreversible investment', MIT Working Paper.

Bertola, G. and R. Caballero (1989), 'Target zones and realignments', Working Paper.

Dixit, A. (1987), 'Intersectoral capital reallocation under price uncertainty'. Mimeo, Princeton University.

(1988), 'A simplified exposition of some results concerning regulated Brownian motion'. Mimeo, Princeton University.

Flood, R.P. and P.M. Garber (1980), 'An economic theory of monetary reform', *Journal of Political Economy* **88**, 24–58.

(1983a), 'A model of stochastic process switching', *Econometrica* **51**, 537–52.

(1983b), 'Process consistency and monetary reform: further evidence', *Journal of Monetary Economics* **12**, 279–96.

(1984a), 'Gold monetization and gold discipline', *Journal of Political Economy* **92**, 90–107.

(1984b), 'Collapsing exchange rate regimes: some linear examples', *Journal of International Economics* **18**, 1–13.

Froot, K.A. and M. Obstfeld (1989), 'Exchange rate dynamics under stochastic regime shifts: a unified approach', Working Paper.

Grilli, V. (1986), 'Buying and selling attacks on fixed exchange rate systems', *Journal of International Economics* **20**, 143–56.

Harrison, J.M. (1985), *Brownian Motion and Stochastic Flow Systems*, New York: John Wiley and Sons.

Krugman, P.R. (1979), 'A model of balance-of-payments crises', *Journal of Money, Credit and Banking* **11**, 311–25.

(1987), 'Trigger strategies and price dynamics in equity and foreign exchange markets', NBER Working Paper No. 2459.
(1988), 'Target zones and exchange rate dynamics', NBER Working Paper No. 2841.
(1989), 'Target zones with limited reserves', Working Paper.
Miller, M. and P. Weller (1989), 'Solving stochastic saddlepoint systems: a qualitative treatment with economic applications', CEPR Discussion Paper No. 308.
Obstfeld, M. (1984), 'Balance-of-payments crises and devaluation', *Journal of Money, Credit and Banking* **16**, 208–17.
(1986), 'Rational and self-fulfilling balance of payments crises', *American Economic Review* **76**, 72–81.
Obstfeld, M. and A.G. Stockman (1985), 'Exchange rate dynamics', in R.W. Jones and P.B. Kenen (eds.) *Handbook of International Economics*, Vol. 2, Amsterdam: North-Holland.
Salant, S.W. and D.W. Henderson (1978), 'Market anticipations of government policies and the price of gold', *Journal of Political Economy* **86**, 627–48.
Smith, G.W. (1987), 'Stochastic process switching', Queen's University Working Paper.
Smith, G.W. and T. Smith (1990), 'Stochastic process switching and the return to gold, 1925', *Economic Journal* **100**, 164–75.
Svensson, L. (1989), 'Target zones and interest rate variability', Seminar Paper No. 457, Institute for International Economic Studies, University of Stockholm.
Williamson, J. and M. Miller (1987), *Targets and Indicators: a Blueprint for the International Coordination of Economic Policy*, Washington: Institute for International Economics.

Discussion

PAUL WELLER

This paper presents a very useful and interesting extension of the target zone model of Krugman (1988) to encompass the case where the monetary authorites use a fully credible discrete intervention rule to defend a currency band.

In my discussion I shall begin by comparing the analysis of Flood and Garber to related work on a model with sluggish price adjustment that I have done with Marcus Miller (see Miller and Weller, 1989, 1990). In particular, I will show how discrete intervention rules of the form analysed by Flood and Garber can be used to support a *real* exchange rate band of the type advocated by John Williamson (1985). I shall then discuss how the treatment of permanent collapse of a currency band can be extended to the case of temporary collapse, analysed by Krugman and Rotemberg (1990) in the context of a model with infinitesimal rather than discrete intervention.

The model I shall use is a stochastic version of that presented in Dornbusch (1976) and consists of the following equations:

$$m - p = \kappa y - \lambda i \qquad (1) \text{ Money market}$$

$$y = -\gamma(i - \pi) + \eta(x - p) \qquad (2) \text{ Goods market}$$

$$E(dx) = (i - i^*)\,dt \qquad (3) \text{ Currency arbitrage}$$

$$dp = \phi(y - \bar{y})\,dt + \sigma\,dz \qquad (4) \text{ Price adjustment}$$

$$\pi = E(dp)/dt \qquad (5) \text{ Inflation expectations}$$

The first equation describes the equilibrium condition for the domestic money market, where m is the log of the money supply, p the log of the price level, y the log of GNP and i the domestic interest rate. The second equation is an *IS* curve which captures the dependence of output on the real exchange rate, $x - p$, and on the real interest rate, $i - \pi$, where x represents the log of the price of foreign currency and π is the instantaneous expected rate of inflation. The uncovered interest parity condition is captured by (3) and (4) reflects the assumption of gradual price adjustment, where $\bar{y}$ is full employment output. In place of shocks to the velocity of money I assume the existence of (supply-side) shocks to the level of prices.

By contrast, the model underlying the reduced form equations (1) and (2) in the paper of Flood and Garber can be thought of as some variant of the following system:

$$m - p = \kappa\bar{y} - ai - v \qquad (6)$$

$$x = p - p^* \qquad (7)$$

$$E(dx) = (i - i^*)\,dt \qquad (8)$$

$$dv = \eta\,dt + \sigma\,dz \qquad (9)$$

The variable v in (6) represents a cumulative velocity shock which follows the Brownian motion process specified in (9). The model assumes that output is always at its full employment level, $\bar{y}$, and that the real exchange rate is fixed at PPP (equation (7), where p^* is the log of the foreign price level). Subsuming constant terms into the velocity shock term, we obtain the reduced form equation:

$$x = m + v + aE[dx]/dt \tag{10}$$

So equations (9) and (10) correspond to the equations (1) and (2) in Flood and Garber, where k corresponds to the composite fundamental $m + v$. Breaking down the fundamental into its component parts enables one to see more clearly how m is used as a 'regulator'.

Returning now to the stochastic Dornbusch model, one can show that it has a reduced form in the real variables $c \equiv x - p, l \equiv m - p$, of the following form:

$$dl = (a_{11}l + a_{12}c)dt + \sigma dz \tag{11}$$

$$c = a_{21}l + a_{22}E[dc]/dt \tag{12}$$

Equations (10) and (12) are formally identical. The important difference comes in comparing (9) and (11). In the stochastic Dornbusch model the fundamental $l(t)$ has an endogenously determined drift, which depends both upon its own current value and, more importantly, upon that of the (log of the) real exchange rate.

This means that closed-form solutions are not available, but one can show that the qualitative features of the solutions to the two models are similar in a number of respects (see Miller and Weller, 1989); and, most importantly, the variable l can be regulated by discrete adjustments to the money supply m in precisely the same manner as is assumed to be the case for the fundamental k in the monetary model.

Thus, within the framework of the stochastic Dornbusch model, if the authorities wish to impose a limit upon the range of variation of the *real* exchange rate, they can achieve this objective by announcing suitably chosen upper and lower limits for l, at which discrete adjustments to the money supply occur.

It is instructive to consider the effect of the following simple intervention rule: increase the money supply by Q when p exceeds its current long-run equilibrium level by Q, and reduce it by the same amount when p lies below its long-run equilibrium level by Q.

This rule specifies *intermittent* full accommodation of inflationary shocks. It will determine a band for the real exchange rate symmetrically positioned about PPP. The solution will be such that, paradoxically, intervention only occurs when the exchange rate is at PPP. As Q is reduced, the band will narrow and intervention will occur more frequently, until in the limit continuous intervention will perfectly stabilize the real exchange rate at PPP. An analogous result is obviously true in the Flood and Garber model.

Next I examine the effects of such a discrete intervention rule upon nominal variables. This is illustrated in Figure 3A.1. The edges of the real

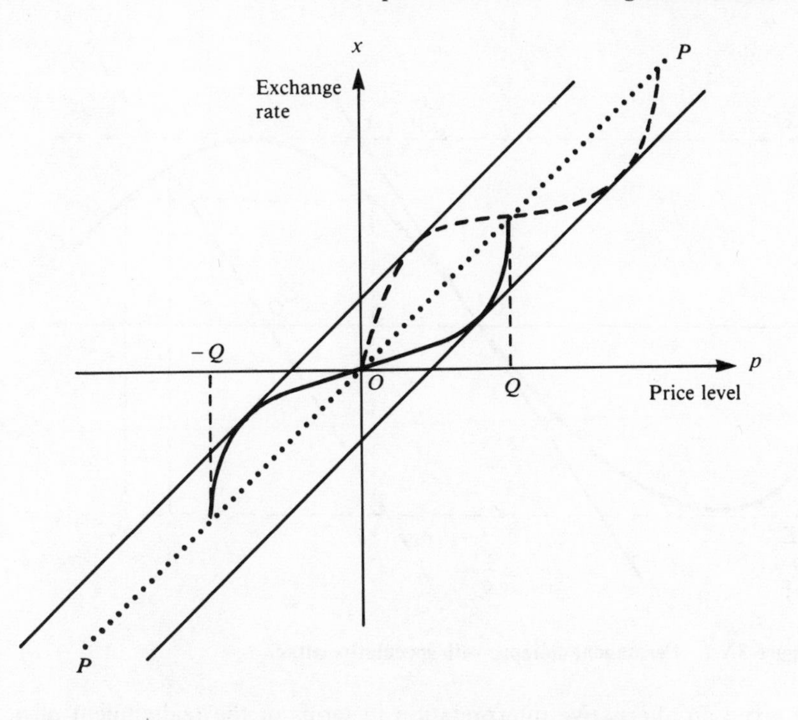

Figure 3A.1 A real exchange rate band with discrete intervention

band run parallel to *POP*, which is the line of purchasing power parity. Intervention occurs when $p = \pm Q$. As the price level rises above its long-run equilibrium level, the real exchange rate falls, as does competitiveness. However, there is a point beyond which further increases in p generate an increase in competitiveness. This 'paradoxical' response is in fact easy to explain. The market anticipates the impact of the intervention at Q, which by lowering interest rates will raise the price of foreign exchange.

If intervention is infinitesimal, then the solution 'smooth pastes' on to the edges of the real band, and checks movement in the real interest rate $i - \pi$. A significant difference in the behaviour of the fundamental in the two models emerges. The cumulative velocity shock is driven by an exogenous non-stationary process, whereas the price level displays a degree of 'local' stability in that its conditional expected movement is always in the direction of the current long-run equilibrium. However, given the periodic accommodation of inflationary shocks, both the price level and the money supply will be 'globally' non-stationary.

It is worth noting that the discrete intervention rule described above can

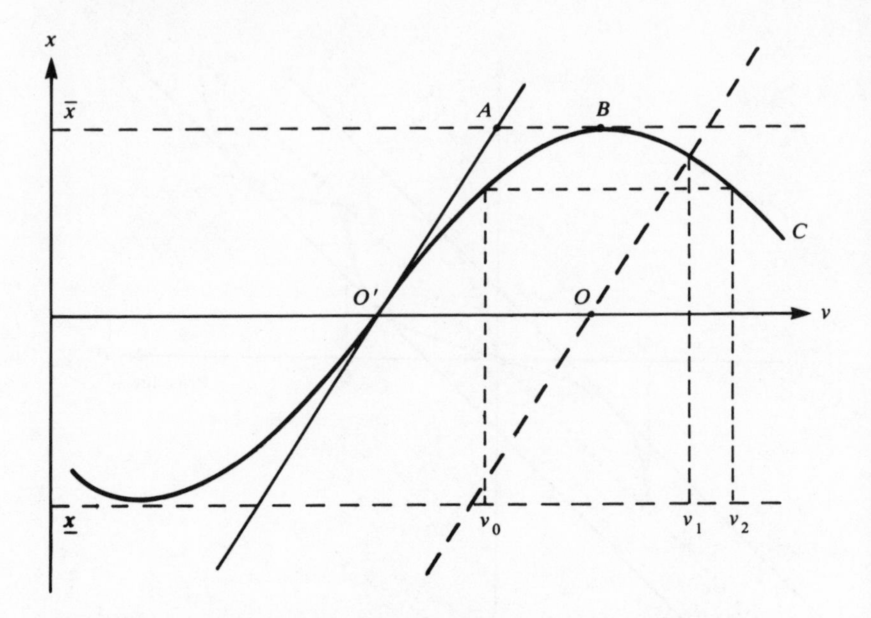

Figure 3A.2 Permanent collapse with speculative attack

be given an alternative interpretation in terms of the realignment of a nominal currency band. Suppose the authorities impose a nominal band $[\underline{x}, \bar{x}]$ where $\underline{x} = -Q$, $\bar{x} = Q$. Assume also that the following rule for realigning the band is announced to the market: the central parity will be shifted upwards (downwards) by Q whenever the exchange rate hits the top (bottom) of the band, and the monetary accommodation necessary to validate the realignment will occur simultaneously.

This rule, if it is fully credible, must, by applying exactly the same logic as Flood and Garber, produce no jump in the exchange rate. It is not difficult to see that the only solution satisfying this condition is the one illustrated in Figure 3A.1 (see Miller and Weller, 1989, for further discussion of such realignment rules).

If we return now to the analysis of the monetary model, the treatment of the case of a permanent collapse of a currency band regime raises an interesting point not brought out in the paper. This is that, in general, when a discrete intervention rule is used to support the regime, a true speculative attack causes the collapse of the regime. In other words, when there exists a sufficient quantity of reserves left for at least one more intervention, there will be a speculative outflow of all remaining reserves triggered at a point before the final intervention would occur.

This is illustrated in Figure 3A.2, for the case where the velocity variable

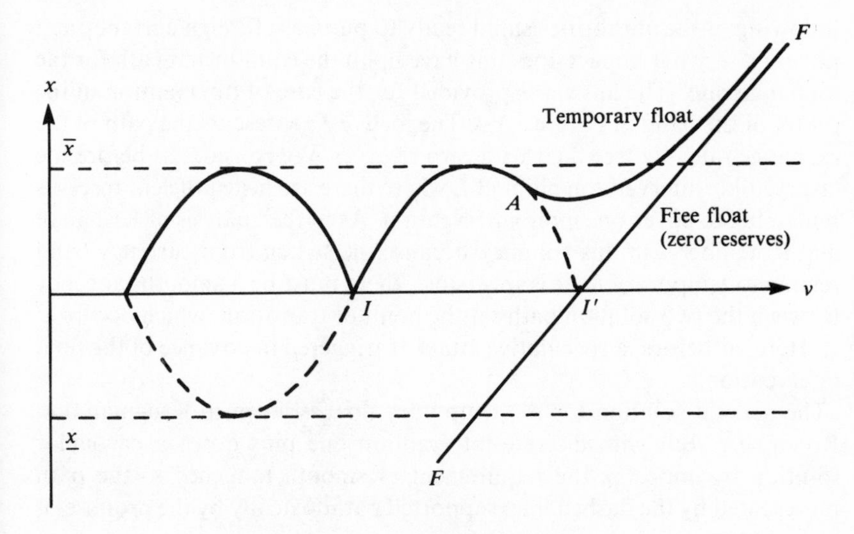

Figure 3A.3 Temporary collapse with speculative attack

v has zero drift, and therefore the path for the exchange rate is symmetric about the centre of the band. The 45° line through O represents the free float with zero reserves. The size of the final intervention is given by $v_2 - v_0$, which is constructed to be equal to the distance between O' and O. Thus the path $O'BC$ is the one which would occur when there are just sufficient reserves remaining for one more intervention. It is immediately clear from Figure 3A.2 that the final intervention at v_2 will not be observed, since it would involve a fully anticipated jump in the exchange rate. What happens in fact is that a speculative attack is triggered when v reaches v_1, all reserves are exhausted, and the exchange rate moves permanently on to the free-float locus through O.

Note that AB measures the minimum quantity of reserves necessary to sustain the regime, regardless of whether intervention is discrete or infinitesimal. Therefore, if the size of discrete intervention is less than AB, and in particular when it is small, collapse of the regime will be caused by a speculative attack which occurs even though the level of reserves is sufficient to support a large number of further interventions.

The above discussion relates to the case of permanent collapse of a currency band regime. But it is arguably more plausible to suppose that the collapse will be temporary. If the currency strengthens substantially after the collapse as a consequence of favourable movements in fundamentals, it seems reasonable to suppose that the authorities would again start to accumulate reserves. The question we can then pose is the following: if the authorities stand ready to purchase foreign currency at a price $x \leqslant \bar{x}$, what impact does this have upon the equilibrium path for the exchange rate? The answer is provided for the case of intervention in the centre of the band in Figure 3A.3. The locus *FF* represents the path of the exchange rate in a free float with zero reserves. We consider as before the last credible intervention point at *I*, where there are just sufficient reserves remaining to cover one more intervention. As in the analysis of Krugman and Rotemberg (in this volume), because the switch from currency band regime to temporary float is reversible, there must be a smooth tangency between the two solution paths at the point of transition, which occurs at *A*. Here, as before, a speculative attack is triggered in advance of the final intervention.

The general solution for the temporary float is given in Krugman and Rotemberg. But with discrete intervention one pins down a particular solution by imposing the requirement of smooth tangency to the path represented by the dashed line, supported paradoxically by the promise of an intervention that is never observed.

REFERENCES

Dornbusch, R. (1976), 'Expectations and exchange rate dynamics', *Journal of Political Economy* **84**, 1161–76.

Krugman, P. (1991), 'Target zones and exchange rate dynamics', NBER Working Paper No. 2481 (forthcoming in *Quarterly Journal of Economics*).

Krugman, P. and J. Rotemberg (1990), 'Target zones with limited reserves', mimeo, July.

Miller, M. and P. Weller (1989), 'Qualitative solutions for stochastic saddlepaths and the analysis of exchange rate regimes', mimeo, University of Warwick.

(1990), 'Exchange rate bands with price inertia', CEPR Discussion Paper No. 421, forthcoming in the *Economic Journal.*

Williamson, J. (1983, 1985), *The Exchange Rate System.* Washington, D.C.: Institute for International Economics.

4 Target zones, broad and narrow

FRANCISCO DELGADO and
BERNARD DUMAS

This paper is an extension of earlier work. In Delgado and Dumas (1990) a general solution technique is used to analyse different contracting arrangements between two central banks who agree to intervene in the foreign exchange market to maintain their currencies within certain limits. In this study we would like to address a different issue, namely the effect on macro variables of the widening and narrowing of the target zone, with special emphasis on changes in the interest rate differential. The experiment of progressively narrowing the target zone is of interest as a representation of the transition between a target zone arrangement and a single currency, assuming that a fully credible fixed exchange rate is identical to a single currency.

Svensson (1989) has already studied this question. He restricted himself to the study of a stochastic process without drift. We extend his work and Delgado and Dumas (1990) by incorporating successively a non-zero drift and a mean-reverting process. As Svensson suggested, it is necessary to study a process that is not characterized by a constant mean. A mean-reverting process has this property. This type of process will be used to model the fact that in the functioning of the EMS about 85% of the intervention is done intramarginally.

The paper is organized as follows: Section 1 lays out the basic framework for both the non-zero drift Brownian motion and the mean-reverting process. The necessary assumptions will be made in this section. Section 2 presents the various solutions for the exchange rate process in the Brownian motion case. Section 3 studies the limiting properties of the zone when the target zone is either very wide or very narrow; this includes the behaviour of the interest rate differential. Section 4 describes the various interpretations of the mean-reverting process and presents the various solutions for the exchange rate function. Section 5 establishes the limiting properties of the mean-reverting case. We conclude in Section 6.

1 The model: differential equation for the exchange rate

The basic equation on which most of the target zone literature is based is:

$$S = m - m^* + v + \gamma E\{dS|\Phi(t)\}/dt \tag{1}$$

where S is the exchange rate between two currencies (the domestic currency value of foreign exchange), $m = ln(R + D)$ and $m^* = ln(R^* + D^*)$ are domestic and foreign measures of *controllable* money supply and v is an *exogenous* monetary shock. In this study m and m^* are deemed controllable because foreign exchange intervention by Central Banks modifies reserves R and R^*; D and D^* stand for domestic credit. γ is a coefficient interpreted as an interest semi-elasticity of money demand and $E\{dS|\Phi(t)\}/dt$ is the conditionally expected instantaneous change in the exchange rate; $\Phi(t)$ is the information set of economic agents acting in the foreign exchange market.

The following assumptions are made:

(A1) Intervention in the foreign exchange market which occurs at the boundaries of the target zone (marginal intervention) is instantaneous and infinitesimal. Intervention which occurs within the band (intramarginal intervention) is proportional in intensity to the deviation from some target, so that we can model it by means of a mean-reverting process. This reflects a policy of 'leaning against the wind'.[1]

(A2) There is full cooperation between central banks to render the target zone completely credible. The burden of intervention is shared. If the country whose currency is weak has run out of reserves, the other central bank intervenes by printing money. The assumption is made in order to avoid the problem of running out of reserves which has been examined elsewhere (Delgado and Dumas, 1990; see, by way of contrast, their Assumption 2).

(A3) Commodity prices are flexible, purchasing power parity and uncovered interest rate parity hold. There is full capital mobility and interventions are not sterilized.

(A4) Both countries share the same money demand function with identical parameters.

Svensson (1989) has examined limiting properties of some solutions of (1) under the assumption that the shock v follows a zero-drift arithmetic Brownian motion. Here we extend the analysis to Brownian motion with a non-zero constant trend and to mean-reverting processes. The *constant-trend* formulation is:

$$dv = \mu dt + \sigma dW \qquad \mu, \sigma \text{ constant and } > 0 \qquad v_0 > 0 \text{ given} \tag{2}$$

In (2), μ and σ are constants and dW is the increment of a standard Wiener process. For $\mu > 0$ – which, for the sake of definiteness, will be assumed – we will say that the domestic currency is inherently *weak* because the trend in fundamentals works against it; without intervention the domestic currency is expected to depreciate.

We also extend the analysis to the case of *mean-reverting shocks* which produces a variable drift:

$$dv = -\rho(v - a_0)\,dt + \sigma\,dz; \qquad \rho, \sigma \text{ constant and } > 0 \quad v_0 > 0 \text{ given} \tag{3}$$

where a_0 is the long-run level of v and ρ is the speed with which the process tends towards this value. In this specification a positive shock to v is detrimental to the domestic currency in the short run but also induces a drift which in the long run is favorable to the domestic currency. Appendix 4A reminds the reader (see also Svensson, 1989; Froot and Obstfeld, 1989b, footnote 2) that it is conceivable to interpret v either as a supply or a demand shock. As long as v follows a constant drift process, the distinction is immaterial. When v is mean-reverting, however, more care must be exercised; we return to the issue in Section 4.

Equation (1) is the basic equation which Krugman (1991) used to study exchange rate target zones. Define the 'fundamentals' X as: $m - m^* + v$. Note that X includes controllable (reserves) and uncontrollable (domestic credit) terms. Equation (1) can be rewritten as:

$$S = X + \gamma E\{dS \mid \Phi(t)\}/dt \tag{4}$$

2 Solutions of the model: the constant-trend case

We are now ready to solve the model for the two basic assumptions about the stochastic process followed by the 'fundamentals'. In the next two sections we analyse the non-zero constant trend case and in the following ones the mean-reverting case.

We interpret the constant-trend case (equation (2)) as one in which intervention occurs at the margins only and is of the instantaneous variety. The stochastic differential equation for the fundamentals can be written as the non-regulated fundamentals plus two terms that take into account the intervention of the central banks, dU and dL:

$$dX = \mu\,dt + \sigma\,dW - dU + dL \tag{5}$$

with initial condition $X(0) = X_0 = m_0 - m^*_0 + v_0$, $U(0) = 0$, $L(0) = 0$, U and L being two non-negative non-decreasing processes, and U increases only when $S = \bar{S}$ while L increases only when $S = \underline{S}$. U and L stand for the cumulative amounts of intervention done by the two countries. Because of Assumption A2 we do not have to specify who performs the intervention. Equation (5) indicates that the same fixed trend drives v and the fundamentals X.

Assume that the value of the exchange rate is a twice continuously differentiable function of X and apply Ito's lemma to calculate $E\{dS|\Phi(t)\}/dt$ explicitly. Substitution of the resulting expression into (4) yields the basic differential equation which must be satisfied by the exchange rate function, irrespective of the particular government policy regarding exchange rates:

$$S = X + \gamma[\mu S'(X) + 0.5\sigma^2 S''(X)] \qquad (6)$$

This equation applies over the domain of X where no intervention takes place.

The *general solution* of (6) is:

$$S(X) = X + \gamma\mu + Ae^{aX} + Be^{-\beta X} \qquad (7)$$

where A and B are constants of integration which must be solved for, using the boundary conditions implied by the exchange rate policy. a and $-\beta$ are the positive and negative roots of the characteristic equation: $1 = \gamma\mu q + 0.5\gamma\sigma^2 q^2$. One property of the roots will prove useful later: $1/a - 1/\beta = \gamma\mu$.

The free-float particular solution: Resorting to a no-bubble argument and considering the fact that X under free float has support in $(-\infty, \infty)$ both exponential terms are eliminated on the grounds that they would generate explosive paths. This implies $A = B = 0$. Therefore, the equation for the exchange rate is:

$$S = X + \gamma\mu \qquad (8)$$

The free-float solution is shown in Figure 4.1 and other figures as the upwards sloping line with intercept at $S = \gamma\mu$.

A fixed-rate regime is, in theory, an exchange rate system in which the government is committed to doing whatever is necessary to maintain the current parity. Because of the full credibility assumption, we can in this study treat a fixed-rate regime and a one-currency world as identical.[2]

If we refer to Figure 4.1, point FX on the diagonal DD' where $S = X$ represents a strict fixed-exchange regime solution. If the exchange rate is not expected to change ($E\{dS|\Phi(t)\}/dt = 0$), Equation (4) implies:

$$S = X \qquad (9)$$

so if the authorities wish to peg the exchange rate at some level S_0, they must strictly maintain the fundamentals at a level $X = S_0$.

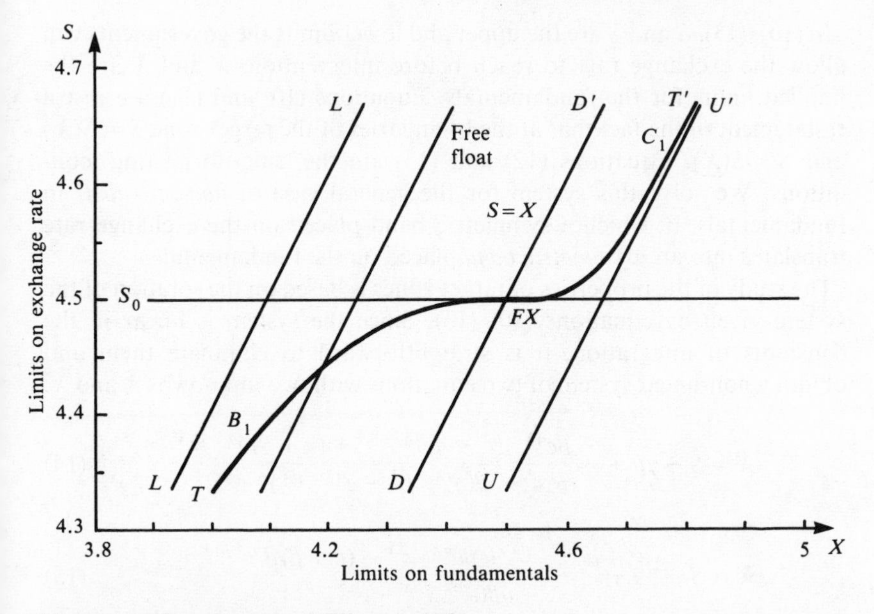

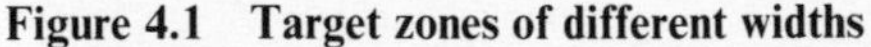

Figure 4.1 Target zones of different widths
The figure is constructed by changing the width of the band around $S_0 = 4.5$. This means solving the system (14)–(15) for different values of $\bar{S}$ and $\underline{S}$ *positioned symmetrically around* S_0. The two straight lines in the middle are the diagonal DD', where $S = X$, containing the fixed exchange points, and the free float line. The thick line TT' is the locus of tangencies implied by the smooth-pasting conditions. Points above S_0 are pairs $(\bar{X}, \bar{S})$; points below S_0 are pairs $(\underline{X}, \underline{S})$. Numerical values of parameters are: $\sigma^2 = 0.25$, $\mu = 0.5$ and $\gamma = 0.5$. Units on the two axes are not the same.

Target zone solutions: Assuming that the target zone policy has been specified by two bounds on the exchange rate and the size of the interventions (infinitesimal in our case), there is a unique solution to the target zone problem. This solution is characterized by smooth pasting conditions at the boundaries.[3]

The determination of the constants of integration A and B and the bounds on fundamentals implied by the bounds on exchange rates is done by solving simultaneously the following system of four equations with four unknowns A, B, $\underline{X}$, and $\bar{X}$.

$$\bar{S} = \bar{X} + \gamma\mu + Ae^{\alpha\bar{X}} + Be^{-\beta\bar{X}} \tag{10}$$

$$\underline{S} = \underline{X} + \gamma\mu + Ae^{\alpha\underline{X}} + Be^{-\beta\underline{X}} \tag{11}$$

$$0 = 1 + \alpha Ae^{\alpha\bar{X}} - \beta Be^{-\beta\bar{X}} \tag{12}$$

$$0 = 1 + \alpha Ae^{\alpha\underline{X}} - \beta Be^{-\beta\underline{X}} \tag{13}$$

In (10)–(13), $\bar{S}$ and $\underline{S}$ are the upper and lower limits the governments will allow the exchange rate to reach before intervention. $\bar{X}$ and $\underline{X}$ are the implied limits for the fundamentals. Equations (10) and (11) are just a restatement of the fact that at the boundaries of the target zone $\bar{S} = S(\bar{X})$ and $\underline{S} = S(\underline{X})$. Equations (12) and (13) are the 'smooth pasting' conditions. We solve this system for the general case of *non-zero drift* in fundamentals, in which a symmetric band placed on the exchange rate translates into an *asymmetric band* placed on the fundamentals.

The study of the properties of target zones is based on the solution of the system given by equations (10)–(13). Since the system is linear in the constants of integration, it is straightforward to eliminate them and obtain a non-linear system of two equations with two unknowns $\bar{X}$ and $\underline{X}$:

$$\bar{X} = \bar{S} - \gamma\mu + \frac{-\beta e^{a\bar{X} - \beta\underline{X}} - a e^{a\underline{X} - \beta\bar{X}} + (a + \beta) e^{(a - \beta)\bar{X}}}{-a\beta(e^{a\bar{X} - \beta\underline{X}} - e^{a\underline{X} - \beta\bar{X}})} \tag{14}$$

$$\underline{X} = \underline{S} - \gamma\mu + \frac{a e^{a\bar{X} - \beta\underline{X}} + \beta e^{a\underline{X} - \beta\bar{X}} - (a + \beta) e^{(a - \beta)\underline{X}}}{-a\beta(e^{a\bar{X} - \beta\underline{X}} - e^{a\underline{X} - \beta\bar{X}})} \tag{15}$$

Part of our exposition of what happens as one changes the width of the band will refer to Figure 4.1. We proceed to explain it at this point. The figure is constructed by changing the width of the band around S_0. This means solving the system (14)–(15) for different values of $\bar{S}$ and $\underline{S}$ *positioned symmetrically around* S_0 (= 4.5 in Figure 4.1). The two straight lines in the middle are the diagonal DD' where $S = X$, which contains the fixed-exchange points, and the free float. As we know, the free float is $S = X + \gamma\mu$, i.e. it is the diagonal translated upwards by the distance $\gamma\mu$. The thick line TT' is the locus of tangencies implied by the smooth-pasting conditions. Points above S_0 are pairs $(\bar{X}, \bar{S})$; points below S_0 are pairs $(\underline{X}, \underline{S})$. Furthermore, in Figure 4.1 – as is clear from the basic equation (4) which indicates that the interest-rate differential is equal to $(S - X)/\gamma$ – iso-interest-rate differential loci would be parallel lines: the diagonal line DD' corresponds to a zero value of the interest-rate differential, for example, while the free-float line corresponds to an interest differential of μ.

As is clear from Figure 4.1, the following holds:

> **Statement # 1**: The locus of tangency points establishes a monotonic (increasing) relationship between the positioning of the bounds on the exchange rate and the positioning of the bounds on the fundamentals.

Proof: See Appendix 4B.

Statement # 1 authorizes us, under the current assumption of infinitesimal intervention, to define a target zone in terms of exchange rate bounds. The assumption of declared bounds imposed on the exchange rate rather than on the fundamentals is preferable because, in practice, exchange rates are directly observable by the financial markets, while fundamentals are less easily observable.

3 Limiting properties of target zones under constant-trend fundamentals

3.1 Widening the band

We now study the behaviour of exchange rates and interest rate differentials for wide bands. The behaviour of the interest rate differential is quite different for wide bands from what it is for narrow ones. We show that:

> **Statement # 2**: For wide enough bands, the distance of $\bar{X}$ from the diagonal line is the same asymptotically as the distance of $\underline{X}$

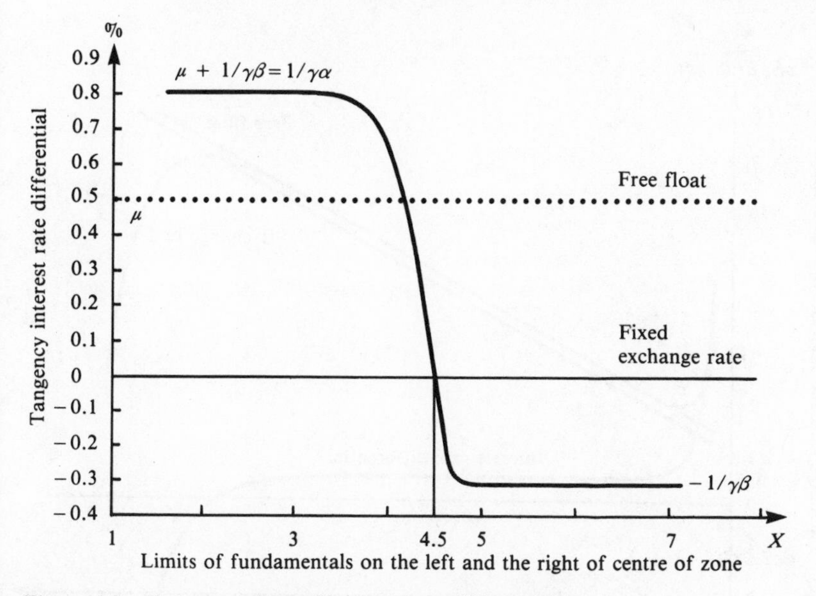

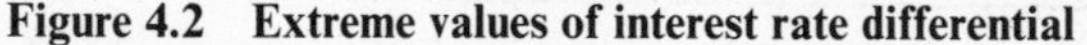
Figure 4.2 Extreme values of interest rate differential
The figure is constructed by changing the width of the exchange rate band symmetrically around $S_0 = 4.5$. Points above S_0 have abscissae equal to $\bar{X}$ and ordinates equal to the interest rate differential (assumed equal to the conditionally expected exchange rate change) reached when $X = \bar{X}$. Points below S_0 have abscissae equal to $\underline{X}$ and ordinates equal to the interest rate differential (assumed equal to the conditionally expected exchange rate change) reached when $X = \underline{X}$. Numerical values of parameters are: $\sigma^2 = 0.25$, $\mu = 0.5$ and $\gamma = 0.5$, which imply $1/\gamma\alpha = 1/(\sqrt{5} - 1) \approx 0.809$ and $-1/\gamma\beta = -1/(1 + \sqrt{5}) \approx -0.309$.

from the free-float line and that both tend to a constant value. (So, in Figure 4.1, UU' is the same distance to the right of DD' as LL' is to the left of the free-float line).

Proof: See Appendix 4C.

The asymptotic behaviour of the band described by statement # 2 has two implications. First, it implies that at points such as B_1 the *expected change in the exchange rate* (and the interest-rate differential) is close to $\mu + 1/\gamma\beta$, which is also $1/\gamma\alpha$. Second, at points such as C_1, it is close to $-1/\gamma\beta$. These are also the limits of the two extreme values of the interest rate differential occurring at the edges of the band (see Figure 4.2).

Figure 4.3 shows in greater detail an example of an exchange rate curve, an interest-rate differential curve and the free-float curve for a given wide band. For values of the exchange rate close to the free-float curve, the interest rate differential is constant and equal to μ. As the band is

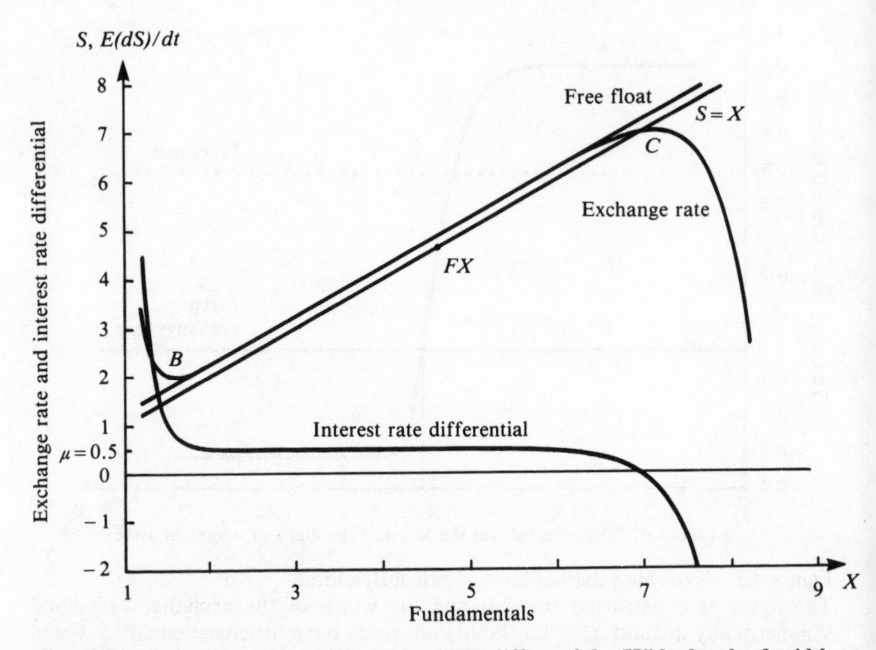

Figure 4.3 Exchange rate and interest rate differential. (Wide band of width 7.001–1.999)

When the band is wide as in the case of this figure ($\underline{S} = 1.999$, $\bar{S} = 7.001$), the exchange-rate curve follows the free-float line and the interest-rate curve is flat over most of the range of allowed variations. Numerical values of parameters are: $\sigma^2 = 0.25$, $\mu = 0.5$ and $\gamma = 0.5$.

widened, this flat section expands because the exchange rate is closer to the free float over a wider range of fundamentals. Hence, interest rate variability would tend to approach zero. This point has been emphasized by Svensson (1989); it is obviously equally valid in the special symmetric case and in the general case; we do not dwell on it further.

3.2 Narrowing the band

Figure 4.1 can again help in visualizing the process of narrowing the band. As one tightens the band around a given exchange rate value S_0, the system converges to the fixed-rate solution ($X = S = S_0$). The interesting aspect, however, is the rate at which this convergence takes place:[4]

> **Statement # 3**: The relationship between the bounds on the exchange rate and the bounds on the fundamentals is cubic.

Proof: See Appendix 4D.

Statement # 3 generalizes a similar result obtained by Svensson (1989) in the zero-mean case. This result has an important policy implication. *Even a very tight target zone provides some room for the fundamentals to move about*: the bounds on the fundamentals are two orders of magnitude wider apart than the bounds on the exchange rate! As compared to a strict fixed-rate system, in which fundamentals would be absolutely immutable, a narrow target zone buys a lot of temporary flexibility. Foreign exchange traders do not move the exchange rate in response to a deviation in the fundamentals precisely because, under the target zone intervention policy, they know that this deviation is temporary. The anticipated reversion in the fundamentals, which is bound to be triggered in the near future, is what keeps the current exchange rate from reacting to the current value of the fundamentals.

As a function of fundamentals, the interest differential, as we narrow the band, has a smaller and smaller flat section over the range within which fundamentals are allowed to oscillate without intervention. In Figure 4.4, drawn for a given narrow band, the interest differential is practically a straight line at an angle equal to $-1/\gamma$. Hence, as in Svensson (1989), fundamentals volatility translates one-for-one into interest-rate volatility, provided the economy is *inside* the band; in fact, the standard deviation of the differential, conditional on being at a given point in the band, grows monotonically as one narrows the band.

But, of course, as the band narrows, the supports of the probability distribution of the fundamentals and the interest rate differential shrink dramatically. The overall, unconditional variability of the differential approaches zero as the band shrinks. This fact is vividly illustrated by

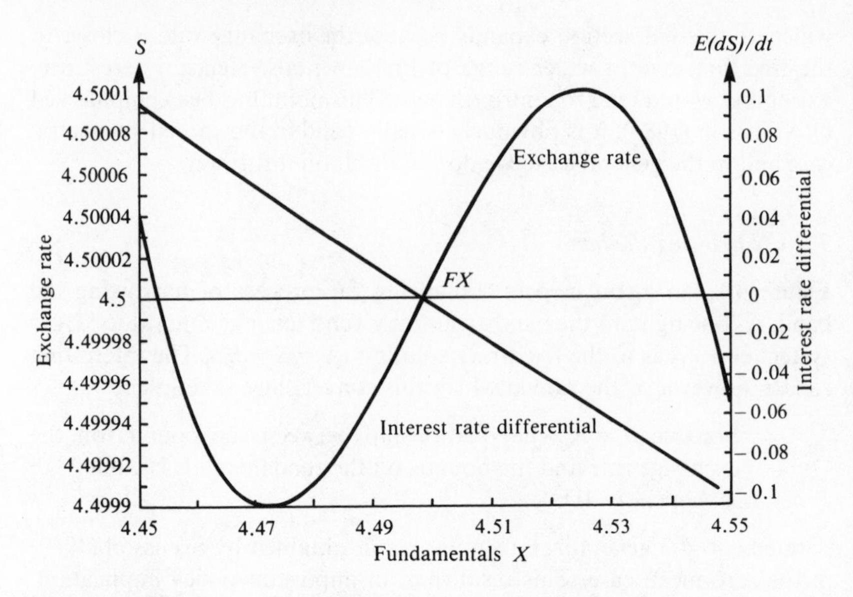

Figure 4.4 Exchange rate and interest rate differential. (Narrow band of width 4.5001–4.4999)
When the band is narrow as in the case of this figure ($\underline{S} = 4.4999$, $\bar{S} = 4.5001$), the exchange-rate curve is S-shaped and is situated far from the free-float line. The interest-rate curve is practically a straight line reflecting the imminent intervention. Numerical values of parameters are: $\sigma^2 = 0.25$, $\mu = 0.5$ and $\gamma = 0.5$.

Figure 4.2, which also illustrates the rate at which convergence to zero variability takes place. Recall that this figure shows the extreme values of the differential against the extreme values of the fundamentals. The range of fluctuations of the differential drops precipitously as the band is tightened.

4 Mean-reverting fundamentals

In this section we set up and solve an exchange rate system similar to the fixed trend fundamentals but with a crucial difference: the assumed process for the cumulative disturbance v is mean-reverting,[5] as in equation (3). A mean-reverting supply disturbance is particularly interesting to study if v is interpreted as a supply shock, as it can represent an error-correction policy on the part of the authorities. In particular, intervention on the part of Central banks within the band, prior to reaching the edges, can be modelled that way. This interpretation would fit the fact that 85% of all EMS intervention is done intramarginally. In the earlier constant-drift specification (Sections 2 and 3), it has been possible to interpret v

interchangeably as a demand or as a supply shock (see Appendix 4A). In the present case, we are going to distinguish the two interpretations carefully.

4.1 The model

Exchange rate Equation (1) remains in force, but, in place of Equation (2), stochastic differential Equation (3) characterizes the process followed by v. a_0 is the long-run level of accumulated shocks and ρ is the speed with which the process tends toward this value. This equation implies that the process followed by $X = m - m^* + v$ is given by:

$$dX = -\rho(X - A_0) + \sigma dW - dU + dL \tag{16}$$

where $A_0 = a_0 + m - m^*$. We now distinguish two interpretations of the model.

Interpretation # 1: v is a demand shock. The mean-reverting process for v translates into a similar mean-reverting process for X. However, while a_0 is a constant, the reversion point A_0 for X is not immutable. U and L have the same interpretation as before. Every time intervention is activated at the boundaries, $m - m^*$ changes value and affects A_0. A_0 becomes in effect a new state variable of the system, one, however, which changes only at the boundaries. The initial condition is still $X_0 = m_0 - m_0^* + v_0$.

Interpretation # 2: v is a supply shock reflecting intramarginal intervention. Here again, the mean-reverting process for v translates into a similar mean-reverting process for X. The difference with interpretation # 1 arises in the joint behaviour of a_0 and A_0. We are no longer forced to consider that A_0 varies over time. If the authorities have decided to enforce, by marginal intervention, a target zone centered on S_0, it would be inconsistent for them to let the target point of the intramarginal intervention wander away from some preset level; they must therefore adjust a_0 as $m - m^*$ changes to keep A_0 constant. This preset level is likely to be precisely $A_0 = S_0$.

Under both interpretations, the differential equation implied by (1) and the process for X given in (16) is:[6]

$$S(X) = X - \gamma\rho(X - A_0)S'(X) + 0.5\gamma\sigma^2 S''(X) \tag{17}$$

A change of variable $Y = \rho(A_0 - X)^2/\sigma^2$ turns equation (17) into Kummer's equation.[7] The general solution of differential equation (17) is:

$$\begin{aligned} S(Y(X)) = {} & (X + A_0\rho\gamma)/(1 + \rho\gamma) + C_1 M[1/2\rho\gamma;\ 0.5;\ Y] \\ & + C_2 M[(1 + \rho\gamma)/2\rho\gamma;\ 1.5;\ Y]\sqrt{\rho}(A_0 - X)/\sigma \end{aligned} \tag{18}$$

where $M[\cdot;\ \cdot;\ \cdot]$ is the confluent hypergeometric function (HGF); C_1 and C_2 are constants of integration to be determined by boundary behaviour as in Section 2.

4.2 Solutions

The *free float* solution – corresponding to a regime of no marginal intervention – is given by the first term in (18), a straight line in Figures 4.5 and 6. Unlike the fixed trend fundamental case, this line is not fixed. Its position (but not its slope) depends, via the variable A_0 on the two money supplies and therefore on the two Central banks' levels of assets (including reserves).

The *target zone policy* implies, as before, the solution of a system of four equations with four unknowns C_1, C_2, $\bar{X}$, $\underline{X}$, given the choice of exchange rate bounds.

$$S(Y(\bar{X})) = \bar{S} \tag{19}$$

$$S(Y(\underline{X})) = \underline{S} \tag{20}$$

$$S'(Y(\bar{X})) = 0 \tag{21}$$

$$S'(Y(\underline{X})) = 0 \tag{22}$$

Consider first *the symmetric case*, in which exchange rate bounds are placed at an equal distance from the mean-reversion point A_0. Direct observation of equation (18) allows one to conclude that the integration constant C_1 must be equal to zero, since it is the coefficient of the only non-symmetric term. Let $S_0 = A_0$, $\bar{X} = A_0 + \delta$, $\underline{X} = A_0 - \delta$ and $\bar{S} = S_0 + \epsilon$, $\underline{S} = S_0 - \epsilon$. The variable δ must be determined as a function of ϵ, the distance of the bounds from $S_0 = A_0$. The system reduces to one of two equations with two unknowns C_2 and δ.

$$\begin{aligned} S_0 + \epsilon = {} & (S_0 + \delta + A_0\rho\gamma)/(1 + \rho\gamma) \\ & - C_2 M[(1 + \rho\gamma)/2\rho\gamma;\ 1.5;\ \bar{Y}]\ \sqrt{\rho}\delta/\sigma \end{aligned} \tag{23}$$

$$\begin{aligned} 0 = {} & 1/(1 + \rho\gamma) - C_2(\sqrt{\rho}/\sigma)\{M[(1 + \rho\gamma)/2\rho\gamma;\ 1.5;\ \bar{Y}] \\ & + 2\bar{Y}[(1 + \rho\gamma)/2\rho\gamma]M[(1 + 3\rho\gamma)/2\rho\gamma;\ 2.5;\ \bar{Y}]\} \end{aligned} \tag{24}$$

where $\bar{Y} = \rho\delta^2/\sigma^2$. Given S_0 and the halfwidth of the band (ϵ) we can obtain C_2 and δ.

Under interpretation # 2 with $A_0 = S_0$ the symmetric case is perfectly natural. Under interpretation # 1, however, it is very special: even if an exchange rate system starts in a symmetric situation, the first time one country intervenes to maintain the exchange rate within the specified bands, the symmetry will have been eliminated because the mean reversion point A_0 will have been shifted.[8]

It is therefore essential to solve the *non-symmetric case* as well. For that purpose we define some functions:

$$Y(X) = \rho(A_0 - X)^2/\sigma^2 \tag{25}$$

$$M_1(Y) = M[1/2\rho\gamma;\ 0.5;\ Y]$$

$$M_2(Y) = M[(1+\rho\gamma)/2\rho\gamma;\ 1.5;\ Y]$$

$$M_3(Y) = M[(1+2\rho\gamma)/2\rho\gamma;\ 1.5;\ Y]$$

$$M_4(Y) = M[(1+3\rho\gamma)/2\rho\gamma;\ 2.5;\ Y]$$

$$M_5(Y) = M[(1+4\rho\gamma)/2\rho\gamma;\ 2.5;\ Y]$$

$$M_6(Y) = M[(1+5\rho\gamma)/2\rho\gamma;\ 3.5;\ Y]$$

$$N_1(Y) = M_1(Y(X))$$

$$N_2(Y) = M_2(Y)\ \sqrt{\rho}(A_0 - X)/\sigma$$

$$NP_1(Y) = -2[(A_0 - X)/\gamma\sigma^2]M_3(Y)$$

$$NP_2(Y) = -(\sqrt{\rho})/\sigma\{M_2(Y) + 2Y[(1+\rho\gamma)/3\rho\gamma]M_4(Y)\}$$

$$NPP_1(Y) = (2/\gamma\sigma^2)M_3(Y) + 4Y[(1+2\rho\gamma)/(3\rho\gamma^2\sigma^2)]M_5(Y)$$

$$NPP_2(Y) = 2\rho\sqrt{Y}[(1+\rho\gamma)/(3\rho\gamma\sigma^2)]\{3M_4(Y) + 2Y[(1+3\rho\gamma)/(5\rho\gamma)]M_6(Y)\}$$

N_1 and N_2 are the last two functional forms in the solution (19); NP_1 and NP_2 are their first derivatives and NPP_1 and NPP_2 their second derivatives.

With these definitions and some algebra to eliminate the constants of integration in the system (19)–(22) we can write a non-linear system of two variables with two unknowns for $\bar{X}$ and $\underline{X}$, to be solved for given values of $\bar{S}$ and $\underline{S}$:

$$\begin{bmatrix} \bar{X} + A_0 - \bar{S}(1+\rho\gamma) \\ \underline{X} + A_0 - \underline{S}(1+\rho\gamma) \end{bmatrix} = \begin{bmatrix} N_1(\bar{X}) & N_2(\bar{X}) \\ N_1(\underline{X}) & N_2(\underline{X}) \end{bmatrix} \begin{bmatrix} NP_1(\bar{X}) & NP_2(\bar{X}) \\ NP_1(\underline{X}) & NP_2(\underline{X}) \end{bmatrix}^{-1} \begin{bmatrix} 1 \\ 1 \end{bmatrix} \tag{26}$$

We now draw the implications of this system.

5 Limiting properties of target zones under mean-reverting fundamentals

The set of target zones of different widths is pictured as the TT' locus in Figures 4.5 and 6. These figures are laid out exactly like Figure 4.1 but under the assumption of a variable drift. Figure 4.5 depicts the 'symmetric' mean-reversion case in which the exchange rate bands are centered, and then widened or narrowed, around the long-run mean-reversion point for fundamentals ($S_0 = A_0$), while Figure 4.6 depicts the general case in which the same is done around an arbitrary point.

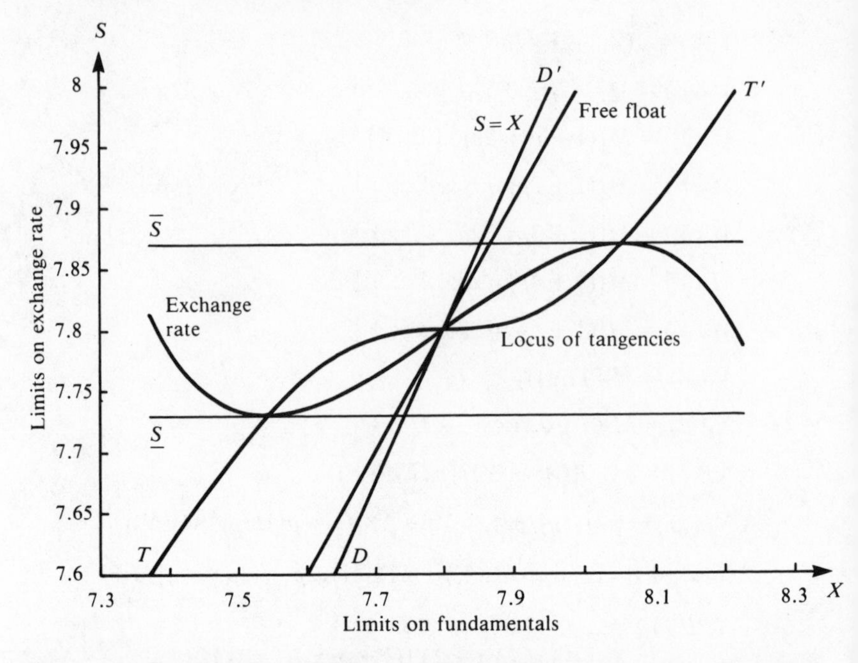

Figure 4.5 Target zones of different widths: mean-reverting case. (Symmetric solution: $A_0 = 7.8$)
The figure is constructed by changing the width of the band around $S_0 = A_0 = 7.8$. This means solving the system (26) for different values of $\bar{S}$ and $\underline{S}$ *positioned symmetrically around* $S_0 = A_0$. The two straight lines in the middle are the diagonal line DD', where $S = X$, which contains the fixed exchange points, and the free float which is flatter than DD' in this case. The s-shaped curve is an example of an exchange rate curve. The curve TT' is the locus of tangencies implied by the smooth-pasting conditions. Points above S_0 are pairs $(\bar{X}, \bar{S})$; points below S_0 are pairs $(\underline{X}, \underline{S})$. Observe the flatness of the locus around 7.8. Numerical values of parameters are: $\rho = 0.5$, $\sigma^2 = 0.2$, $A_0 = 7.8$ and $\gamma = 0.5$. Units on the two axes are not the same.

A comparison with the constant-trend case seems worthwhile at this point. For this purpose, one would calibrate a constant-trend analysis to match the values of the drift at the centre of the band (e.g. we pick $\mu = 0$ in the symmetric case). It would be found that the constant-trend locus so calibrated is not uniformly inside or outside the mean-reversion locus. One might expect that the market would tolerate wider bands – i.e. wider deviations in the fundamentals – when the disturbance is known to have a temporary component than when it is permanent. In fact, the mean-reversion bounds on the fundamentals are inside the mean-reversion bounds for moderate size bands; they are outside them, as expected, only when the band is wide enough.

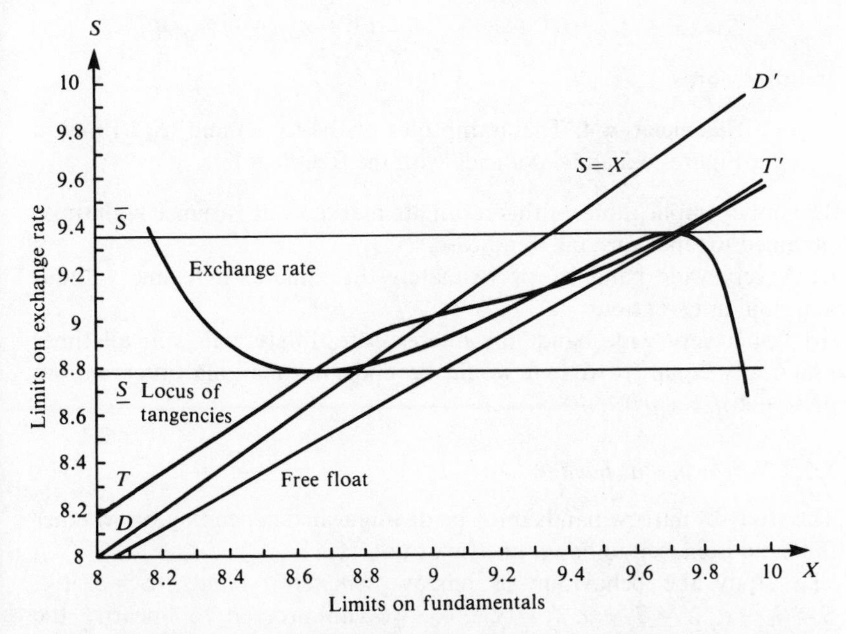

Figure 4.6 Target zones of different widths: mean-reverting non-symmetric case
This figure is similar to Figure 4.5. While the reversion point A_0 is still equal to 4.8, the centre of the exchange rate band is now at $S_0 = 9$. The free-float lines and the diagonal DD', where $S = X$, would intersect at 7.8. The s-shaped curve is an example of an exchange rate curve. The curve TT' is the locus of tangencies implied by the smooth-pasting conditions. Observe that the locus is not flat around the central point $S_0 = 9$.

For the analysis of limiting properties of target zones, the following asymptotic values of the HGF will be useful:[9]

(i) For small Y we can approximate

$$M[a;\, b;\, Y] = 1 + (a/b)\, Y \tag{27}$$

(ii) For large Y we can approximate

$$M[a;\, b;\, Y] = [\Gamma(b)/\Gamma(a)] e^{Y} Y^{a-b}\{1 + o|Y|^{-1}\} \tag{28}$$

5.1 *Widening the band*

The solution of (26) for any band produces a relationship which links the positioning of the band in the fundamentals dimension to the centre and width of the band in the exchange dimension. Using the limiting value of (28) of this HGF, this relationship, at either end, is found to be:

$$\bar{S} = (\bar{X} + A_0\rho\gamma)/(1 + \rho\gamma) \qquad \underline{S} = (\underline{X} + A_0\rho\gamma)/(1 + \rho\gamma) \tag{29}$$

In other words:

> **Statement # 4**: The asymptotes of the $(\bar{S}, \bar{X})$ and $(\underline{S}, \underline{X})$ loci in Figures 4.5 and 6 coincide with the free-float line.

The policy implications of this result are markedly at variance with those obtained for the constant-trend case:[10]
(i) A very wide band is approximately the same as a regime without marginal intervention:
(ii) For a very wide band, the interest-rate differential is at all times practically equal to what it would be under no marginal intervention: $\rho(A_0 - X)/(1 + \rho\gamma)$.

5.2 *Narrowing the band*

The study of narrow bands must be distinguished depending on whether the band is chosen to be symmetric or not.

To study the behaviour of narrow *symmetric* bands ($\bar{S} = S_0 + \epsilon$, $\underline{S} = \underline{S_0} - \epsilon$; $\bar{X} = S_0 + \delta$, $\underline{X} = S_0 - \delta$), we can proceed to linearize the system (19)–(22) using the expansion (27) of the HGF. This will give us a system of two equations with two unknowns. Solving for the constant of integration C_2 from (24) and replacing it in (23) yields the following equation which links the distance δ of the limits on fundamentals with the width ϵ of the band.

$$\epsilon = \frac{\delta}{1 + \rho\gamma} - \frac{\delta + \delta^3(1 + \rho\gamma)/(3\sigma^2\gamma)}{(1 + \rho\gamma)[1 + \delta^2((1 + \rho\gamma)/(\sigma^2\gamma))]} \tag{30}$$

or, simplifying further:

$$\epsilon = (2/3)[(1 + \rho\gamma)/(\gamma\sigma^2)]\delta^3 \tag{31}$$

Hence:

> **Statement # 5**: In the case of narrow symmetric bands, the relationship between the bounds on fundamentals and the bounds on the exchange rate is cubic, as in the case of constant drift.

The fundamentals deviation δ is of order $|\epsilon|^{1/3}$ (witness the flat section of the double-sided locus in Figure 4.5 near point *FX*). The fundamentals, here again, have a lot of room to move about.

A comparison of Figures 4.5 and 6 around point *FX* provides a hint that this result does not survive to an asymmetry in the band. For the *asymmetric case* ($\bar{S} = S_0 + \epsilon$, $\underline{S} = S_0 - \epsilon$; $\bar{X} = S_0 + \bar{\delta}$, $\underline{X} = S_0 - \underline{\delta}$), the full system (26) is needed. Expand around S_0 using the previously defined functions:

$$N_1(\bar{X}) = N_1(S_0) + NP_1(S_0)\bar{\delta}$$

$$N_2(\bar{X}) = N_2(S_0) + NP_2(S_0)\bar{\delta}$$

$$NP_1(\bar{X}) = NP_1(S_0) + NPP_1(S_0)\bar{\delta}$$

$$NP_2(\bar{X}) = NP_2(S_0) + NPP_2(S_0)\bar{\delta}$$

$$N_1(\underline{X}) = N_1(S_0) - NP_1(S_0)\underline{\delta}$$

$$N_2(\underline{X}) = N_2(S_0) - NP_2(S_0)\underline{\delta}$$

$$NP_1(\underline{X}) = NP_1(S_0) - NPP_1(S_0)\underline{\delta}$$

$$NP_2(\underline{X}) = NP_2(S_0) - NPP_2(S_0)\underline{\delta}$$

where NPP_1 (resp. NPP_2) is the derivative of NP_1 (NP_2) with respect to X. Replacing in (26) we can solve for $\bar{\delta}$ and $\underline{\delta}$ and obtain:

$$\bar{\delta} = \underline{\delta} = 2\epsilon(1 + \rho\gamma)$$

or: $$\epsilon = \delta/2(1 + \rho\gamma) \tag{32}$$

This result is to be compared to equation (31) which was cubic in δ.

> **Statement # 6**: As soon as the band is not exactly centered on the reversion point, the relationship between the bounds on fundamentals and the bounds on the exchange rate is linear.

We lose the policy implication which said that fundamentals have room to move about even when the exchange rate band is narrow.

6 Conclusions

This paper has illustrated the trade-offs policy-makers would face when choosing the width of a band, or when converging to an extremely narrow band in order to shift to a single currency. These tradeoffs concern the degree of exchange-rate, interest-rate and fundamentals variability. They depend on the assumed process (constant drift or mean-reversion) for the disturbances which affect money demand and/or supply.

They also depend on the type of coordination which would take place in case of foreign exchange crisis. In this last respect, we have been careful to make Assumption 2 so as to avoid altogether the problem of speculative attacks and needed reserves. We have assumed that central banks credibly and unconditionally intervene so as prevent speculative attacks. Indefinite intervention is possible if the central bank of the currently strong currency supports the other currency by printing money.

We have generalized the result of Svensson (1989) that the variability of the exchange rate is translated into variability in the interest rate differential.

We have also found that the degree of fundamentals variability which would be tolerated by the market when a target zone is extremely narrow is very large (a difference of two orders of magnitude) in the case of a constant drift disturbance and in the case of mean-reversion with a band exactly centered on the reversion point. The result is lost if the band is not precisely centered there.

Appendix 4A: Model interpretation

It is possible to interpret v either as a supply or a demand shock. Consider the following two-country log-linear monetary exchange rate model which has been extensively used in recent work (see for example Delgado and Dumas, 1990, and all the references given there).

$$\tilde{m} = ln(D + R) + z_1 = m + z_1 \tag{A1}$$

$$\tilde{m}^* = ln(D^* + R^*) + z_1^* = m^* + z_1^* \tag{A2}$$

$$\tilde{m} - p = \psi y - \gamma i + z_2 \tag{A3}$$

$$\tilde{m}^* - p^* = \psi y^* - \gamma i^* + z_2^* \tag{A4}$$

$$i = i^* + E\{dS|\Phi(t)\}/dt + z_3 \tag{A5}$$

All starred variables are the foreign variables corresponding to the non-starred domestic variables. Z_1 being a multiplicative shock which affects $(D + R)$ and is assumed to follow a geometric Brownian motion process, z_1 is the log of Z_1.[11] $\tilde{m}$ is the total money supply, that can be broken down into two components, m the controllable money supply, and z_1 the uncontrollable component. The right-hand sides of equations (A3) and (A4) are money demands; z_2 and z_2^* are money demand shocks, p is the price level, y is domestic output and i is the domestic interest rate.

E is the expectations operator. $\Phi(t)$ is the information set used by economic agents to form their expectations. It includes, as Froot and Obstfeld (1989a, b) put it, all information regarding not only the evolution of the variables in the system (A1)–(A5), but the implicit as well as explicit government policies regarding exchange rate regimes in particular and monetary policy in general. Of importance for our purposes is the market perception that once the central bank whose currency is weak runs out of reserves, the other central bank will continue intervention to support the weak currency.

Subtracting (A3) from (A4) and replacing (A1), (A2) and (A3) we can obtain equation (1), where $v = (z_1 - z_1^*) + \psi(y - y^*) + (z_2 - z_2^*) + z_3$ is a cumulative shock. Given that v includes terms in z_1 and z_1^* it can be interpreted either as a demand or a supply shock to money.

Appendix 4B: Monotonic relationship between the band on fundamentals and the band on the exchange rate

For simplicity let us define the following functions:

$$NF(\bar{X}, \underline{X}) = -\beta e^{\alpha\bar{X} - \beta\underline{X}} - \alpha e^{\alpha\underline{X} - \beta\bar{X}} + (\alpha + \beta)e^{(\alpha - \beta)\bar{X}} \tag{B1}$$

$$NG(\bar{X}, \underline{X}) = \alpha e^{\alpha\bar{X} + \beta\underline{X}} + \beta e^{\alpha\underline{X} - \beta\bar{X}} - (\alpha + \beta)e^{(\alpha - \beta)\underline{X}} \tag{B2}$$

$$DF(\bar{X}, \underline{X}) = -\alpha\beta(e^{\alpha\bar{X} - \beta\underline{X}} - e^{\alpha\underline{X} - \beta\bar{X}}) \tag{B3}$$

$$F(\bar{X}, \underline{X}; \bar{S}, \underline{S}) = -\bar{X} + \bar{S} - \gamma\mu + NF(\bar{X}, \underline{X})/DF(\bar{X}, \underline{X}) = 0 \tag{B4}$$

$$G(\bar{X}, \underline{X}; \bar{S}, \underline{S}) = -\underline{X} + \underline{S} - \gamma\mu + NG(\bar{X}, \underline{X})/DF(\bar{X}, \underline{X}) = 0 \tag{B5}$$

Using the implicit function theorem for $F(\cdot) = 0$ and $G(\cdot) = 0$ we can obtain the two derivatives $\partial\bar{X}/\partial\bar{S}$ and $\partial\underline{X}/\partial\underline{S}$ which we are looking for.

Defining the following functions

$$F_{x1}(\cdot) = \partial F(\cdot)/\partial\bar{X} \tag{B6}$$

$$F_{x2}(\cdot) = \partial F(\cdot)/\partial\underline{X} \tag{B7}$$

$$G_{x1}(\cdot) = \partial G(\cdot)/\partial\bar{X} \tag{B8}$$

$$G_{x2}(\cdot) = \partial G(\cdot)/\partial\underline{X} \tag{B9}$$

$$F_{s1}(\cdot) = \partial F(\cdot)/\partial\bar{S} \tag{B10}$$

$$F_{s2}(\cdot) = \partial F(\cdot)/\partial\underline{S} \tag{B11}$$

we can determine the signs of the following expressions

$$\partial\bar{X}/\partial\bar{S} = \begin{bmatrix} F_{s1} & F_{x2} \\ G_{s1} & G_{x2} \end{bmatrix} / J \geq 0 \tag{B12}$$

$$\partial\underline{X}/\partial\underline{S} = \begin{bmatrix} F_{x1} & F_{s2} \\ G_{x1} & G_{s2} \end{bmatrix} / J \geqslant 0 \tag{B13}$$

where:

$$J = \begin{bmatrix} F_{x1} & F_{x2} \\ G_{x1} & G_{x2} \end{bmatrix} > 0 \tag{B14}$$

Replacing all definitions in (B12) and (B13), and remembering that $1/\alpha - 1/\beta = \gamma\mu$, we obtain the signs of the partial derivatives. Q.E.D.

Appendix 4C: Asymptotic behaviour for wide bands under constant drift

Let us call δ the joint asymptotic value of the distance of $\bar{X}$ from the diagonal line and of the distance of $\underline{X}$ from the free-float line; let us also call 2ϵ the width of the exchange rate band, $\bar{S} = S_0 + \epsilon$ and $\underline{S} = S_0 - \epsilon$. We have:

$$\bar{X} = S_0 + \epsilon + \delta$$

$$\underline{X} = S_0 - \epsilon - \gamma\mu - \delta \qquad \text{and}$$

$$\underline{X} = \bar{X} - 2(\epsilon + \delta) - \gamma\mu$$

To study the behaviour of wide bands we can substitute these relationships into (14), simplify, and neglect terms that approach zero as we make $\delta, \epsilon \to \infty$. We obtain a simple relationship:[12]

$$\delta = \epsilon - \gamma\mu + 1/a = \epsilon + 1/\beta \tag{C1}$$

Q.E.D.

Appendix 4D: Cubic relationship for narrow bands under constant drift

To obtain the relationship between the band on fundamentals and on the exchange rate we shall for narrow bands use a linear approximation to the exponential function:

$$e^{\lambda x} \approx 1 + \lambda x + (\lambda x)^2/2! + (\lambda x)^3/3! + \ldots \tag{D1}$$

The expansion is carried out as far as is needed. Additional terms are added if the prior order terms vanish or lead to an identity.

We proceed with the linearization around S_0. The four variables with respect to which the linearization is to be performed can be written as:

$$\bar{S} = S_0 + \epsilon \tag{D2}$$

$$\underline{S} = S_0 - \epsilon \tag{D3}$$

$$\bar{X} = S_0 + \bar{\delta} \tag{D4}$$

$$\underline{X} = S_0 - \underline{\delta} \tag{D5}$$

Replacing (D2)–(D5) in (14)–(15) the system is written as:

$$\bar{\delta} = \bar{\epsilon} - \gamma\mu + \frac{-\beta e^{a\bar{\delta} + \beta\underline{\delta}} - a e^{-(a\underline{\delta} + \beta\bar{\delta})} + (a + \beta) e^{(a - \beta)\bar{\delta}}}{-a\beta(e^{a\bar{\delta} + \beta\underline{\delta}} - e^{-(a\underline{\delta} + \beta\bar{\delta})})} \tag{D6}$$

$$\underline{X} = \underline{S} - \gamma\mu + \frac{a e^{a\bar{\delta} + \beta\underline{\delta}} + \beta e^{-(a\underline{\delta} + \beta\bar{\delta})} - (a + \beta) e^{-(a - \beta)\underline{\delta}}}{-a\beta(e^{a\bar{\delta} + \beta\underline{\delta}} - e^{-(a\underline{\delta} + \beta\bar{\delta})})} \tag{D7}$$

The last two equations can also be written in matrix form as

$$\begin{bmatrix} \epsilon \\ -\epsilon \end{bmatrix} = \begin{bmatrix} \gamma\mu + \bar{\delta} \\ \gamma\mu - \underline{\delta} \end{bmatrix} + \begin{bmatrix} e^{a\bar{\delta}} & e^{-\beta\bar{\delta}} \\ e^{-a\underline{\delta}} & e^{\beta\underline{\delta}} \end{bmatrix} \begin{bmatrix} 1/a & 0 \\ 0 & -1/\beta \end{bmatrix} \begin{bmatrix} e^{a\bar{\delta}} & e^{-\beta\bar{\delta}} \\ e^{-a\underline{\delta}} & e^{\beta\underline{\delta}} \end{bmatrix}^{-1} \begin{bmatrix} -1 \\ -1 \end{bmatrix} \tag{D8}$$

Using $\gamma\mu = 1/a - 1/\beta$ and expanding (D8), the following expression is obtained:

$$\epsilon \approx (a + \beta)^2 (\bar{\delta} + \underline{\delta})^3 / 12 \tag{D9}$$

Q.E.D.

NOTES

Parts of this paper were presented at a CEPR/NBER conference on 'Exchange Rate Targets and Currency Bands' held at the University of Warwick on 10 and 11 July 1990. We are grateful to participants at this conference and especially Leonardo Bartolini, Vittorio Grilli and Paul Krugman for their remarks.

1 Lewis (1990) models 'leaning against the wind' in a different manner.
2 We show below that the fixed rate regime is also the limit of a sequence of narrower and narrower bands.
3 Flood and Garber (1989) present a model in which the policy is not specified by infinitesimal interventions but by discrete ones. This implies the same exchange rate function for the same bounds placed on the exchange rate. The type of regulation implied by discrete interventions is called impulse control.
4 We also find below for the mean-reversion case that the relationship is cubic.
5 Other researchers have used this process: Dumas (1989), Miller and Weller (1988), Krugman and Rotemberg (1990) and Froot and Obstfeld (1989a).
6 This is, of course, after applying Ito's lemma, and assuming that $S(X)$ is twice continuously differentiable.
7 See Abramowitz and Stegun (1972), page 504.
8 For the same reason, the free-float locus moves whenever a country intervenes.
9 See Abramowitz and Stegun (1972), especially equations 13.1.2 and 13.1.4, page 504.
10 Also, under imperfect credibility (as in Delgado and Dumas, 1990), a very wide band would require no reserves, as there would be practically no risk of speculative attacks: under mean-reversion, reaching the edges of a very wide band becomes a zero-probability event. But this observation falls outside the topic of the present paper.
11 In the classic speculative attack literature (Krugman, 1979, and Flood and Garber, 1983; see also Dornbusch, 1984, and Claessens, 1986), shocks came from growth in domestic credit. In our formulation, the terms Z_1 and Z_1^* are shocks applied to the sum of R and D, not to D.
12 Svensson (1989) obtained a similar relationship for the special case of zero drift ($\mu = 0$) in which the two roots are of equal magnitude: $a = \beta$. The distance from the free-float (confounded in his case with the 45° line) was $1/a = -1/\beta$.

REFERENCES

Abramowitz, M. and I.A. Stegun (editors) (1972). *Handbook of Mathematical Functions*, New York: Dover.

Claessens, C. (1986). 'Balance of payments crises', Unpublished Dissertation, University of Pennsylvania.

Delgado, F. and B. Dumas (1990). 'Monetary contracting between central banks and the design of sustainable exchange-rate zones', Working Paper No. 3440, NBER. September.

Dornbusch, R. (1984). 'Collapsing exchange rate regimes', Working Paper, MIT.

Dumas, B. (1989). 'Hysteresis in capital formation', Wharton School working paper, July 1988, revised as: 'Perishable investment and hysteresis in capital formation', Working Paper No. 2930, NBER.

Flood, R.P. and P.M. Garber (1983). 'A model of stochastic process switching', *Econometrica* **51**, 537–52.

(1989). 'The linkage between speculative attack and target zone models of exchange rate', Working Paper No. 2918, NBER.

Froot, K.A. and M. Obstfeld (1989a). 'Stochastic process switching: some simple solutions', Working Paper No. 2998, NBER, also this volume, and *Econometrica* forthcoming.

(1989b). 'Exchange rate dynamics under stochastic regime shifts: a unified approach', mimeo, IMF.

Krugman, P. (1979). 'A model of balance-of-payments crisis', *Journal of Money Credit and Banking* **11**, 311–25.

(1991). 'Target zones and exchange rate dynamics', *Quarterly Journal of Economics*, forthcoming.

Krugman, P. and J. Rotemberg (1990). 'Target zones with limited reserves', NBER Working Paper No. 3418.

Lewis, K. (1990). 'Occasional interventions to target rates with a foreign exchange application', Working Paper, New York University.

Miller, M. and P. Weller (1988). 'Target zones, currency options and monetary policy', mimeo, University of Warwick.

Svensson, L.E.O. (1989). 'Target zones and interest rate variability: where does the variability go, and is a fixed exchange rate regime the limit of a narrow target zone?', mimeo, Institute for International Economic Studies, University of Stockholm.

Discussion

LEONARDO BARTOLINI

Delgado and Dumas' paper focuses on extending previous results on the asymptotic behaviour of target zones to a Brownian motion process with non-zero drift and to the case of a mean-reverting process.

With respect to the extension to the case of non-zero drift Brownian motion, I am left with the impression that the advance is essentially technical. It is true that when μ is different from zero, one faces the situation of a currency which is inherently weak (or strong); but this does not seem to lead to qualitative analytical changes. Things would be different if we were considering the case of a country endowed with limited reserves – the subject of a related paper by the same authors – but not here, under the maintained assumption that concerted intervention will sustain the target zone indefinitely.

The case of a mean-reverting process is, however, both analytically more interesting and empirically more relevant. As the authors suggest, a mean-reverting process for fundamentals may be a reasonably realistic and analytically tractable way to capture that conglomerate of rules of thumb which European Central Banks follow when intervening intramarginally. I found the discussion of the two possible interpretations of the model – in terms of either supply or demand shocks – illuminating. I have myself used mean-reverting processes for fundamentals, while routinely assuming that invariance of the attractor for the exchange rate would imply invariance of the attractor for fundamentals: the paper's discussion has convinced me that I was implicitly assuming supply-side shocks.

From an empirical point of view, it is an unfortunate feature of the model that for several countries in the EMS (most notably France, Italy and – the standard of reference – Germany) simply increasing the degree of reversion towards the central parity makes it more difficult for the model to match the observed pattern of forward premia. If the assumed uncontrolled process for fundamentals is already mean-reverting, superimposing the control of a credible target zone – within which a weak currency is expected to appreciate, and vice versa – will generate an increasingly downward sloped curve for interest rate differentials, which is in many cases unrealistic. So the imposition of a mean-reverting process for fundamentals makes more pressing the need to consider models of non-credible target zones, or of stochastic devaluation (to cite only two possible solutions to the interest rate differential puzzle).

From an analytical standpoint, on the other hand, it is indeed remarkable that characterisation results of the type of statements #4 and #5 can be obtained; more often than not a closed-form solution is all that can be hoped for. In this respect, this paper should represent a useful reference for related research.

More specifically, I find that the result that, for mean-reverting fundamentals, the relationship linking the bounds on fundamentals to those on the exchange rate is still cubic, the most interesting in the paper. Related work by Svensson and by Dixit (the latter in the context of investment hysteresis) had already obtained this for the case of simple Brownian motion; but the extension to the mean-reverting case is novel. It is a pity that this property is lost in the more general case of non-symmetric bands; this should – if nothing else – serve as a warning that the cubic relationship may in many cases be a peculiar offspring of the model's specification.

A topic for further research, implicitly suggested by this paper, would be to examine the asymptotic properties of *finite-maturity* interest rate differentials, so as to verify which of the results obtained for *instantaneous* interest rate differentials hold for this empirically more relevant case. (Capital flows have been observed to be most sensitive to changes in the one- to three-month interest rates.) In this case, however, the differential equation characterising the interest rate differential becomes a partial differential equation (which includes the time-to-maturity of the forward contract as an additional variable). But the authors' proofs may possibly be mimicked for the case of perfectly credible target zones, since upon separation of variables the differential equation characterising the forward rate can still be integrated by confluent hypergeometric functions, and set up as infinite Fourier series, subject to the same smooth-pasting boundary conditions. Substantially more difficulty will arise in the case of imperfectly credible target zones (of the type discussed by Bertola and Caballero, for instance), as closed-form solutions for the forward rate appear in general elusive when jumps at the barrier are assumed.

As a contribution to the target zone literature, this paper will doubtless prove a useful reference for those seeking the effects of making alternative hypotheses about the process governing fundamentals.

PART III
REGIME SHIFTS: THE RETURN TO GOLD AND EMS ENTRY

5 Stochastic process switching: some simple solutions

KENNETH A. FROOT and
MAURICE OBSTFELD

1 Introduction

Economists have recently begun to explore the effects of prospective regime changes on forward-looking variables. In an example inspired by Britain's return to the gold standard in 1925, Flood and Garber (1983) study the case in which an asset price (specifically, the exchange rate) floats freely until it reaches a pre-announced level, at which time the government intervenes to keep it fixed thereafter. They show how a first-stopping time methodology can be applied to their problem, but are unable to derive a closed-form solution using that relatively cumbersome technique.

In this paper we apply techniques of regulated Brownian motion to derive easy solutions for a large class of regime-switching problems, including the one posed by Flood and Garber (1983).[1] The technical approach we use has several advantages over the alternatives. First, and most important, the method is both simpler and more helpful for understanding the intuition behind the mathematics. Second, it clarifies the economic similarities between Flood–Garber process switches and other types of stochastic regime change. Finally, the approach allows us to be precise about potential indeterminacies in asset prices that can crop up when policy makers do not fully specify how they intend to achieve their economic targets.[2]

The rest of the paper is structured as follows. In Section 2 we lay out a very general exchange-rate model. Section 3 contains solutions to several specific process-switching examples, and it also discusses how some formulations of future policy intentions may leave asset prices underdetermined.

2 The model

To keep the analysis simple, we use the standard flexible-price monetary model of the exchange rate.[3] In this framework, the (log) spot exchange rate at time t, $x(t)$, is the sum of a scalar indicator of macroeconomic fundamentals, $k(t)$, plus a speculative term proportional to the expected percentage change in the exchange rate:

$$x(t) = k(t) + aE(dx(t) \mid \phi(t))/dt \tag{1}$$

Above, the exchange rate $x(t)$ is the domestic-currency price of foreign currency. Included among the fundamental factors that affect $k(t)$ is a variable measuring the domestic money supply relative to the foreign money supply. Money supplies are assumed to be controlled directly by monetary authorities; but other, exogenous determinants of exchange rates that the authorities cannot control directly may influence $k(t)$ as well.

The parameter a in (1) can be interpreted as the semi-elasticity of money demand with respect to the interest rate; E is the expectations operator; and $\phi(t)$ is the time-t information set, which includes the current value of fundamentals, $k(t)$, as well as any explicit or implicit restrictions the authorities have placed on the future evolution of fundamentals. For example, if the authorities have announced that they will fix the exchange rate once it reaches a certain level, this information would be incorporated into $\phi(t)$.

The monetary authorities may intervene to influence exchange rates by altering the stochastic process governing (relative) money-supply growth. This in turn will alter the process driving the fundamentals, $k(t)$. A regime of freely floating exchange rates is said to be in effect when the authorities refrain from intervening to offset shocks to fundamentals. Under a free float, we assume that the fundamentals evolve according to the process

$$dk(t) = \eta\, dt + \sigma\, dz(t) \tag{2}$$

where η is the (constant) predictable change in k, dz is a standard Wiener process, and σ is a constant. Equation (2) is just the continuous-time version of a random walk with trend.[4] As noted above, the authorities can control k through intervention, so k need not follow (2) under regimes other than a free float.

In a rational-expectations equilibrium with no speculative bubbles, there is a unique exchange-rate path that satisfies (1). This path has the integral representation

$$x(t) = a^{-1} \int_t^{\infty} e^{(t-s)/a} E(k(s) \mid \phi(t))\, ds \tag{3}$$

a representation valid under *any* policy regime or sequence of policy regimes. In words, (3) equates the current exchange rate to the present discounted value of expected future fundamentals (the discount rate is $1/a$). We refer to the equilibrium exchange rate, given by the present-value formula (3), as the *saddlepath* exchange rate.[5]

Given (2) and the types of regime change we will consider, it is reasonable to suppose that the saddlepath exchange rate can be written as a twice continuously differentiable function of a single variable, the current fundamental

$$x(t) = S(k(t)) \tag{4}$$

Naturally, the precise form of the function $S(k)$ depends (as is demonstrated below) on the nature of the regime shifts that the market thinks are possible.

A well-known special case is the one in which the authorities are committed to a *permanent* exchange-float, so that fundamentals are expected to follow process (2) forever. In this case, the conditional expectations in (3) are easy to evaluate, since they depend exclusively on current fundamentals, and not on possible future regime shifts. The saddlepaths exchange rate $S(k(t))$ is given by

$$a^{-1}\int_t^\infty e^{(t-s)/a}E(k(s)\,|\,k(t))\,ds$$

$$= a^{-1}\int_t^\infty e^{(t-s)/a}(k(t) + (s-t)\eta)\,ds = k(t) + a\eta \tag{5}$$

If, however, the market expects the authorities to alter (2) in the future, the exchange rate need not satisfy (5), even while allowed to float. In such cases, direct computation of the sequence of conditional expectations in the present-value formula (3) is likely to be burdensome. We therefore follow an alternative, two-step approach to determine $S(k)$ when a regime switch from (2) to some other process is possible. First, we characterize the family of functions of form $x = G(k)$ that satisfy the equilibrium condition (1) so long as fundamentals evolve according to (2). Second, we find the member of this family that satisfies boundary conditions appropriate to the stochastic regime switch under consideration. This last function is the saddlepath solution, $S(k)$.

To implement step one of the procedure outlined above – finding the general solution $x = G(k)$ – use Ito's lemma and equation (1) to express expected depreciation during the float as[6]

$$E(dx\,|\,\phi)/dt = E(dG(k)\,|\,\phi)/dt = \eta G'(k) + \frac{\sigma^2}{2}G''(k) \tag{6}$$

where we have assumed $G(k)$ is twice continuously differentiable. Combining (1) and (6) yields a second-order differential equation that the exchange rate in (1) and (3) must satisfy:

$$G(k) = k + a\eta G'(k) + \frac{a\sigma^2}{2} G''(k) \tag{7}$$

The general solution to (7) is

$$G(k) = k + a\eta + A_1 e^{\lambda_1 k} + A_2 e^{\lambda_2 k} \tag{8}$$

where $\lambda_1 > 0$ and $\lambda_2 < 0$ are the roots of the quadratic equation in λ,

$$\lambda^2 a\sigma^2/2 + \lambda a\eta - 1 = 0 \tag{9}$$

where A_1 and A_2 are constants of integration. Equation (8) forms the basis of our analysis below. As just discussed, a lone member of the family defined by (8) will turn out to be equivalent to the present-value formula for x in (3), and this function is just the saddlepath function, $S(k)$.

Notice that the general solution (8) consists of two components: one is linear, and the other is nonlinear, in k. The linear part, $k + a\eta$, would be the standard linear saddlepath solution if no change in the fundamentals process (2) were possible, so that a free float were permanently in effect (see equation (5)). When there is a possibility of regime switching, however, fundamentals may *not* remain permanently a random walk with trend, and the present-value formula (3) therefore need *not* equal (5). Under prospective regime switches, the exchange rate's saddlepath value will generally depend on the nonlinear terms in (8). Just which initial conditions A_1 and A_2 are appropriate depends on the boundary conditions associated with the regime switch, conditions to be determined in step two of the two-step solution procedure outlined above.

3 Stochastic process switching

This section carries out the second step of the solution method outlined in the last section. As an example of the simplicity of the technique, we solve the problem posed by Flood and Garber (1983). In terms of the mathematics, all that is involved is the appropriate choice of the two arbitrary constants in (8), A_1 and A_2.

3.1 Deriving a closed-form solution

Suppose that the authorities wish to let the exchange rate float until it reaches a lower or an upper level, $\underline{x}$ or $\bar{x}$, at which time they plan to fix x permanently. How does the rate behave prior to pegging? This class of problems is a generalization of that posed by Flood and Garber (1983), who are concerned with the behaviour of a floating exchange rate when the authorities plan to switch to a fixed-rate regime at a single, predetermined level of the exchange rate. We return to a more detailed discussion of their formulation at the end of this subsection. Our rationale for looking at a more general problem first is that its solution will clarify the economics of more specialized (and realistic) cases.

One way for the authorities to enforce their policy is to place lower and upper limits, $\underline{k}$ and $\bar{k}$, on the *fundamentals*, and to freeze fundamentals when one of these bounds is reached. This policy implies that $\underline{k}$ and $\bar{k}$ must be *absorbing* barriers on the fundamentals. Thus, if $S(k)$ is monotonically increasing in k (as turns out to be the case in equilibrium), then as long as k moves between the absorbing barriers $\underline{k}$ and $\bar{k}$, the exchange rate will float between the lower and upper values $\underline{x} = S(\underline{k})$ and $\bar{x} = S(\bar{k})$ until it reaches one of them.

Expectations about the way future regime shifts will be implemented are actually quite important in determining the exchange rate's saddlepath. For now we stay with the formulation of the previous paragraph, which is the same as the one used by Flood and Garber in their calculations. In particular, the assumption that the absorbing barriers are set as just described implies that the fundamentals will not jump at the moment of transition. As the next subsection shows, this restriction may be relaxed, but doing so will change the equilibrium exchange-rate path.

To determine exchange-rate behaviour during the initial float, we solve for the exchange-rate path that satisfies (1), given that (2) holds for $k \in (\underline{k}, \bar{k})$ and that $\underline{k}$ and $\bar{k}$ are absorbing barriers. The saddlepath solution is a special case of (3)

$$
\begin{aligned}
x(t) &= S(k(t)) \\
&= a^{-1} \int_t^{\infty} e^{(t-s)/a} E(k(s) \mid k(t),\, k(s) \in [\underline{k}_a, \bar{k}_a])\, ds \qquad (10)
\end{aligned}
$$

where the a subscript denotes that the barriers on fundamentals are absorbing. As noted in Section 2, direct evaluation of the conditional expectation in (10) is much more difficult than for the permanent free float (equation (5)): the bounds on fundamentals imply that the saddlepath exchange rate $S(k)$ generally is no longer a purely linear function of k.

We have already taken the first step toward solving the problem by deriving the general nonlinear solution $x = G(k)$ given by (8). Some member of this family of solutions must characterize exchange-rate behaviour when k is *in the interior of* $[\underline{k}, \bar{k}]$, where (1) and (2) hold simultaneously. A nontrivial logical gap must be bridged, however, before concluding that equation (8) is also relevant *at the boundary* of this interval, that is, at the barriers $k = \underline{k}$ and $k = \bar{k}$. The needed bridge is supplied by the fact that the saddlepath solution $S(k)$ is *continuous* on the entire interval $[\underline{k}, \bar{k}]$. Continuity of $S(k)$ ensures that if that function coincides with a continuous function of form $G(k)$ on the interior of an interval, it coincides with the same function at the edges.[7]

All that remains, then, is to determine the boundary conditions on $G(k)$, which deliver unique values for the undetermined coefficients A_1 and A_2 in (8), and therefore tie down uniquely the member of the class $G(k)$ that coincides with $S(k)$. But the boundary values of integral (10) are easily found; by our choice of the barriers, they are[8]

$$S(\underline{k}) = a^{-1} \int_t^{\infty} e^{(t-s)/a} E(k(s) \mid k(t) = \underline{k}_a)\, ds$$

$$= a^{-1} \int_t^{\infty} e^{(t-s)/a} \underline{k}\, ds = \underline{k} = \underline{x} \tag{11}$$

$$S(\bar{k}) = a^{-1} \int_t^{\infty} e^{(t-s)/a} E(k(s) \mid k(t) = \bar{k}_a)\, ds$$

$$= a^{-1} \int_t^{\infty} e^{(t-s)/a} \bar{k}\, ds = \bar{k} = \bar{x} \tag{12}$$

Combining (8) with (11) and (12) leads to the desired equations for A_1 and A_2

$$a\eta + A_1 e^{\lambda_1 \underline{k}} + A_2 e^{\lambda_2 \underline{k}} = 0 \tag{13}$$

$$a\eta + A_1 e^{\lambda_1 \bar{k}} + A_2 e^{\lambda_2 \bar{k}} = 0 \tag{14}$$

These two expressions give the following proposition:

Proposition 1. When fundamentals follow (2) within the absorbing barriers $\underline{k}$ and $\bar{k}$, the saddlepath solution (10) is

$$x = S(k)$$

$$= k + a\eta \left(1 + \frac{e^{\lambda_2 \bar{k} + \lambda_1 k} - e^{\lambda_2 \underline{k} + \lambda_1 k} + e^{\lambda_1 \underline{k} + \lambda_2 k} - e^{\lambda_1 \bar{k} + \lambda_2 k}}{e^{\lambda_2 \underline{k} + \lambda_1 \bar{k}} - e^{\lambda_2 \bar{k} + \lambda_1 \underline{k}}}\right) \tag{15}$$

If we let the lower bound, $\underline{k}$, go to minus infinity, (15) simplifies to:

$$x = k + a\eta(1 - e^{\lambda_1 (k - \bar{k})}) \tag{16}$$

If in addition the upper bound, $\bar{k}$, goes to infinity, we get the familiar linear solution (5):

$$x = k + a\eta \tag{17}$$

When both boundaries are infinitely distant the exchange rate is linear in fundamentals.

The saddlepath solution given in the proposition is of the form hypothesized earlier: it is a function of the current state k and the two barriers. It is also straightforward to verify that $S(k)$ is monotonically increasing over its domain, as claimed earlier.

To understand the economics of the foregoing proposition, consider first the simple case in which fundamentals have no trend, $\eta = 0$. The exchange rate then is simply equal to current fundamentals: $x = k$. To understand why, notice that when $\eta = 0$, the expected growth of fundamentals always is zero – at as well as within the absorbing barriers. Thus, the best forecast of all future fundamentals is just today's value of k; and the conditional expectations in (3), as well as the exchange rate, all equal current k.

Matters are more complicated when $\eta > 0$, so we use Figure 5.1 to illustrate. The line labelled *FF* indicates the linear solution given by (5), which corresponds to the case $A_1 = A_2 = 0$. (*FF* is the saddlepath under a permanent free-float regime.) The figure shows two exchange rate paths with the same upper bound, but different lower bounds. Path 1 depicts the behaviour of x when the absorbing barriers are the points $\underline{k}$ and $\bar{k}$. Path 2 is drawn to correspond to the extreme case in (16), where the lower bound is at minus infinity. It is clear from (11) and (12) that the exchange rate must lie on the 45-degree line through the origin at both absorbing barriers. The free-float saddlepath, *FF*, is relevant when both boundaries are infinitely distant.

The intuition behind the bent curves in Figure 5.1 is as follows. On the saddlepath, the exchange rate is the present discounted value of fundamentals, and the evolution of fundamentals is governed in part by their deterministic trend growth rate, which depends on η. Suppose that $\eta > 0$ (the case shown in the figure). As k approaches either $\bar{k}$ or $\underline{k}$, the probability that the exchange rate will still be floating on any given future date declines; and since η is set permanently to zero at the moment of pegging, the expected rate of fundamentals growth on any future date also declines as either absorbing barrier is approached. As a result, there is a progressive currency appreciation (fall in x) relative to *FF* as k moves towards a barrier. For $\eta < 0$, *FF* would lie below the 45-degree line and the saddlepath solution would be the mirror image of the one in Figure 5.1. As we have seen, when $\eta = 0$ the bending effects are absent because absorption of k has no effect on the expected change in fundamentals. Think of the saddlepath as being trapped between *FF* and the 45-degree line, which collapse into a single line when η shrinks to zero.[9]

The path given by (16), whose derivation implies setting $A_2 = 0$ in (8), is

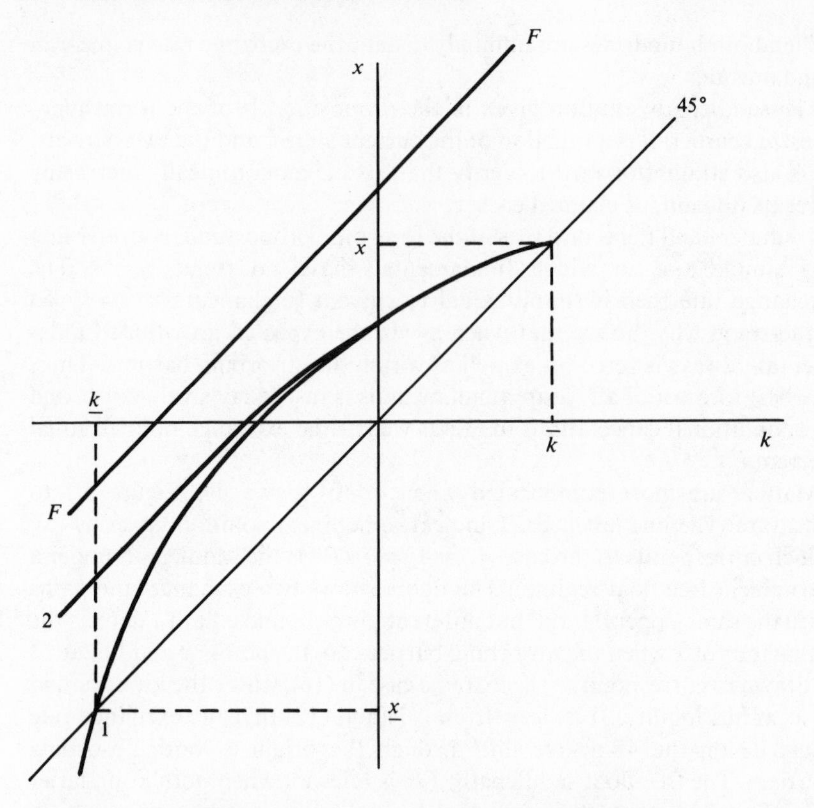

Figure 5.1 Stochastic exchange rate pegging in fundamentals space

the unique path for the stochastic-process-switching problem of Flood and Garber (1983). They attempt to solve directly the integral representation for the exchange rate when pegging occurs at $x = \bar{x}$ with no jump in fundamentals at the moment of pegging

$$x(t) = a^{-1}\int_t^{\infty} e^{(t-s)/a} E(k(s)\,|\,k(t),\, k(s) \leq \bar{k}_a = \bar{x})\, ds \qquad (18)$$

Equation (16) is the unique solution to this integral.[10]

3.2 Policy announcements and exchange-rate indeterminacy

In the foregoing discussion, we assumed that the authorities announced bounds on the fundamentals, and that their policy was a passive one until one of the bounds was reached. In practice, policy makers are unlikely to make future policy contingent on the level of a policy instrument such as the money supply. They are more likely to announce bounds on the exchange rate itself. Indeed, in their verbal description of the process-switching problem, Flood and Garber (1983) assumed that the British authorities committed themselves simply to peg the exchange rate once it reached a target level $\bar{x}$. [Editors' note: for Flood and Garber, the home country is the US, so x represents the dollar price of sterling (in logarithms).] Only in their calculations did they add the supplementary – but crucial – assumption that fundamentals cannot jump at the instant of pegging. In the last section, we solved the Flood–Garber problem assuming explicitly that this additional information had been conveyed to the market.

If policy-makers are less explicit in their announcements that we have assumed so far, however, the market may have too little information to calculate an equilibrium exchange rate. We now show that a unique equilibrium will exist if the authorities announce *both* a future exchange-rate peg *and* the size of the intervention they will undertake at the moment of transition. But prospective interventions of different size give rise to different exchange-rate paths. It follows that exchange-rate information alone does not generally suffice to determine an equilibrium. Our basic point is a familiar one: a determinate market outcome requires that different expectations not be validated by accommodating official behaviour.[11]

We can see how a prospective transitional intervention affects the equilibrium by imagining that the authorities make the following announcement: 'When the exchange rate reaches $\bar{x}$, we will peg it by means of an intervention that instantaneously raises the fundamental k by the amount $\bar{I}$. From then on, we will do whatever is necessary to hold the exchange rate of $\bar{x}$.' To solve, it is easiest to work backwards from the moment after the intervention, when the exchange rate has already been fixed. At this time, and forever after, it must be the case that $k = \bar{k} = \bar{x}$. The intervention that brings k to $\bar{k}$ occurs at the moment x reaches $\bar{x}$, so at that moment, fundamentals move discontinuously from $\bar{k} - \bar{I}$ to $\bar{k}$. Note that investors fully anticipate this large change in fundamentals when x reaches its boundary level; but, if there are to be no riskless profit opportunities, the exchange rate must remain steady at $\bar{x}$ as the anticipated intervention is carried out. This condition is another application of asset-price continuity. In terms of our earlier notation, it can be written as

$$S(\bar{k} - \bar{I}) = \bar{k} = \bar{x} \tag{19}$$

As before, the appropriate boundary conditions, applied to (8), yield a closed-form solution. Since the barrier is one-sided, one condition is $A_2 = 0$, which forces the saddlepath to approximate the linear solution for k far below $\bar{k} - \bar{I}$. Given that $A_2 = 0$, continuity condition (19) is

$$\bar{k} - \bar{I} + \alpha\eta + A_1 e^{\lambda_1(\bar{k} - \bar{I})} = \bar{k} = \bar{x} \tag{20}$$

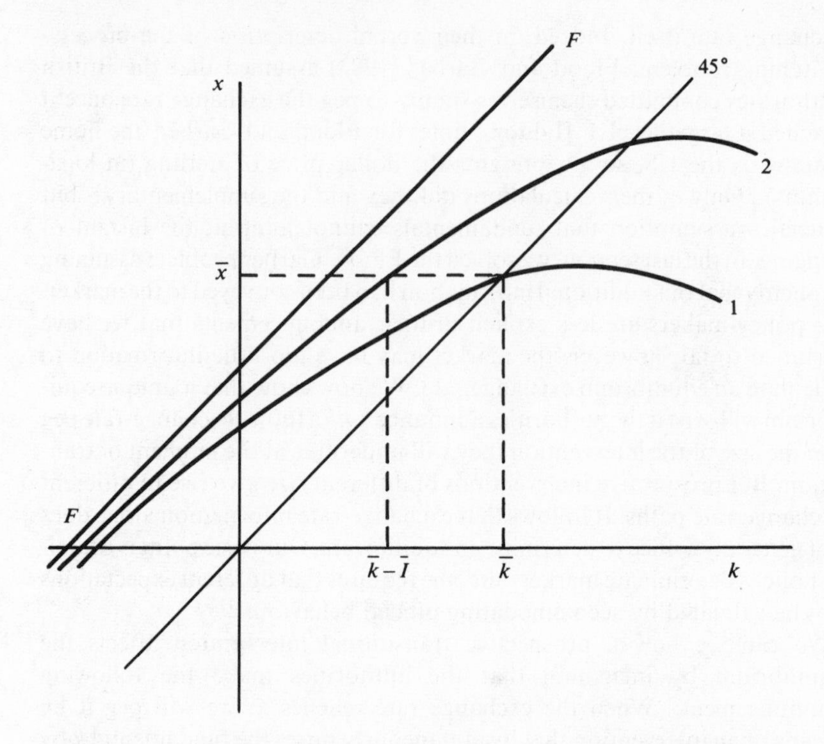

Figure 5.2 Stochastic exchange rate pegging with a discrete transitional intervention

This second boundary condition leads to:

Proposition 2. Assume that fundamentals are expected to rise discontinuously by the amount $\bar{I}$ at the moment the exchange rate is pegged at $\bar{x}$. While floating, the equilibrium exchange rate is given by:

$$x = k + a\eta + (\bar{I} - a\eta)e^{\lambda_1(k - \bar{k} + \bar{I})} \tag{21}$$

Figure 5.2 illustrates how the prospect of a discrete intervention alters the equilibrium. Path 1 depicts the equilibrium with $\bar{I} = 0$ described by (16) and shown previously (as path 2) in Figure 5.1. Path 2 in Figure 5.2, by contrast, graphs the relationship described by (21), where the authorities undertake an intervention of $\bar{I} > 0$ at $x = \bar{x}$. Path 2 lies above and is steeper than path 1: near the upper bound $\bar{k} - \bar{I}$, where a large positive intervention is imminent, the greater discounted value of expected future fundamentals increases the exchange rate.[12]

Equation (21) underscores the main point: when the authorities commit themselves *only* to peg the spot rate once it reaches $\bar{x}$, they are implicitly committing themselves to perform whatever intervention the market happens to conjecture will occur at that moment. Indeed, in the extreme case, suppose that when the policy is first announced at $t = 0$, with $k(0) < \bar{k} = \bar{x}$, the market immediately pushes the exchange rate to $\bar{x}$. If the authorities are to fulfill their commitment, they would be forced to adjust fundamentals instantly by the amount $\bar{k} - k(0)$.

To rule out multiple equilibria, the authorities can announce both the size of the intervention they are willing to undertake and the exchange-rate peg. Alternatively, as was assumed in the previous subsection, they can announce that they will remain passive while fundamentals follow (2), until absorption occurs at the fundamental $\bar{k} = \bar{x}$. This last policy corresponds to an announced transitional intervention of size zero.

3.3 *More complex forcing processes*

The techniques above are practical only when the driving process in (2) is relatively simple; it is usually impossible to find closed-form general solutions to the analogues of (7) when k follows more complicated forcing processes. Nonetheless, some special cases do have solutions. Suppose, for example, that fundamentals are mean-reverting, following the Ornstein–Uhlenbeck process

$$dk(t) = (\eta - \theta k(t))\,dt + \sigma\,dz(t) \tag{22}$$

where η, θ and σ are known constants. Use of (1) and application of Ito's lemma lead to the differential equation:

$$G(k) = k + a(\eta - \theta k)G'(k) + \frac{a\sigma^2}{2}G''(k) \tag{23}$$

The following proposition gives the general solution to (23):

Proposition 3. When fundamentals follow (22), any solution to equation (1) must satisfy

$$x = G(k) = \frac{k + a\eta}{1 + \theta} + A_1 M\left(\frac{1}{2\theta a}, \frac{1}{2}, \frac{2(\eta - \theta k)^2}{\theta\sigma^2}\right) + A_2 M\left(\frac{1 + \theta a}{2\theta a}, \frac{3}{2}, \frac{(\eta - \theta k)^2}{\theta\sigma^2}\right)\frac{(\eta - \theta k)}{\sigma\sqrt{\theta}} \tag{24}$$

where A_1 and A_2 are arbitrary constants and $M(.,.,.)$ is the confluent hypergeometric function.[13]

Using the procedures discussed above, it is straightforward to rederive all the propositions when fundamentals evolve according to (22). Naturally, for values of k such that $\theta k \approx \eta$ the mean-reversion component of (22) is unimportant, so that the solutions appear qualitatively very similar to those shown in the graphs. For values of k where mean-reversion is important, the mean-reversion introduces a new source of bending (toward the unconditional mean of k, η/θ) into the paths above.

Appendix: A flexible-price model of exchange rates

The model consists of four equations. First, there is a domestic money demand equation for the country we study

$$m(t) - p(t) = \psi y(t) - ai(t) + v(t), \quad \psi, a > 0 \tag{A1}$$

where m is the log of the domestic money supply, p is the log of the domestic price level, y is the log of real income, i is the nominal interest rate, and v is a random money-demand shock. Money demand by the rest of the world is given by

$$m^*(t) - p^*(t) = \psi y^*(t) - ai^*(t) + v^*(t) \tag{A2}$$

where the asterisks denote the rest-of-the-world counterparts to the variables in (A1). The model assumes that purchasing power parity holds up to an exogenously varying real exchange rate shock q, so the log of the nominal exchange rate is

$$x(t) = p(t) - p^*(t) + q(t) \tag{A3}$$

The model also assumes that domestic and foreign assets are perfect substitutes up to an exogenously varying risk premium on domestic-currency assets, ρ. Expected depreciation is thus the sum of the nominal interest-rate differential and the risk premium

$$E(dx(t) | \phi(t))/dt = i(t) - i^*(t) - \rho(t) \tag{A4}$$

Subtracting (A2) from (A1), and using (A3) and (A4), we obtain equation (1) in the text with

$$k(t) = \psi(y^*(t) - y(t)) + m(t) - m^*(t) + q(t) + a\rho(t) + v^*(t) - v(t) \tag{A5}$$

NOTES

A somewhat shorter version of this paper appeared in *Econometrica* **59** (1991). The authors are grateful to Bob Flood, Rob Porter and an anonymous referee for helpful comments, and to the John M. Olin, Henry Ford and National Science Foundations for generous financial support.

1 Smith (1991) has shown how to derive an explicit solution to the Flood–Garber problem using the methods those authors suggested. Naturally, our solution agrees with that found by Smith. Smith and Smith (1990) apply this result to the 1925 British episode.
2 Froot and Obstfeld (1991) present a detailed discussion of the relationship between the process-switching examples in this paper and some others, including systems of exchange-rate 'target zones'. Under a target zone, the policy-maker keeps an asset price from moving out of some predetermined range, but she does not intervene when the price is within the range. The original target-zone solution is due to Krugman (1991); see Miller and Weller (1988), Flood and Garber (1989), and Klein (1990) for other studies of exchange-rate zones.
3 The single-equation formulation assumed below is derived from underlying behavioural relationships in the appendix. We assume continuous trading, but a discrete-time binomial setup yields comparable results. Miller and Weller (1988) analyse numerically a stochastic sticky-price exchange-rate model. Their methods are easily extended to the types of process switches we study here.
4 Propositions 1 and 2 below can be rederived using more complex forcing processes. See Section 3.3.
5 This terminology is meant to differentiate the present-value exchange rate from other solutions to (1), which include extraneous bubble components driven by self-fulfilling expectations. We assume that such explosive bubble solutions are ruled out by market forces.
6 Where it does not create confusion, we drop the time-dependence notation. It is worth noting that while we refer to $G(k)$ as a 'general' solution, it is general only if attention is restricted to solutions that depend on current fundamentals alone. In fact, (1) has even more general solutions, for example, solutions that are functions not only of current fundamentals, but also of variables extraneous to the model; see Froot and Obstfeld (1990). Such solutions are not considered in this paper. This exclusion is not restrictive given the economic problem we are considering.
7 Formally, taking limits as (say) k approaches $\bar{k}$ from below, continuity implies that $S(\bar{k}) = S(\lim_{k \to \bar{k}} k) = \lim_{k \to \bar{k}} S(k) = \lim_{k \to \bar{k}} G(k) = G(\lim_{k \to \bar{k}} k) = G(\bar{k})$. Asset-price continuity reflects the arbitrage process that prevents the exchange rate from taking anticipated discrete jumps.
8 The boundary conditions given here generalize easily to other types of regime change. For example, suppose that the authorities announce that at $k = \bar{k}$, the stochastic process driving fundamentals will switch permanently from (2) to $dk = \eta' \, dt + \sigma' \, dz$. Then the boundary condition corresponding to (12) is $S(\bar{k}) = \bar{k} + \alpha\eta' = \bar{x}$. (Note that under this switching scenario, only the expected future trend growth of fundamentals, and not their variability, matters for the boundary condition and therefore also for the exchange-rate process under the pre-switch regime.) As another example, suppose that the authorities wish to implement a target-zone exchange-rate regime by keeping fundamentals within reflecting barriers $\underline{k}$ and $\bar{k}$. Then if policy interventions are infinitesimal and occur only at the margins, conditions (11) and (12) above are replaced by the value-matching conditions $G'(\underline{k}) = G'(\bar{k}) = 0$. (See the appendix of Froot and Obstfeld, 1991, for a formal proof.) The saddlepath solution for the exchange rate combines these new boundary conditions with (8).

9 Naturally, the exchange-rate paths shown in Figure 5.1 do *not* have zero slopes at the regime boundaries, as would be the case under a credible target zone with infinitesimal marginal interventions (see footnote 8 above).
10 See also Smith (1991).
11 Obstfeld (1984, page 209), points out this indeterminacy. Flood and Garber (1989) use a boundary condition identical to the one invoked below to study target zones with discrete interventions at the margins.
12 If we think of the authorities as intervening by a sharp increase in the domestic money supply when x reaches $\bar{x}$ along path 2, then equilibrium is maintained by a discontinuous fall in the domestic nominal interest rate. The counterpart of this fall in the domestic interest rate is a fall to zero in the expected rate of domestic currency depreciation, which depends on the curvature of path 2. In general, the exchange-rate path (21) can be either convex or concave, depending on whether $\bar{I}$ is greater or less than $\alpha\eta$, respectively. A negative value of $\bar{I}$ (an intervention that reduces the domestic money supply) would imply an exchange-rate path lying to the right of path 1.
13 See Slater (1965) for the properties of confluent hypergeometric functions.

REFERENCES

Flood, R.P. and P.M. Garber (1983), 'A model of stochastic process switching', *Econometrica* **51**, 537–52.

(1989), 'The linkage between speculative attack and target zone models of exchange rates', NBER Working Paper No. 2918.

Froot, K.A. and M. Obstfeld (1990), 'Intrinsic Bubbles: the Case of Stock Prices', NBER.

(1991), 'Exchange-rate dynamics under stochastic regime shifts: a unified approach', *Journal of International Economics*, forthcoming.

Klein, M.W. (1990), 'Playing with the band: dynamic effects of target zones in an open economy', *International Economic Review* **31**, 757–72.

Krugman, P. (1991), 'Target zones and exchange rate dynamics', *Quarterly Journal of Economics*, forthcoming.

Miller, M. and P. Weller (1988), 'Target zones, currency options and monetary policy', University of Warwick.

Obstfeld, M. (1984), 'Balance-of-payments crises and devaluation', *Journal of Money, Credit and Banking* **16**, 208–17.

Slater, L. (1965), 'Confluent hypergeometric functions', in M. Abramowitz and I. Stegun (eds.), *Handbook of Mathematical Functions*. New York: Dover Publications.

Smith, G.W. (1991), 'Solution to a problem of stochastic process switching', *Econometrica* **59**, forthcoming.

Smith, G.W. and R.T. Smith (1990), 'Stochastic process switching and the return to gold, 1925', *Economic Journal* **100**, 164–75.

6 Entering a preannounced currency band

MASAKI ICHIKAWA, MARCUS MILLER and
ALAN SUTHERLAND

1 Introduction

What are the dynamics of a freely floating exchange rate in circumstances where entry into a currency band is widely anticipated? The answer will surely depend *inter alia* upon whether the transition is expected only 'when conditions are right' or if it is to take place at a given date, irrespective of such conditions. The former case (that of a *state-dependent* switch from a floating to a managed rate) has been examined for a stochastic environment first by Flood and Garber (1983) and more recently by Smith and Smith (1990) and Froot and Obstfeld (1989).[1] (The specific episode they focus on is, in fact, sterling's return to the gold standard in 1925.) As far as we are aware the latter case, that of a purely *time-dependent* switch, has not been analysed; it is the subject of this paper.

In the context of a monetary model with flexible prices, continuous Purchasing Power Parity and a 'random walk' in the velocity of money, it is found that the exchange rate satisfies a partial differential equation (PDE) before the date of entry. The relevant boundary condition applying at that time is the stationary solution obtained by Paul Krugman (1988) for such a model – see Section 2 below. By transforming the model into the 'heat equation of physics', we are able to obtain an explicit general solution; and we provide an intuitive explanation of the integrals involved. An illustration for the special case of an anticipated return to a fixed rate (i.e. a band with zero width) is given, for which the formula takes a much simpler exponential form.

2 The monetary model and the stationary solution within the band

The monetary model and its stationary solution inside a currency band in Krugman (1988) may briefly be summarised. There are three equations

$$m(t) + v(t) = p(t) - \lambda \frac{E[ds(t)]}{dt} \tag{1}$$

$$p(t) = s(t) \tag{2}$$

$$dv(t) = \sigma\, dz(t) \tag{3}$$

where $s(t)$ is the log of the exchange rate, $p(t)$ is the log of the price level, $m(t)$ is the log of the domestic money supply and $v(t)$ is the disturbance affecting the velocity of money. (For notational convenience the time 'subscripts' are typically dropped in what follows, except where they are essential to the argument.) Inside the band the money supply is constant, but the random evolution of the velocity shock (equation (3)) has an impact on both the exchange rate and the price level (equation (2)) as they evolve so as to satisfy money market equilibrium (equation (1)).

The required solution is obtained as a stationary function relating the exchange rate to the 'velocity-adjusted money stock' $(m + v)$ of the form

$$s = f(m + v) = m + v + Ae^{\rho(m+v)} + Be^{-\rho(m+v)} \tag{4}$$

where $\rho = (2/\lambda\sigma^2)^{1/2}$. The coefficients A and B are determined by boundary conditions which, for a fully credible band, are

$$\begin{aligned} f(\overline{m + v}) &= \bar{s} \\ f(\underline{m + v}) &= \underline{s} \\ f'(\overline{m + v}) &= f'(\underline{m + v}) = 0 \end{aligned} \tag{5}$$

where $\overline{m + v}$ and $\underline{m + v}$ are the values of the fundamental at which the rate is driven onto the edges of the band, $\bar{s}$ and $\underline{s}$ respectively. This solution, for the symmetric case $A = -B$, is shown as the familiar S-shaped curve labelled KK in Figure 6.1 where the boundary conditions ensure that the exchange rate 'smooth pastes' onto the edges of the band. At the edges of the band, the money supply is varied (by 'infinitesimal intervention') as necessary to offset any velocity shocks that would take the velocity-adjusted money stock outside the range shown, see Krugman (1988).

Note that, if there is no band and the currency floats freely with the money supply held constant, then the exchange rate moves *pari passu* with the velocity shock, as shown by the 45° line in Figure 6.1, marked FF.

3 Anticipations of managed exchange rates

Consider now how the exchange rate will depart from the freely floating solution FF under the impact of an announcement at time 0 that the monetary authorities are to defend the band $(\bar{s}, \underline{s})$ after time T. Assume

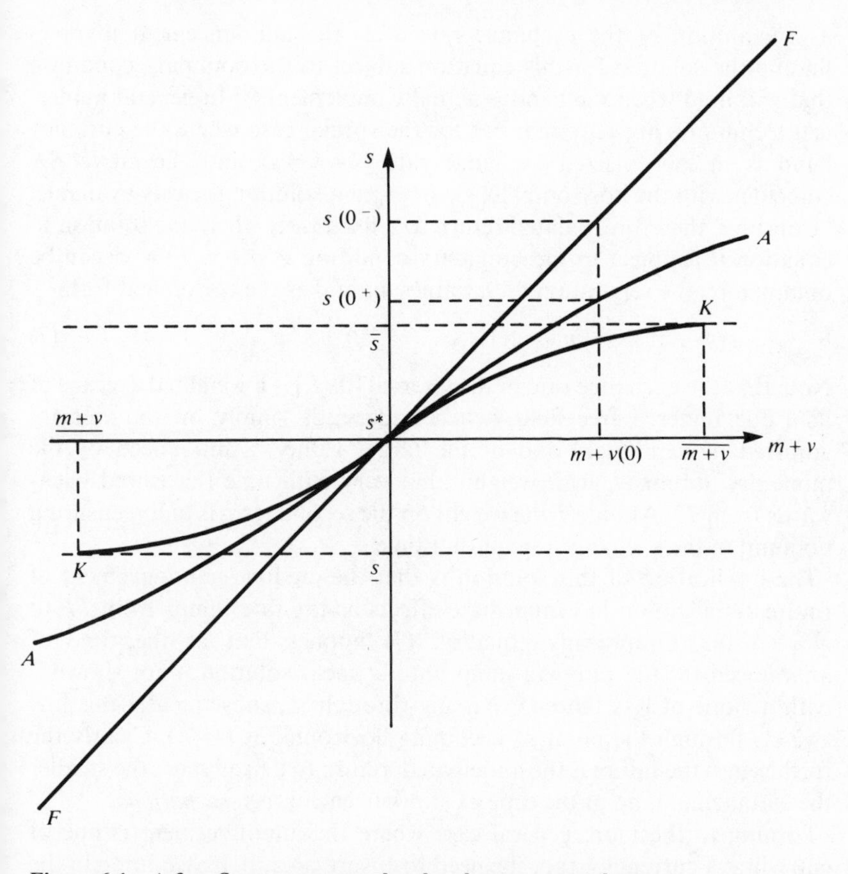

Figure 6.1 A free float, a currency band and preannounced entry

for convenience that the announcement is fully credible, and that the currency band can be successfully defended, so that the solution at time T is the curve KK itself; and no further regime shifts are anticipated.

Given that the solution for the rate at time T (and after) is known, the solution between 0 and T may be obtained by introducing a time-varying element into the relationship between the exchange rate and economic fundamentals, so (4) becomes

$$s = g(m + v, t) \tag{4'}$$

and the application of Ito's lemma produces a partial differential equation of the form

$$\frac{\sigma^2}{2} g_{11}(m + v, t) + g_2(m + v, t) = \frac{1}{\lambda}(s - m - v) \tag{6}$$

The evolution of the exchange rate after the announcement involves finding the solution for this equation subject to the boundary condition that will hold when the band is actually implemented. In general numerical techniques are required; but for the special case where the currency band is in fact a fixed exchange rate ($\bar{s} = \underline{s} = s^*$ and the curve KK coincides with the horizontal axis), an explicit solution is easily available.

Consider, therefore, a dated return to a fixed rate, where the solution to equation (6) subject to the boundary condition $g(m + v, T) = s^*$ can be obtained by the separation of variables and takes the convenient form

$$g(m + v, t) = (m + v)(1 - e^{-\frac{1}{\lambda}(T - t)}) + s^* e^{-\frac{1}{\lambda}(T - t)} \tag{7}$$

Note that the exchange rate in the interval $[0, T]$ is a weighted average of its value under a free float (when it depends simply on the velocity adjusted money stock) and of the target value s^* announced by the monetary authority, with weights that vary with time (measured backwards from T). At time T the weight on the second term is unity, ensuring no jump in the exchange rate at that time.

The implication of this solution is that the credible announcement of future stabilization has immediate effects as the rate jumps from FF to $g(m + v, 0)$. (Graphically equation (7) implies that at the time of announcement the rate will jump onto a linear solution – not shown – with a slope of less than 45° passing through s^*; subsequently this line swivels through the point s^* becoming horizontal at $t = T$). Clearly the further into the future is the anticipated 'return to a fixed rate', the smaller the stabilizing jump at the time of announcement, *ceteris paribus*.

Turning to the more general case where the announcement is one of entry into a currency band, the need to ensure no anticipated jump in the exchange rate requires the solution to (6) coincide with Krugman's stationary S-shaped solution at the time of implementation. Formally the relevant boundary (or terminal) condition is

$$\begin{aligned} g(m + v, T) &= \bar{s} && \text{for} \quad m + v > \overline{m + v} \\ g(m + v, T) &= f(m + v) && \text{for} \quad \underline{m + v} < m + v < \overline{m + v} \\ g(m + v, T) &= \underline{s} && \text{for} \quad m + v < \underline{m + v} \end{aligned} \tag{8}$$

where, as before, $\overline{m + v}$ and $\underline{m + v}$ are the values of the fundamental (the velocity adjusted money stock) at which the stationary solution is tangent to the edges of the currency band. Note that the money stock will be constant before T, but may require *discrete* adjustment at that time, if $m + v$ lies outside the range consistent with the currency band. So, if $m + v > \overline{m + v}$ at T, for example, the money stock will have to be reduced by just enough to keep the exchange rate at the upper edge of the band. Once the band is established its support will from time to time require the marginal adjustment to the money stock already mentioned.

There is a close parallel between the analysis of a preannounced band and the analysis of option prices in Black and Scholes (1973). In the case of options, Black and Scholes used Ito's lemma to obtain a PDE in the option pricing function which (if allowance is made for their use of levels rather than logs) is identical in form to (6). Similarly, there is a terminal condition at the date the option expires (provided by the need for the option price to coincide with the underlying stock price less the strike price or zero whichever is the greater).

Black and Scholes solve their PDE by a change of variables which transforms the equation into the heat equation of physics, for which solutions can be obtained by Fourier transform methods (see Guenther and Lee, 1988, pp. 166–178). The same approach is applied to the solution of (6) subject to condition (8) and the solution that emerges is

$$g(m+v,t) = (m+v) - \frac{e^{-\frac{1}{\lambda}(T-t)}}{\sqrt{2\pi\sigma^2(T-t)}} \times \int_{-\infty}^{\infty} \exp\left[-\frac{(x-m-v)^2}{2\sigma^2(T-t)}\right][(m+v)-\phi(x)]\,dx \tag{9}$$

where $\phi(x) = \bar{s}$ for $x > \overline{m+v}$

$\phi(x) = f(x)$ for $\underline{m+v} < x < \overline{m+v}$

$\phi(x) = \underline{s}$ for $x < \underline{m+v}$.

Note that while v is a stochastic process evolving through time, the money supply is kept constant until T.

Equation (9) has a simple interpretation. To see this, observe that the distribution of $(m+v(T))$ conditional on $(m+v(t))$ is $N(m+v(t), \sigma^2(T-t))$, bearing in mind that m is constant before T. This implies that the expected value of the exchange rate at time T, conditional on the level of the fundamental at time t, is obtained as

$$E(s(T)\,|\,m+v(t),t) = \frac{1}{\sqrt{2\pi\sigma^2(T-t)}} \times \int_{-\infty}^{\infty} \exp\left[-\frac{(x-m-v(t))^2}{2\sigma^2(T-t)}\right]\phi(x)\,dx \tag{10}$$

It is therefore possible to rewrite (9) as follows

$$g(m+v,t) = (m+v)(1 - e^{-\frac{1}{\lambda}(T-t)}) + E(s(T)|m+v,t)e^{-\frac{1}{\lambda}(T-t)} \quad (11)$$

(where once again $v(t)$ is written simply as v.) The similarity between this solution and that obtained for the case of a move to a fixed rate is clear. The only difference is the appearance of the conditional expectation of $s(T)$ in (11) in the place of s^* in (7). The explanation for this is obvious – in the case of a move to a fixed rate the value of the exchange rate at time T is known with certainty, while in the case of a preannounced band the exchange rate at time T is uncertain, so its expected value is used instead.

We have evaluated equation (11) numerically, but rather than report these numerical results, we show that the qualitative nature of the solution can be deduced directly from the formula itself, as follows. Suppose the level of the velocity adjusted money stock at time 0 is given by $m + v(0)$ as shown in Figure 6.1. Immediately before the announcement the exchange rate lies on the free float line FF and is thus $s(0^-)$. When the announcement is made agents use their knowledge of the distribution of $m + v(T)$ to form their expectation of the exchange rate that will hold at time T. Since velocity follows Brownian motion without drift, their expectation of $m + v(T)$ is simply its current level, $m + v(0)$. But the curvature of the S-shaped stationary solution (marked KK) at this level of $m + v$ implies that the expectation of $s(T)$ is slightly below that given by KK. Equation (11) tells us that the level of the current exchange rate is a weighted average of the expected exchange rate at time T and the current free float solution. This is shown by the point marked $s(0^+)$ in Figure 6.1. If this procedure is carried out for each possible level of $m + v(0)$ the curved line marked AA – the isochronous solution to the PDE at time 0 – is traced out. It is apparent that a credible announcement of a band has an immediate stabilizing effect.

The passage of time has two effects on the solution. Firstly the variance of $m + v(T)$ decreases as time T approaches, thus the expectation of $s(T)$ moves closer to KK. The second and much larger effect is the increase in the weight attached to the expectation of $s(T)$ in equation (11). The isochronous solution therefore moves closer to KK, and the stabilizing effect of the anticipated band increases.

4 Conclusions

Where an anticipated transition from floating to managed exchange rates is treated as state-contingent, others have shown that the solution for the exchange rate as a function of fundamentals is stationary. This is not the case where the commitment to stabilize rates is to take effect from a fixed future time. The partial differential equation describing the rate can, however, be solved using the appropriate stationary solution as a boundary or terminal condition. An explicit solution is available for the case of a credible return to a fixed rate. Although numerical methods are necessary for evaluating the exchange rate when entry to a currency band is anticipated, a qualitative interpretation of the path of the rate is available.

Two possible extensions of the techniques developed here are worth mentioning: first is the idea of *combining* state- and time-contingent elements; second is that of allowing for lack of credibility in the commitment to stabilize the rate.

NOTES

This paper has been produced as part of an ESRC project on The International Monetary System, and resources supplied (under grant number R000231417) are gratefully acknowledged. Masaki Ichikawa is indebted to the Economic Planning Agency, Tokyo for leave to do research at Warwick. We have benefited from discussions with Andrew Carverhill of the Financial Options Research Centre at the University of Warwick; but responsibility for any errors remains with us. This paper is reprinted, with permission, from *Economics Letters* **34**, (4), 1990.

1 See also their contribution to this volume.

REFERENCES

Black, Fischer and Myron Scholes (1972), 'The valuation of options and corporate liabilities', *Journal of Political Economy* **81**, 637–54.

Flood, Robert P. and Peter M. Garber (1983), 'A model of stochastic process switching', *Econometrica* **51**, 537–51.

Froot, Kenneth A. and Maurice Obstfeld (1989), 'Exchange-Rate Dynamics under Stochastic Regime Shifts: A Unified Approach', mimeo, MIT and University of Pennsylvania.

Guenther, Ronald B. and John W. Lee (1988), *Partial Differential Equations of Mathematical Physics and Integral Equations*, Prentice Hall, Englewood Cliffs, New Jersey.

Krugman, Paul (1988), 'Target Zones and Exchange Rate Dynamics', NBER Working Paper No. 2481.

Smith, G.W. and T. Smith (1990), 'Stochastic Process Switching and the Return to Gold, 1925', *Economic Journal* **100**, 164–75.

7 Britain's return to gold and entry into the EMS: joining conditions and credibility

MARCUS MILLER and
ALAN SUTHERLAND

1 Introduction

In studying changes of monetary regime Flood and Garber (1983) treated them as irreversible switches in the stochastic process determining prices and the exchange rate, and showed how the *anticipation* of such a regime change could affect the economy *ex ante*. As an application of these ideas they cited the behaviour of the pound sterling in the 1920s, when the return to the gold standard was widely anticipated; and in order to highlight the novel aspect of their study, they adopted 'the simplest exchange rate model popular in the current literature – the monetary model'.

Even with this simple model, the formal analysis was rather forbidding; but subsequent studies have derived closed-form solutions which are much easier to interpret, see Smith (1989) and Froot and Obstfeld (1989) and their contribution to this volume. Smith and Smith (1990) have used these solutions to spell out a surprising implication of the analysis, which is that the desire of the authorities to restore sterling back up to its pre-war peg of $4.86 had the effect of *weakening* sterling relative to what would have emerged from a clean float.

We begin our discussion of the return to gold by arguing that this paradoxical conclusion is probably due to misspecifying the nature of monetary policy. It is shown that treating the trends in money in the 1920s, not as exogenous, but as part and parcel of the planned return to gold radically changes one's interpretation of the effect of the anticipated regime switch. We also note that the stationary solutions proposed by the authors cited give no role to the fixed time limit implied by the expiration of the Gold and Silver (Export Control) Act at the end of 1925. Since its significance was stressed by those centrally involved in the decision to return, we indicate how non-stationary solutions can be obtained for the monetary model which allow a role for such time-dependent features.

As the contemporary debate was to a very large extent focused on the problems of securing the adjustment of British prices necessary to remain internationally competitive as sterling was pushed back to $4.86, it seems distinctly inappropriate to analyse events with a 'monetary model' which assumes perfect flexibility of prices and continuous purchasing power parity. As an alternative, we therefore consider the same issues in a model where there is inertia in the price level. Postulating inertia in prices and not in monetary policy offers, we argue, a more convincing interpretation of the state-contingent condition for return to gold than does the monetary model; and we note how it can generate endogenous time trends leading sterling towards its planned parity. However, the fact that British prices were widely thought to be *uncompetitive* (by about 10%) when sterling actually went back on gold in 1925, suggests the relevance of a non-stationary solution, which allows for return by a planned date (without regard to PPP being achieved). This solution, we believe, captures the role of 'speculative anticipations' promoted by Sir Charles Addis, a director at the Bank of England, and lamented by Keynes, a vociferous critic of early return.

The last part of the paper, written before Britain joined, addresses some issues in the debate on UK entry into the European Monetary System. We note, for example, that the contrast between state-contingent and time-dependent conditions again played a role.

What we focus on, however, is a key difference between 1990 and 1925, namely the perceived credibility of the exchange rate peg after the regime switch. Mrs Thatcher played an active role in opposing and delaying entry, and explicitly indicated that realignments of sterling would be allowed within the Exchange Rate Mechanism. So we suggest that UK entry with Mrs Thatcher as Prime Minister could be thought of as a switch to a 'peg with a peso problem'. Where there are forward-looking labour contracts, we show how a realignment probability can undo some or all of the benefits of 'locking' onto a hard currency like the DM; and we note that even when there is a serious commitment to locking currencies, the *perceived* probability of realignment will raise the output cost of maintaining the peg.

2 The return to gold in the monetary model: a reinterpretation

In this section we spell out three key reservations concerning the existing analysis of the return to gold using the monetary model. The first concerns the role of the time trend in fundamentals assumed by both Flood and Garber and Smith and Smith. We show that if this trend is viewed as policy action implemented to speed the return to gold then, contrary to

Smith and Smith's assertion, the appropriate interpretation of their results is that sterling was strengthened, not weakened. The second criticism is of the interpretation Flood and Garber place on their choice of state-contingent joining condition. We dispute their suggestion that it represents a return to gold 'when purchasing power parity is achieved' but show that it arises from an implicit assumption that the money supply does not make discrete adjustments – an assumption which is given no justification. Our third reservation concerning the existing analysis results from the emphasis put on state-contingent joining conditions. We suggest that, in fact, expectations in 1925 were strongly affected by events *fixed in calender time* which were reckoned to set a time limit on floating. We use the monetary model to show how this kind of joining condition tends to pull sterling towards its known future value.

The two-country model used by Flood and Garber to analyse the effect of a state-contingent commitment to stabilize sterling at \$4.86 (listed in Appendix 7A) implies a linear 'structural semi-reduced form' relationship between the current exchange rate ($s(t)$, measured in logs), its own expected rate of change and economic fundamentals $k(t)$. This takes the form

$$s(t) = k(t) + \lambda \frac{E[ds(t)]}{dt} \tag{1}$$

where fundamentals are represented by

$$k(t) \equiv m(t) - m^*(t) + v(t) - v^*(t) - \phi[y(t) - y^*(t)]$$

λ is the interest semi-elasticity of demand for money, and $E_t[ds(t)]/dt$ is the expected rate of change of the exchange rate conditioned on the time t information set containing the structure of the model and all variables dated t or earlier. For Flood and Garber, the home country is the US, so s represents the dollar price of sterling (in logarithms). Unstarred variables refer to the US, starred to the UK. (For simplicity, structural parameters are assumed to be the same in the US and the UK.)

If fundamentals follow a Brownian motion process with instantaneous variance σ^2 and drift η, then, as Froot and Obstfeld (1989) show, the general stationary solution for the exchange rate is

$$s(t) = f[k(t)] = k(t) + \lambda\eta + A_1 e^{\rho_1 k(t)} + A_2 e^{\rho_2 k(t)} \tag{2}$$

where $\rho_1 > 0$ and $\rho_2 < 0$ are the roots of

$$\rho^2 \lambda \frac{\sigma^2}{2} + \rho\lambda\eta - 1 = 0$$

and where A_1 and A_2 are constants to be determined by boundary conditions.

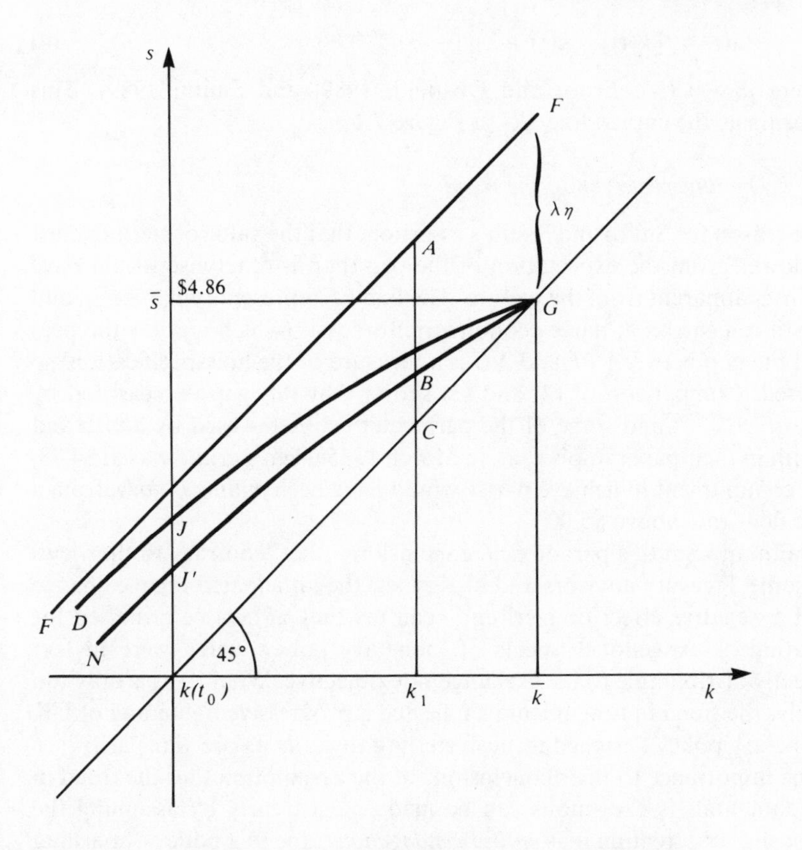

Figure 7.1 A state-contingent return to gold in the monetary model

The 'free float' solution with no bubbles ($A_1 = A_2 = 0$)

$$s(t) = k(t) + \lambda\eta \tag{3}$$

is shown by the line FF in Figure 7.1 for the case where the trend is positive (due, for example, to the faster growth rate of velocity adjusted money, $m + v$, in the US).

If $\bar{s}$ is the desired parity then fixing the exchange rate at this level implies stabilizing the fundamental at $\bar{k}$, where $\bar{k} = \bar{s}$. If discrete jumps in the money stock are ruled out (a point discussed below) then one obtains the boundary condition that a currently floating rate must pass through the point $\bar{s}$, $\bar{k}$. A second boundary condition is provided by the requirement that the solution should asymptotically approach the free float line as k diverges progressively below $\bar{k}$. So the following solution is obtained for the behaviour of the sterling/dollar rate in the period before the return to the gold standard,

$$s(t) = f[k(t)] = k(t) + \lambda\eta(1 - e^{\rho_1(k(t) - \bar{k})}) \quad (4)$$

where $\rho_1 > 0$ (see Froot and Obstfeld, 1989, and Smith, 1989). This appears as the curved line *NG* in Figure 7.1.

2.1 The interpretation of the trend

The reason for Smith and Smith's assertion, that the value of sterling must be lower given the expectation of the peg than it otherwise would have been, is apparent from the picture. The line *FF* represents what Smith and Smith refer to as a 'naive econometric forecast' (which ignores the peg) and the gap between *FF* and *NG* is a measure of the 'misspecification' so caused. Comparison of (2) and (3) shows that this gap is measured by $-\lambda\eta e^{\rho_1(k(t)-\bar{k})}$: and some of the parameter estimates used by Smith and Smith in their paper imply that, in March 1925 when sterling was at \$4.78, the commitment to achieve parity would have been *pulling it down* from a free float rate above \$5.00!

Smith and Smith's paradoxical conclusion – that 'contrary to the views of some Treasury advisors and of Keynes, the anticipated regime change had a negative effect on sterling' – can (as they admit) be criticised for treating as exogenous aspects of monetary policy which were in fact directly attributable to the exchange rate objective. What if, as is only too likely, the trend in fundamentals reflected a progressive tightening of UK monetary policy designed to push sterling towards its pre-war parity?[1]

The importance to their conclusions of the assumption that the trend in fundamentals is exogenous can be made most clearly by assuming the opposite – by treating it as *entirely endogenous*, due to a policy of pushing sterling back to \$4.86. As we will show, this essentially reverses their interpretation of events: for in these circumstances the monetary model implies that sterling would have jump-appreciated much earlier (when it was realised what the policy was) and would only be sustained by the perceived culmination of the policy.

The easiest way to demonstrate this is to forget the noise in fundamentals and also to assume that, prior to the decision to go back to \$4.86, the composite fundamental k had no trend. In the absence of actual or expected policy changes the solution for the exchange rate would be the 45° line passing through the origin (see equation (3), setting $\eta = 0$). In these circumstances let the UK monetary authorities announce at time t_0 their intention to introduce a trend reduction in the UK money stock (relative to the US money stock) for as long as necessary to get sterling back to its pre-war parity – and no further. Under present assumptions, this would imply a predictable trend increase in k from $k(t_0)$ to $\bar{k}$, where it would stop.

What about sterling? Conveniently the solution is available from equations (1) and (2) by setting $\sigma = 0$ ($\rho_1 = 1/\lambda\eta$) and the result is shown by the curve *DG* in Figure 7.1. At time t_0, when the plan is first announced (but before fundamentals have actually changed!) sterling must appreciate onto the line *DG* (see point *J* in Figure 7.1). Note that it does *not* appreciate as far as *FF*; that would only be appropriate if the trend were thought to be permanent. The subsequent trajectory (*JG*) for sterling is the combined result of the steady rise in the fundamental and the progressive unwinding of the jump appreciation as the end of the policy of monetary tightening gets closer.

The economic rationale for these movements is simply that changes in monetary trends lead (via their effects on the rate of interest) to changes in desired real balances. But if discrete jumps in the level of fundamentals are ruled out (see below) then it is the price level, and (by PPP) the exchange rate, which have to adjust. But from time t_0 onwards everything is perfectly predictable, so any jumps in the exchange rate must occur at the beginning.

How does this account depend on the omission of noise? It is obvious that adding back the noise to the evolution of fundamentals makes the date of return endogenous, but it does not change the story in any essential way. The size of the initial appreciation is somewhat reduced, however, as can be seen from Figure 7.1. Starting again at $k(t_0)$, the rate will only jump to J' on the line *NG* giving the solution for $\sigma > 0$. (The reason why the 'noisy' solution *NG* lies below the deterministic curve *DG* is because the latter is concave. Adding noise thus imparts a downward bias to the expected value of sterling and arbitrage considerations imply the need for a higher interest rate for sterling; in this model this is achieved by lowering the value of sterling which raises the price level and tightens monetary conditions.)

Treating the trend as policy-induced does of course have dramatic effects on one's interpretation of the movements in sterling, as can be seen from Figure 7.1. Consider, for example, the case when fundamentals have reached the point k_1, quite close to $\bar{k}$ (where all trends and noise are to be 'switched-off' by policy adjustment) and where sterling is at *B* on the path *NG* leading to \$4.86. For Smith and Smith, the market's recognition that pegging sterling involves 'switching off' an exogenous trend is responsible for weakening sterling from *A* to *B*. The contrary interpretation is that sterling lies above *C* only because of the market's perception that the policy induced trend in fundamentals will continue a little longer! (Imagine for example that it were to be ended immediately, leaving fundamentals to 'wander' randomly the rest of the way to $\bar{k}$, then the rate would fall to *C* on the 45° line.)

2.2 The interpretation of the state-contingent joining condition

In deriving their results Flood and Garber assert that 'the timing of [sterling's return to the gold standard] depended on achieving purchasing power parity at the pre-war exchange rate'. Below, we take issue with this as an accurate interpretation of history. First, however, it is important to point out that, on a purely technical level, such a joining condition is not particularly meaningful in the monetary model. Since in that model PPP holds in all states of the world and at all levels of the exchange rate, 'achieving PPP' cannot provide a guide to the selection of a unique solution for the exchange rate!

To see that this is so consider Figure 7.2 where three possible solutions are illustrated. The Flood and Garber/Smith and Smith solution is, as before, marked NG. The second solution is marked FG' and coincides with the free-float line. The latter solution is sustained by the anticipation of a *discrete reduction* of the UK money supply by amount $\lambda\eta$ to take place at the moment sterling is restored to gold. Notice that no bending takes place and that, by definition, at the point of joining 'purchasing power parity at the pre-war exchange rate has been achieved'. This is also true of the third solution marked $N' G''$ which bends up from the free-float line FG' and involves a larger discrete reduction of UK money at the point of joining (measured by the distance $G'' G'$). Indeed it can be seen that any solution can be sustained provided there is the anticipation of an appropriately sized discrete monetary adjustment at the time of joining, and all these solutions involve achieving 'purchasing power parity at the pre-war exchange rate'.

It appears therefore, that PPP considerations themselves are playing no part in the selection of the Flood and Garber/Smith and Smith solution. Instead the crucial assumption being made is the ruling out of discrete adjustments to the money supply. (The role of this assumption in determining exchange rate behaviour within a currency band is discussed in Flood and Garber, 1989.) It is only by assuming this form of 'monetary inertia' that they are able to select their unique solution. We feel however, that the important source of inertia in the UK economy at that time was in goods prices, not monetary policy! It is for this reason that later we use a model of price inertia to investigate sterling's return to gold.

2.3 The role of 'speculative anticipations'

In their interpretation of events surrounding the return to gold both Flood and Garber and Smith and Smith dispense with the notion that there might have been any fixed 'end date' by which the market was

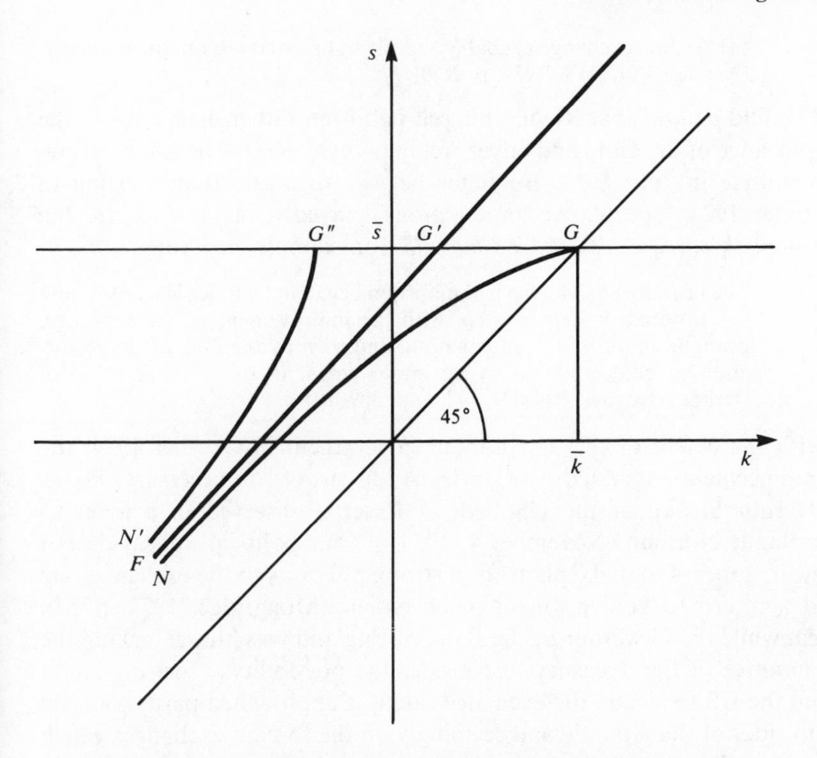

Figure 7.2 Effects of a discrete tightening of money at the time of return

certain that return would be achieved, in favour of the idea that the timing was essentially endogenous. This is rather a surprising position to adopt for two reasons. First, because there was a natural 'end date' for floating, namely the expiry at the end of 1925 of the Gold and Silver (Export Control) Act of 1920. Second, because this strict antithesis (between state-contingent and time-dependent) versions is unnecessary. As in the pricing of dated options, the two factors can be combined – so that the timing may be endogenous but only within a fixed horizon for example.

On the first point it is worth quoting from a letter (dated July 1924) to Keynes from Sir Charles Addis giving the latter's plan for exploiting the existence of the 'end point' to secure an appreciation of sterling.

> Had I a magician's wand I would cause a definite statement to be made, probably in reply to a question in the House of Commons, that HM Government has no present intention of interfering with the ordinary course of events by which on the expiry of the Prohibition Act the free export of gold would be resumed on the 1st January 1926 . . . The effect of such an announcement if people really believed it would tend to raise

> the sterling exchange probably sharply at first and later more gradually. (Keynes, Vol. XIX, 1973, p. 268)

It should be said that Keynes himself had been rather dismissive of the importance of the Gold and Silver Act in his evidence to the Chamberlain Committee in July 1924. But later he was to argue that, starting in October 1924, 'speculative anticipations' played a major role. In *The Economic Consequences of Mr Churchill*, for example, he wrote

> The movement away from equilibrium began in October last [1924] and has proceeded, step by step, with the improvement of the exchange, brought about by the anticipation, and then by the fact, of the restoration of gold, and not by an improvement in the intrinsic value of sterling' (Keynes, Vol. IX, 1972, pp. 209–10)

With the defeat of the first Labour government in October 1924, the announcement suggested by Charles Addis proved unnecessary; for as Governor Strong of the US Federal Reserve observed in a letter to Montague Norman (November 4, 1924). 'Your political upheaval, as I view it, appears to make plans for a strong policy as to the exchange rate and a return to gold payment much easier' (Moggridge, 1972, p. 57). Meanwhile the Governor of the Bank of England was himself asking the Committee of the Treasury to consider the possibility of getting credit from the US to steady the exchange rate if it approached parity. So, 'on both sides of the Atlantic and seemingly on the foreign exchanges which rose sharply after the election, thinking was moving towards a speedy restoration of the gold standard in England'. (Moggridge, 1972, p. 57).

To see formally how this 'speculative anticipation' could operate in the monetary model it is simplest to ignore the time trend (i.e. set $\eta = 0$). Assuming there is an announcement that the authorities are to return to a fixed rate $\bar{s}$ at time T which is taken to be a fully credible expression of intent (and that the currency peg can be successfully defended) then one obtains a non-stationary solution to equation (1) of the form

$$s(t) = k(t)(1 - e^{-\frac{1}{\lambda}(T-t)}) + \bar{s}e^{-\frac{1}{\lambda}(T-t)} \tag{5}$$

so the exchange rate over the interval $[t, T]$ is a weighted average of the value under a free float (given simply by $k(t)$) and of the target value $\bar{s}$ with weights that vary over time (measured backwards from T), see Ichikawa *et al.* (1991).

The implied result of a credible announcement, illustrated in Figure 7.3, is almost exactly as described in Addis's plan. At the time of the announcement the floating rate jumps from the 45° line onto the flatter line passing through the point B (where $\bar{s}$ cuts the 45° line). Then this sharp movement is followed by a more gradual movement as the line

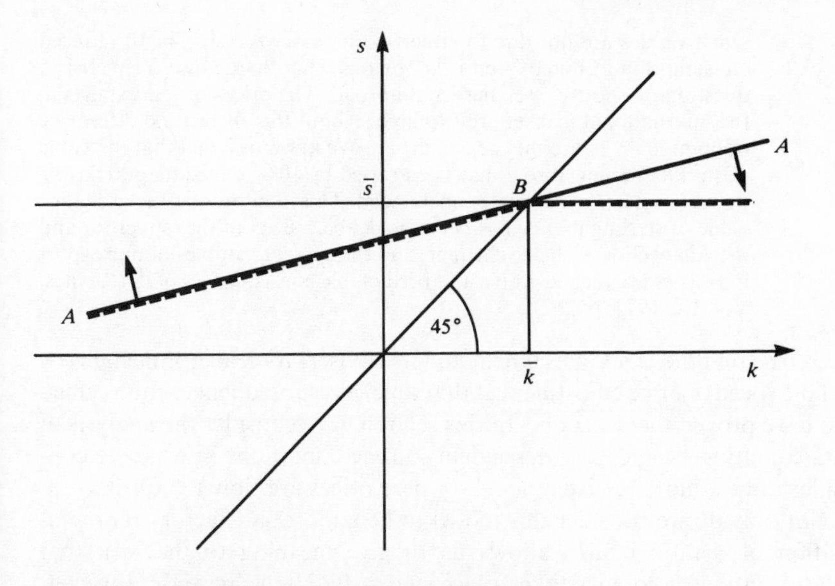

Figure 7.3 A time-dependent return to gold ($\eta = 0$)

showing the solution swivels until it coincides with $\bar{s}$ at T. (For present purposes we ignore the fact that the spread between the gold points means that the final equilibrium is a narrow band rather than simply a fixed value $\bar{s}$.)

What has been outlined is a purely time-dependent version of events, with the rate fixed for sure at time T, but not before. It implies, however, that if fundamentals were to go above $\bar{k}$ before T, for example, then sterling would be allowed to rise above \$4.86. As this seems to rule out the known desire to return sterling to its pre-war parity as soon as reasonably possible, the obvious answer is to combine both the time-dependent and state-contingent elements; so sterling is assumed to return by a fixed end point for sure, but earlier if fundamentals happen to carry it to \$4.86. This compromise can be seen in Figure 7.3 as the combination of the time-dependent solution already discussed to the left of $\bar{k}$, but the fixed value of $\bar{s}$ to the right of $\bar{k}$.

3 A model with price inertia

We now turn to the fundamental question of price flexibility. The problem of securing price adjustment is stressed in Skidelsky's account of the return to gold (Skidelsky, 1988); and it was made abundantly clear by Keynes in the following passage from *The Economic Consequences of Mr Churchill*

> Our troubles are not due to either world wide recession or to reduced consumption at home. And it is obvious what does cause them. It is a question of *relative price* here and abroad. The prices of our exports in the international market are too high. About this there is no difference of opinion. Why are they too high? . . . We know as a fact that the value of sterling money abroad has been raised by 10%, whilst its purchasing power over British labour is unchanged. This alteration in the exchange value of sterling money has been the deliberate act of the Governor and the Chancellor of the Exchequer, and the present troubles of our export industries are the inevitable and predictable consequences of it. (Keynes, Vol. IX, 1972, p. 207)

It is true that the UK Government and its advisers took an optimistic view of the speed of price adjustment at that time, but subsequent events seemed to have proved them wrong.[2] In this section we reconsider the analysis of state-contingent and time-dependent joining conditions in what we consider to be a more realistic model – where prices are slow to adjust.

Not only do we consider this model to be a more satisfactory representation of reality, it also allows us to give meaning to the idea that state-contingent joining takes place 'when PPP is achieved'. However, after analysing this case we still consider the time-dependent account to be the more accurate reflection of historical events.

The sluggish price model has a further advantage over the monetary model in that it provides a more reasonable explanation of the trend increase in sterling which Flood and Garber and Smith and Smith attempt to model by an exogenous time trend in the fundamental. It is the dynamics of sluggish price adjustment which generates systematic trends in the exchange rate in the model we use here. The case of 'overshooting' exchange rates in the Dornbusch (1976) model illustrates this point; there the response to an (unanticipated) change in the money supply is an initial 'jump' followed by an exponential convergence to equilibrium.

The equations of the two county model of price inertia are summarised in Appendix 7B, but the modifications it involves (relative to Appendix 7A)) may be briefly summarised. The principal change comes from replacing the assumption of price flexibility in favour of a type of Phillips curve relating inflation to the level of output. (A.W. Phillips did after all fit his equations to UK data from 1861 to 1915 and tested it out of sample on the inter-war data being considered here!) The inflation process is subject to zero mean white noise disturbances which are the only stochastic element in the model. Output is demand determined where demand depends on the real interest rate, the real exchange rate and activity overseas. The equations for international currency arbitrage and money market equilibrium are as for the monetary model – except that the velocity of money is taken as a constant.

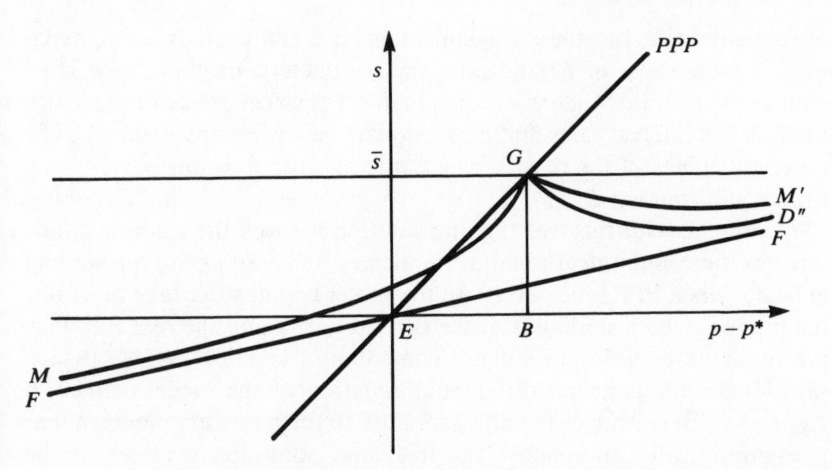

Figure 7.4 A state-contingent return to gold with price inertia

As in the monetary model, the impact of state-contingent commitments can be determined by comparing the unconstrained 'free floating' rate with the solution which is constrained to satisfy the relevant point boundary condition (as well as the fundamental differential equation of the model). Except for special cases, however, there are no closed-form representations of the solutions for models which have inherent dynamics.[3] Numerical results can be obtained for specific parameter values: but as an alternative a qualitative treatment has been developed and this is used in Figure 7.4.

The dollar value of sterling is measured on the vertical axis, while the horizontal axis shows $p - p^*$, the log of the ratio of US to UK prices, measured at an 'equilibrium' exchange rate, s_e. The desired parity of $4.86 is shown at $\bar{s}$ which is higher than s_e. In the absence of any commitment to peg at a high level, the equilibrium is shown at E where the price differential is zero and the nominal rate is s_e. Hence the latter quantity represents the equilibrium *real* exchange rate for this model; and the 45° line shows all other combinations of nominal rates and relative prices which give the same real rate. (This 45° line is referred to as the 'PPP line' in what follows, although, since exports and imports are different goods, it is not strictly a locus of Purchasing Power Parity.)

The upward sloping line labelled *FF* is the stable eigenvector of the system and represents the (no-bubbles) free floating solution for the currency as a function of the relative prices (assuming all other forcing variables are constant, including in particular the ratio of money stocks $m - m^*$). Movements in $p - p^*$ can, therefore, be thought of as movements in fundamentals; but these fundamentals have endogenous stable dynamics. As the slope of *FF* indicates the parameters are those associated with exchange rate 'undershooting': higher US prices are associated with a fall in US interest rates and in the dollar – via what are assumed to be powerful effects of the real exchange rate on output as one moves away from equilibrium at *E*.

To compare with this free floating solution we seek the solution which satisfies the commitment to adjust monetary policy so as to keep sterling at $4.86 'when PPP is achieved'. In the present context we take this to be the point *G* where sterling is at the desired parity and the real exchange rate is at its equilibrium value.[4] The solution labelled *MGM'* (which satisfies the fundamental differential equation of the model defined in Appendix 7B) resembles the noisy solution to the monetary model in that it asymptotically approaches the free float solution as values of the fundamental diverge from those associated with the regime switch point *G*. The effect of the expected future contingent monetary tightening on the exchange rate is apparent, *MGM'* lies everywhere above *FF*. (The kink observed at point *G* itself signifies that this is seen as an irreversible switch of policy: otherwise stochastic smoothing would be expected.)

Once again it may be instructive to suppress the noise and consider the deterministic equivalent. (For which of course an exact exponential representation is available). To the right of *G*, this is shown by the line *GD''*. Like the noisy solution this approaches *FF* asymptotically to the right, but it remains closer to the stable manifold for reasons analogous to those which applied in the monetary model. For points to the left of *G*, the state-contingent announcement has *no* effect since in the absence of noise relative prices will never trigger the tightening: so the deterministic solution coincides with the line *FF*.

Returning to the stochastic case we note that the switch in policy required at *G* must evidently be a (relative) tightening of monetary policy in the UK. This will be achieved by a flow of gold across the Atlantic as necessary to equalise interest rates in the UK and the US. (The necessary adjustment of relative money stocks is essentially given by the distance *EB* which shows the movement of prices that needs to be 'accommodated'.) Note that the flow of money at fixed exchange rates will immediately restore equilibrium in both countries. The anticipation that monetary policy will only be changed when the real exchange rate is in equilibrium means that *all* the adjustment comes before the exchange rate is pegged!

We have already argued that Smith and Smith's conclusion (about sterling being weakened) could be reversed once it is recognised that monetary tightening was part and parcel of the policy of returning to gold. While this illustration confirms the idea that anticipated tightening

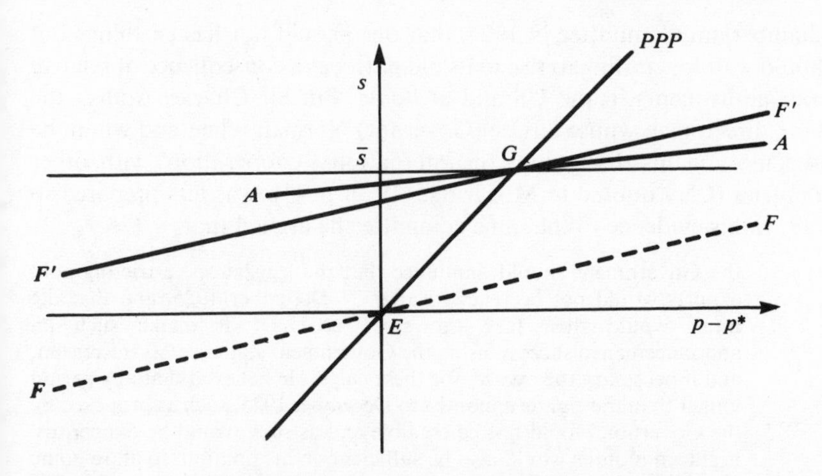

Figure 7.5 A time-dependent return to gold following a tightening of monetary policy

of money strengthens the currency (and the boundary condition seems to correspond more closely to what Flood and Garber describe than those that are imposed in a monetary model with constant PPP) we do not advance it as the most plausible reason for sterling's strength just before 1925. The reason essentially is that monetary policy adjustment was not deferred until the rate was pegged. Money was deliberately tightened ahead of time in the UK and eased in the US; to such an extent indeed that to observers like Keynes in 1924 it seemed as though the necessary monetary shift had already been accomplished and it was only a matter of waiting until it achieved the consequential price changes needed to make $4.86 consistent with PPP.

The case where the monetary adjustment comes first and prices follow after seems to us more plausible and it is illustrated in Figure 7.5. The shift of monetary policy required to move the equilibrium from *E* to *G* (a relative tightening in the UK) shifts the free-float solution from *FF* to *F′ F′* (passing through *G*) and would of course cause an immediate appreciation of sterling. From a point like *E* for example sterling would 'jump appreciate' and then be expected to adjust towards *G*, (subject of course to stochastic noise). Since, by construction, all the necessary monetary tightening has been done, adding a state-contingent commitment 'to do what is necessary when the peg is put in' has no impact on market sentiment. Formally the boundary condition (to pass through *G*) is satisfied by the free floating solution.

The solution described (some might say caricatured) in Figure 7.5 is consistent with the position taken by Keynes in his evidence to the

Chamberlain Committee in 1924, that one should not hasten things but should wait for sterling to rise to its old parity as a consequence of relative price adjustments in the US and at home. But Sir Charles Addis, 'the Bank director on whose advice (Governor) Norman relied and whom he used most in his discussions on international cooperation' with other countries (Clay quoted in Moggridge, 1972, p. 41), was less prepared to wait. In his evidence to the same committee he argued that

> the Government should announce that the legislation restricting gold exports would not be renewed after 31 December 1925, and that the Bank would then take the steps necessary to make such an announcement a success, using the Government statement as the reason, and if necessary the excuse, for these steps. He believed that any period longer than the eighteen months to December 1925, such as proposed by the Governor, would not be credible and as such would be dangerous. Eighteen months would also be sufficient, in his opinion, to allow some adjustment in contracts and take some of the sting out of the price falls implicit in the return to parity. The amount of deflation necessary for a successful return to parity was uncertain, for he expected some rise in American prices to reduce the existing gap of 10 per cent between American and British price levels. (Moggridge, 1972, p. 41)

It has already been shown how, in the monetary model, a credible time-dependent promise to peg affects the rate. Much the same logic applies even when prices are not perfectly flexible, in that the announcement of the dated commitment causes a jump in the exchange rate towards the announced target. The schedule labelled *AA* in Figure 7.5 shows how this swivels the schedule *F′ F′* towards $4.86 at the time of announcement. As time passes the schedule *AA* swivels further until it coincides with the horizontal line passing through parity at the announced time of joining. (The formal solution is given in Appendix 7B). The consequence is that for points to the left of *G*, parity will be reached at a high real exchange rate; and it was largely for this reason that Keynes was to say 'the proposals you outline do terrify me considerably' (Letter to Sir Charles Addis, Keynes, XIX, p. 270).

4 Credibility and the EMS

At the time of writing Britain was, once again, contemplating an exchange rate commitment. On this occasion it was entry into the Exchange Rate Mechanism of the EMS rather than a return to gold; so establishing a fixed rate *vis-à-vis* the DM rather than the US dollar was in prospect.

It is tempting to see whether the methods developed earlier might not be applied to these circumstances. To do this properly would require another paper, so what we do in this section is to indicate some of the key points of similarity and difference; and we use a model with a Poisson process to capture the lack of credibility.

As for points of similarity, on this occasion, as in 1924–5, there was a conflict between 'state-contingent' conditions for entry and those implied by picking a fixed date. The so-called Madrid Conditions spelled out by Mrs Thatcher were a clear statement of the former – those economic conditions which needed to be satisfied before the UK would join. At the time of writing, the conditions concerning the evolution of the EMS itself had been met (for example, the end of capital controls and moves towards financial liberalization), but the requirement that UK inflation should have converged to that in Europe had not. Nevertheless the market was convinced that early entry was in prospect and sterling rose strongly against the DM on this expectation. Evidently the momentum of European monetary integration itself (and the inter-governmental conferences arranged to further this) together with the approach of the next general election in the UK, imposed a time-frame on expectations much tighter than the flexible timetable associated with the Madrid Conditions.

The major difference between the 1920s and 1990 lay in the credibility to be attached to the commitment itself. The return to gold was, in City opinion, a return to the normal order of things; and none doubted the sincerity of Montagu Norman, the Governor of the Bank of England, in his ambition to achieve this.[5] Even the Chancellor of the Exchequer's doubts about the wisdom of elevating the interests of finance above those of industry were regrets about a *fait accompli*, not suggestions that the commitment was to be broken. And Keynes was a lone voice, crying against an irresistible tide of influential opinion.

At the time of writing there was also a flood tide leading Britain towards an exchange rate commitment. The City and the CBI were keen to stabilize the currency against those of European partners; the Governor had signed the Delors Report and both the Treasury and the Foreign Office were believed to be in favor of UK membership of the EMS. But the lone voice on this occasion was none other than that of Mrs Thatcher, the Prime Minister. Because she wished to retain national sovereignty over the conduct of monetary policy, and because the EMS had until recently relied heavily on exchange controls, she opposed membership. (When Mr Lawson, an erstwhile proponent of free floating, had become converted to managed exchange rates and tried to shadow the DM, it was known to be against the wishes of his superior; and ultimately he had been forced to resign over the issue.)

Even when entry into the ERM was a matter of months away, Mrs Thatcher insisted that it would involve no 'locking of currencies'. At the Dublin Summit she said 'should you come up against the upper limit it is also possible, or the lower limit for that matter, to have one of those weekend sessions when you alter the valuation of the currency. So there is no locking at all and it would not work if there were' (*The Financial Times*, 2 July 1990).

In analysing the effects of entry one must surely take account of any such lack of commitment, and its effects on both interest rates and wages.[6] For nominal interest rates the risk of 'realignments' will show up in interest differentials, but to capture adequately the effect on wages one needs an explicit model of wage setting. To allow for the direct impact of future events on current wages while retaining the notion of nominal inertia we have adopted the continuous time model proposed by Calvo (1983). The lack of commitment to a currency peg affects current forecasts of future prices and demand pressure, and current contracts which embody these forecasts.

Formally the Calvo model with a fixed exchange rate consists of the following equations

$$Dp = \delta(x - p) \quad \text{or} \quad p(t) = \delta \int_{-\infty}^{t} x(\tau) e^{-\delta(t-\tau)} d\tau \tag{6}$$

$$Dx = \delta(x - p - \beta y) \quad \text{or} \quad x(t) = \delta E_t \int_{t}^{\infty} [p(\tau) + \beta y(\tau)] e^{-\delta(\tau - t)} d\tau \tag{7}$$

$$E_t[Ds] = (i - i^*) = 0 \tag{8}$$

$$y = -\gamma(i - E_t[Dp]) + \eta(\bar{s} - p + p^*) \tag{9}$$

In equation (6) the current price level is given as an average of all outstanding contracts. The current new contract, denoted x, is a forward-looking integral of expected future prices and demand pressure as shown in equation (7). Equation (8) is the usual international arbitrage equation while equation (9) is the *IS* relationship. The exchange rate is fixed at $\bar{s}$.

The model can be reduced to the following set of two dynamic equations

$$\begin{bmatrix} Dp \\ Dx \end{bmatrix} = A \begin{bmatrix} p \\ x \end{bmatrix} + \begin{bmatrix} 0 \\ -\beta\delta\eta \end{bmatrix} \bar{s}$$

$$A = \begin{bmatrix} -\delta & \delta \\ -\delta[1 - \beta(\delta\gamma + \eta)] & \delta[1 - \beta\delta\gamma] \end{bmatrix} \tag{10}$$

where it is assumed that $i^* = p^* = 0$.

Figure 7.6 illustrates the solution for $\bar{s} = 0$ where the forward looking contract lies on the stable manifold marked *CC* (given by the stable eigenvector of *A*). The stable manifold may be either upward or downward sloping depending on the parameters of the model. *CC* passes through the point of equilibrium at *E*.

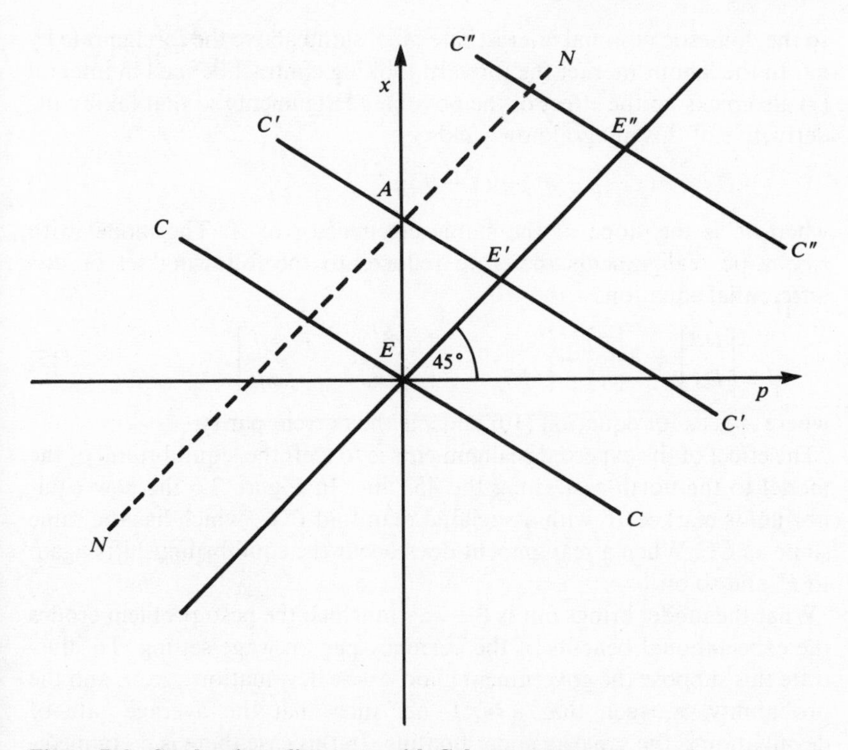

Figure 7.6 Stochastic realignments with Calvo contracts

Before considering realignments, consider the effect of a fully credible peg in this model. Assume that prior to pegging there is an inflationary equilibrium with constant money growth at rate μ. In Figure 7.5 this is represented by a steady crawl up the 45° line marked *NN*. (*NN* is given by the expression $Dp = \mu = \delta(x - p)$.) If the government imposes an unanticipated but permanent and fully credible peg at $\bar{s} = 0$ (at the time prices reach point *E*) the immediate effect is a drop in the contract to point *E* and a fall in inflation to zero.

We represent the lack of full credibility in this model by assuming that there is a constant probability, denoted π, per unit time that the exchange rate will be devalued to a new parity which is *J* from the current parity; which is why it may be referred to as a peg with a 'peso problem'. This approach has recently been applied in connection with currency bands (see for example Miller and Weller, 1989, and Svensson, 1989) but in neither case are the effects on labour contracts considered.[7]

In the currency market the arbitrage equation becomes

$$\pi J = (i - i^*) \tag{11}$$

so the domestic nominal interest rate must stand above the foreign rate by πJ. In the labour market the forward looking contract defined in integral (7) also picks up the effect of the possible realignments so that taking the derivative of this integral now yields

$$Dx = \delta(x - p - \beta y) - (1 - \theta_s)\pi J \tag{12}$$

where θ_s is the slope of the stable eigenvector of A. The model with stochastic realignments therefore reduces to the following set of two differential equations

$$\begin{bmatrix} Dp \\ Dx \end{bmatrix} = A \begin{bmatrix} p \\ x \end{bmatrix} + \begin{bmatrix} 0 \\ (\beta\delta\gamma - 1 + \theta_s)\pi J \quad - \beta\delta\eta\bar{s} \end{bmatrix} \tag{13}$$

where A is as for equation (10) and $\bar{s}$ is the current parity.

The effect of the expected realignments is to shift the 'equilibrium' of the model to the north-east along the 45° line. In Figure 7.6 the new equilibrium is marked E' with associated manifold $C'C'$ which has the same slope as CC. When a realignment does occur the equilibrium shifts again to E'' and so on.

What the model brings out is the way in which the peso problem erodes the expectational benefits of the currency peg on wage setting. To illustrate this suppose the government chooses the devaluation size, J, and the probability, π, such that $\mu = \pi J$, i.e. such that the average rate of devaluation is the same as under floating. In this case there is no immediate fall in inflation as the contract will be given by the displaced manifold $C'C'$ at point A.

It is true that as time passes competitiveness will be eroded in the absence of a realignment and inflation will slow as point E' is approached – but when the realignment comes the contract will jump onto $C''C''$ and inflation is likely to rise above μ.

The fact that there is no immediate fall in inflation by pegging in this case is due to the choice of average devaluation at the same rate as past money growth. If a lower rate of devaluation is chosen, which is credible, then there will be some immediate fall in inflation to the new average.

An interesting feature of this model is that a peg which is in fact fixed can lose some of its benefits if doubts exist about its permanence. Specifically the idea that it might be adjusted encourages wage claims which lead to unemployment as the higher domestic price level reduces competitiveness. In terms of Figure 7.6 the economy converges on E'. This unemployment will only be permanent if there is no learning. But even if people ultimately learn (that there is to be no realignment) the lack of credibility in the meantime means that the cost of reducing inflation is higher than need be.

The model can perhaps also be applied to analyse the issues raised by a split between the DM bloc (now including France?) and the other EMS members. If one treats the second group as those whose pegs are subject to stochastic realignment one may obtain a characterisation of a 'two-speed Europe' with no capital controls[8] where (on average) the rate of inflation in the weak countries remains stubbornly above that in the DM bloc.

5 Conclusions

The convenience of using the monetary model to analyse the anticipatory effects of a regime switch is not to be denied, particularly now that explicit exponential solutions are available (solutions which encompass both temporary switches at the edge of currency bands, see Krugman, 1988, as well as the 'irreversible' switches which Flood and Garber first discussed). In defence of this model we have argued that the implausible result noted by Smith and Smith (that sterling was weakened by the commitment of the British government to return to the Gold Standard) is not an essential feature; it can be reversed by reinterpreting the role of the trend in monetary data, and also by allowing for discrete changes in monetary policy or by nonstationarity in the solution.

But the appeal of such explicit solutions must not be pushed too far. Reference to issues under debate in the 1920s suggests that, at a minimum, some attention should be paid to the dynamics of adjusting prices; and models with endogenous dynamics do not (except in special cases) have explicit solutions. A qualitative treatment is nevertheless possible (at least for low order systems) and generalised regime switching conditions are also available (see Whittle, 1982). So the approach pioneered by Flood and Garber may in fact be applied to models with inherent dynamics as we have shown in the paper. We are inclined however to ascribe a greater role to explicit time-dependent features than are the other contributors we discuss.

UK entry into the EMS under Mrs Thatcher implied a less-than-fully-credible commitment; and the effects of this on labour markets need to be taken into account. The approach taken here is to include a Poisson process to cover realignment of the peg and forward-looking labour contracts to endogenise expectations. The potential for temporary discrepancy between the true Poisson process and what is perceived in financial and labour markets suggests a role for learning (see Lewis, 1988).

Evidence of short-term interest differentials in Europe implies that Britain would not be alone in having a less than fully credible peg *vis-à-vis* the DM. So the issues discussed here surely have relevance to the operation of a two-speed EMS, as well.

Appendix 7A: The monetary model

The model used by Flood and Garber (1983) is as follows

$$m(t) - p(t) = \phi y(t) - \lambda i(t) - v(t) \quad \text{(i)}$$

$$m^*(t) - p^*(t) = \phi y^*(t) - \lambda i^*(t) - v^*(t) \quad \text{(ii)}$$

$$s(t) = p(t) - p^*(t) \quad \text{(iii)}$$

$$\frac{E_t[ds(t)]}{dt} = i(t) - i^*(t) \quad \text{(iv)}$$

Lower case letters denote logarithms (except for i and i^*) and the asterisk indicates a UK variable, others being US variables. The first two equations specify equilibrium in the money market, where m denotes the money supply, p the price level, y is full employment GNP and i is the nominal interest rate. Equation (3) states that purchasing power parity always holds, where s denotes the exchange rate (here the US dollar cost of sterling). Equation (3) is (approximately) a risk-neutral arbitrage condition, in which the expected depreciation is set equal to the interest differential.

By substitution one obtains equation (1) in the text, namely

$$s(t) = k(t) + \lambda \frac{E_t[ds(t)]}{dt} \quad \text{(v)}$$

In the absence of efforts to fix the exchange rate, the forcing function k is assumed to be a Brownian motion process with drift

$$dk(t) = \eta\, dt + \sigma\, dz \quad \text{(vi)}$$

where z is trend free Brownian motion with unit variance.

Application of Ito's lemma establishes that a stationary solution for the exchange rate as a function of fundamentals, $s = f(k)$, must satisfy the second order differential equation

$$f(k) = k + \lambda \eta f'(k) + \lambda \frac{\sigma^2}{2} f''(k) \quad \text{(vii)}$$

which has a general solution of the form

$$f(k) = k + \lambda \eta + A_1 e^{\rho_1 k} + A_2 e^{\rho_2 k} \quad \text{(viii)}$$

Froot and Obstfeld (1989) who show how different boundary conditions expressed in terms of the fundamental k determine the parameters A_1 and A_2.

Note that the requirement that s be a stationary function of fundamentals precludes direct effects of time on the exchange rate, though the latter can nevertheless reflect the trend in fundamentals.

Boundary conditions involving time itself, call for a nonstationary solution of the form $s = g(k, t)$. This leads to the replacement of the ordinary differential equation above with the following partial differential equation

$$g(k,t) = k + g_t(k,t) + \lambda\eta g_k(k,t) + \lambda\frac{\sigma^2}{2} g_{kk}(k,t) \tag{ix}$$

Equation (5) in the text is obtained by solving this PDE (with $\eta = 0$) subject to the boundary condition that the exchange rate coincide with the target rate ($\bar{s}$) at the time of joining (T) for all levels of the fundamental, formally

$$g(k, T) = \bar{s}, \quad -\infty < k < +\infty.$$

The solution is obtained using the method of separation of variables.

Appendix 7B: The model with price inertia

The sticky price model used in Section 2 is a two-country version of that described in Miller and Weller (1990) and consists of the following equations

$$m - p = \phi y - \lambda i - v$$

$$m^* - p^* = \phi y^* - \lambda i^* - v^*$$

$$y = -\gamma(i - E_t[dp]) + \eta(s - p + p^*) + \delta y^*$$

$$y^* = -\gamma(i^* - E_t[dp^*]) - \eta(s - p + p^*) + \delta y$$

$$dp = \psi y\, dt + \sigma\, dz$$

$$dp^* = \psi y^*\, dt + \sigma\, dz^*$$

$$E_t[ds(t)] = (i - i^*)\, dt$$

The assumption that structural parameters are identical in both countries allows the model to be split into two independent sets of equations, one describing global averages and the other describing intercountry differences. Only the differences system involves the exchange rate and it can be reduced to the following set of two stochastic differential equations

$$\begin{bmatrix} d(p - p^*) \\ E_t[ds] \end{bmatrix} = A \begin{bmatrix} (p - p^*) \\ s \end{bmatrix} dt + B(m - m^*)\, dt + \begin{bmatrix} \sigma \\ 0 \end{bmatrix} dz$$

where

$$A = \begin{bmatrix} a_{11} & a_{12} \\ a_{21} & a_{22} \end{bmatrix} = \frac{1}{\Delta}\begin{bmatrix} -\psi(\gamma+\eta) & 2\eta\lambda\psi \\ (1+\delta-\gamma\psi-2\eta\phi) & 2\eta\phi \end{bmatrix}$$

$$B = \frac{1}{\Delta}\begin{bmatrix} \psi\gamma \\ -1-\delta+\gamma\psi \end{bmatrix}$$

and $\Delta = \gamma\phi + 1 + \delta - \gamma\psi$.

As in Miller and Weller (1990), a solution to the exchange rate for non-time-dependent boundary conditions must be a function $f(p - p^*)$ which satisfies the following ordinary differential equation

$$a_{21}(p-p^*) + a_{22}f = [a_{11}(p-p^*) + a_{12}f]f' + \sigma^2 f''$$

When the boundary conditions do involve time, however, the exchange rate is a time-varying solution, $g(p-p^*, t)$, and the fundamental differential equation becomes the following partial differential equation

$$a_{21}(p-p^*) + a_{22}g = [a_{11}(p-p^*) + a_{12}g]g_1 + g_2 + \sigma^2 g_{11}$$

(where g_i is the partial derivative of function g with respect to argument i). The time-dependent solution discussed in Section 3 is obtained by solving this equation subject to the boundary condition

$$g = (p-p^*, T) = \bar{s}, \quad -\infty < p-p^* < +\infty$$

Using the method of separation of variables the following solution is obtained

$$s = g(p-p^*, t) = \bar{s}[1-h(t)] + (p-p^*)h(t)$$

where

$$h(t) = \left[\frac{1-e^{(\rho_s-\rho_u)(T-t)}}{\theta_u - \theta_s e^{(\rho_s-\rho_u)(T-t)}}\right]\theta_s\theta_u$$

and ρ_s and ρ_u are the stable and unstable eigenvectors of A and θ_s and θ_u are the slopes of the corresponding eigenvectors.

(This solution can also be obtained by treating the model as deterministic and solving for the level of the exchange rate for each level of the fundamental and at each point in time given an anticipated regime change at time T.)

NOTES

We are most grateful to Robert Skidelsky and Paul Weller for extensive discussions on both historical and theoretical issues to do with sterling's return to the Gold Standard. We are also happy to acknowledge the financial support of the ESRC (grant no. R000231417). Responsibility for errors remains with us.

1 The authors appear to accept the relevance of this point (p. 170); and in their conclusion they go so far as to divide the causes of the appreciation of sterling into two categories (i) contemporary policy and other fundamentals, and (ii) the anticipation of the return to gold. While they claim to have shown the latter to be negative, they conclude that 'fruitful empirical extensions of the story would involve abandoning our agnosticism about the identity of the fundamentals (in $k(t)$) . . . monetary policy is one possibility'.

2 Those expecting wages and prices to adjust quickly may well have drawn comfort from the dramatic fall in money wages observed in the slump of 1921–22. But there were good reasons for treating this as an exceptional episode and not an appropriate precedent for the mid-1920s. Moggridge (1972, p. 110) points out that 'a large proportion of these reductions were accomplished under sliding agreements through which money wages were adjusted to the cost of living. After the experiences of 1921–22 such agreements naturally became less popular and this meant that this 'easy' route [to deflation] could be less relied on in the future'. In his observations on British wage history, Hicks (1974, pp. 66–9) argues that the wage falls, coming as they did after a large increase in the previous year, were evidence that 'the confidence in money was impaired'; and he concluded that 'when that confidence was restored prices became sticky again'.

3 The principal exception to this is where there is no feedback between the asset price and the evolution of fundamentals ($a_{12} = 0$): in which case the solutions are Confluent Hypergeometric Functions. The attraction of using such solutions is in our view offset by the implausibility of assuming that the exchange rate has no effect of the evolution of prices.

4 The case where there are two possible parities at which one may switch to fixed rates was examined in Miller and Weller (1989).

5 The subtitle of Moggridge's book on the topic is 'The Norman Conquest of $4.86'!

6 See, for example, the comment by S. Brittan 'joining the EMS amid talk of realignments would undo much of the benefit of membership. For which wage negotiators are going to be influenced by a currency peg which Mrs Thatcher insists can readily be withdrawn?' (*Financial Times*, 2 July 1990)

7 The formal methods we adopt here were used in an earlier paper where a Poisson process is embodied in a model of forward looking exchange rates, see Miller and Sutherland (1989).

8 The simple 'peso problem' approach described here is one in which there is essentially no convergence in the speeds – but in research currently in progress at Warwick Luisa Lambertini is using more realistic partial realignment rules such as are described by Giavazzi and Spaventa (1990) to obtain convergence.

REFERENCES

Calvo, G. (1983), 'Staggered prices in a utility-maximizing framework', *Journal of Monetary Economics* **12**, 383–98.

Dornbusch, R. (1976), 'Expectations and exchange rate dynamics', *Journal of Political Economy* **84**, 1161–76.

Flood, R.P. and P.M. Garber (1983), 'A model of stochastic process switching', *Econometrica* **51**, 537–52.

(1989), 'The linkage between speculative attack and target zone models of exchange rates', NBER Working Paper No. 2918.

Froot, K.A. and M. Obstfeld (1989), 'Exchange rate dynamics under stochastic regime shifts: a unified approach', Working Paper.

Giavazzi, F. and L. Spaventa (1990), 'The "new" EMS', CEPR Discussion paper No. 369, January.

Hicks, J. (1974), *The Crisis in Keynesian Economics*, Oxford: Basil Blackwell.

Ichikawa, M., M. Miller and A. Sutherland (1991), 'Entering a preannounced currency band', this volume.

Keynes, J.M. (1972), *The Collected Writings of J.M. Keynes*, Vol. IX, *Essays in Persuasion*. London: Macmillan.

(1973), *The Collected Writings of J.M. Keynes*, Vol. XIX. Activities, 1922–29, The Return to Gold and Industrial Policy I. London, Macmillan.

Krugman, P. (1988), 'Target zones and exchange rate dynamics', NBER Working Paper no. 2481 (forthcoming in the *Quarterly Journal of Economics*).

Lewis, K.K. (1988), 'The persistence of the "Peso Problem" when policy is noisy', *Journal of International Money and Finance* **7**, 5–21.

Miller, M. and A. Sutherland (1989), 'Monetary targets, exchange rate targets and after: a stochastic hard landing for sterling?' Warwick Economic Research Paper No. 336 (forthcoming in V. Argy and P. De Grauwe (eds), *Choosing an Exchange Rate Regime: The Challenge for Smaller Industrial Countries*, IMF, 1990).

Miller, M. and P. Weller (1989), 'Qualitative solutions for stochastic saddlepoints and analysis of exchange rate regimes', mimeo, University of Warwick (presented to NBER Summer Institute, August).

(1990), 'Exchange rate bands with price inertia', Warwick Economic Research Paper No. 337, February (also available as CEPR Discussion Paper No. 421).

Moggridge, D.E. (1972), *British Monetary Policy 1924–31*, Cambridge University Press.

Skidelsky, R. (1988), 'The return to the gold standard', mimeo, Department of International Studies, University of Warwick, (draft chapter from vol. 2 of his life of Keynes).

Smith, G.W. (1989), 'Solutions to a problem of stochastic process switching', revised 1987 mimeo, Queen's University.

Smith, G.W. and R.T. Smith (1990), 'Stochastic process switching and the return to gold, 1925', *Economic Journal* **100**, 164–75.

Svensson, L.E.O. (1989), 'Target zones and interest rate variability', CEPR Discussion Paper No. 372.

Whittle, P. (1982), *Optimisation Over Time: Dynamic Programming and Stochastic Control*, Vol. 2, New York: John Wiley and Sons.

Discussion

GREGOR W. SMITH

Economists have had relatively little success in accounting for movements of contemporary floating exchange rates. It is not surprising that accounts of the interwar float also are controversial. In reexamining the behaviour of the sterling/dollar rate in the 1920s Marcus Miller and Alan Sutherland hold themselves to a strict standard in seeking a model which is consistent with (a) policy announcements and contemporary views in the 1920s, in addition to (b) the behaviour of the exchange rate and some other macroeconomic variables. I shall discuss Sections 1 and 2 of their chapter, dealing with the return to gold in the UK in 1925. Following the organization of the chapter, I first comment on their three criticisms of the model of Flood and Garber (1983), as interpreted by Smith and Smith (1990). I then discuss the sticky-price model proposed by Miller and Sutherland.

1 *Three criticisms of the 'monetary' model*

Some of Miller and Sutherland's criticisms of existing models apply to the general form of the models and some apply only if the unobservable fundamental is interpreted as arising from the monetary model of the exchange rate. Their three criticisms are as follows:

(a) The trend arose as part of a policy to return to parity

A policy can be thought of as consisting of a barrier-drift pair $(\bar{k}, \eta)$ (ignoring randomness and issues of credibility). Given η, lowering $\bar{k}$ (from ∞, say) lowers the path. Given $\bar{k}$, raising η raises the path. Of these two the latter seems more consistent with interwar policy, as Miller and Sutherland argue, since it was the aim of achieving $\bar{k}$ that gave rise to η. Various counterfactual policies may be studied for various reasons. If the alternative to pegging is continuing η then the effect of the peg is to lower s and if the alternative is zero η then the effect is to raise s. The former alternative was of interest because it was involved implicitly in standard applications of floating rate empirical models (as Flood and Garber, 1983, argued). Those (monetary) models assumed implicitly that the madmen in authority were contracting the money supply while uncommitted to a peg; had that been the case then the exchange rate would have been even higher. Miller and Sutherland's lucid discussion has clarified these questions about the counterfactual exchange rates paths. Their next two criticisms deal with alternative models of the actual rate.

(b) Flood and Garber (1983) rule out discrete jumps in k at T

If one interprets k as a money supply differential then the usual path involves the assumption that there is no discrete reduction in UK money at T. This point also has been made by Obstfeld and Stockman (1984) and Obstfeld (1984). More generally, a variety of expected changes in the elements of the composite variable k could support the various paths in Miller and Sutherland's Figure 7.2. Discrete changes in the real exchange rate also are allowed, since one can write the monetary model with PPP and a shock (which can be very persistent). Movements in some individual elements of k (such as currency and bank deposits) could be checked empirically. Unfortunately, there seem to be no data available on the interventions in the spring of 1925 (including forward ones) so it is difficult to examine interventions directly.

However, this criticism and the next one may have statistically testable implications for the path of the exchange rate itself. A simple attempt to study the path directly for the appropriate nonlinearity is described below.

(c) The rule was time- as well as state-dependent

Charles Addis hoped that the authorities would announce that they would let the Gold and Silver (Export Control) Act expire at the end of 1925, effectively putting the UK back on the gold standard at the time. I am not sure whether in the event such a return would have occurred at $4.86. In any case, Addis did not get his wish: to my knowledge Ministers did *not* state that the Act would be allowed to expire. Presumably Addis wished for such a statement precisely because he thought (or thought that market participants thought) that the government might not be determined to let the act expire.

If Ministers did spread word that parity would be attained by the end of 1925, what effect would that have had on the exchange rate? As Miller and Sutherland show, the effect of this anticipation would have been to make the exchange rate a mix of the floating rate and the higher fixed rate, with the weights tilting to the latter over time (as in their equation (5)). They suggest that this may rationalise Keynes's view on the positive speculative effect on sterling.

Miller and Sutherland's model of time dependency has implications which can be tested statistically. Take the general case of their equation (5):

$$s(k(t),t) = [k(t) + \lambda\eta]\cdot[1 - \exp(-\lambda^{-1}(T-t)] + (\bar{s} - \eta(T-\mathrm{t}))[\exp(-\lambda^{-1}(T-t)] \quad (1)$$

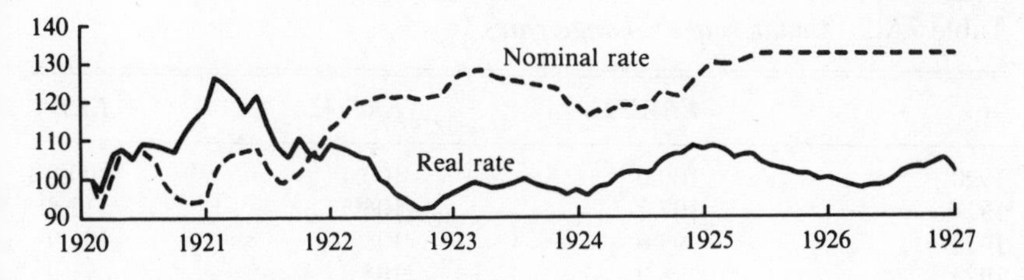

Figure 7A.1 The monthly real exchange rate

election) but earlier ones are clouded by price and capital controls. Gauging jumps may be difficult.

2 *Price inertia*

In Section 3 of their chapter, Miller and Sutherland outline a model with sluggish price adjustment. One of the appealing features of their model is that it seeks to mimic some views of Addis and Keynes on price adjustment (though not those of Governor Norman, who did not believe in calculations of PPP) as well as properties of data. An informal argument in favour of a sticky price model is that the return to gold would have been accomplished much more rapidly and at lower cost with price flexibility. Monetary contraction was early (e.g. see Capie and Collins, 1983; tables 6.15 and 6.17) and Miller and Sutherland allow for this in their Figure 7.5. There, tight money leads to a jump nominal appreciation and then slower appreciation as prices slowly adjust. Thus the model has some intrinsic dynamics, other than those imparted to the nominal exchange rate by η.

Is this view consistent with historical price adjustment? Figure 7A.1 gives the monthly real exchange rate defined as the nominal exchange rate in dollars per pound times the ratio of UK to US wholesale price indexes, with January 1920 = 100, and not seasonally adjusted. The dotted line gives the nominal exchange rate, again scaled so that January 1920 = 100. Table 7A.2 gives annual exchange rates defined using wholesale price indexes (*ERWPI*), cost-of-living indexes (*ERCOL*), and wages in manufacturing (*ERW*) in the two countries. In each case 1920 = 100.

The second column in Table 7A.2 is based on indexes of the cost of living and gives the result expected by students either of postwar floats or of the historiography of the return to gold: the nominal appreciation was a real appreciation. The first and third columns and Figure 7A.1 are more surprising. In those data there does seem to be fairly rapid mean-reversion

Table 7A.2. *Annual real exchange rates*

	ERWPI	*ERCOL*	*ERW*
1920	100.0	100.0	100.0
1921	107.2	106.5	112.8
1922	99.6	108.7	105.9
1923	98.9	105.0	91.0
1924	102.5	102.5	84.9
1925	101.8	109.2	94.4
1926	98.6	107.6	94.9

in the real exchange rate, which seems inconsistent with sluggish price adjustment's being a central part of the story.

3 *Conclusions*

Miller and Sutherland have suggested that time-dependence and price inertia are important in understanding the interwar history of sterling. On the basis of the empirical exercises here I have some doubts about those suggestions. But I have no doubts about the fruitfulness of their developing models without anonymous fundamentals. It is precisely that development which allows most tests, whether based on real exchange rates or, as in the case of their discussion of entry into the exchange-rate mechanism, on wages and interest rates across countries. I hope that Miller and Sutherland also will apply their tools to other interwar process switches such as those of 1926 in France and 1931 in the UK.

Data sources

The spot dollar-sterling rates are found in Lawrie (1924) and *The Commercial and Financial Chronicle* (1925). The UK price indexes come from the tables in Capie and Collins (1983): Board of Trade wholesale price index (Table 2.1); Ministry of Labour retail price index cost of living (Table 2.13); index of 11 weekly wage rates (Table 4.1). The US wholesale price index is from the *Federal Reserve Bulletin*. Other US price indexes are from US Dept. of Commerce (1957) *Historical Statistics of the United States*: Burgess cost-of-living index, series E157–160 p. 127; average hourly earnings in manufacturing, series D626-634 p. 62. I was unable to find reliable export price indexes.

NOTES

I gratefully acknowledge the financial support of the Social Science and Humanities Research Council of Canada and of the CEPR. Peter Garber and Marcus Miller have explained certain points to me but are not responsible for this discussion.

REFERENCES

Capie, F. and M. Collins (1983), *The Interwar British Economy: A Statistical Abstract*. Manchester: Manchester University Press.

Hájek, J. (1969), *Nonparametric Statistics*. San Francisco: Holden-Day.

Hájek, J. and Z. Šidak (1967), *Theory of Rank Tests*. New York: Academic Press.

Flood, R.P. and P.M. Garber (1983), 'A model of stochastic process switching', *Econometrica* **51**, 537–51.

Lawrie, H.N. (1924), *Foreign Currency and Exchange Investigation, Commission of Gold and Silver Inquiry, United States Senate*. Serial 8. Washington: Government Printing Office.

Obstfeld, M. (1984), 'Balance of payments crises and devaluation', *Journal of Money, Credit, and Banking* **16**, 208–17.

Obstfeld, M. and A.C. Stockman (1984), 'Exchange-rate dynamics', in P.B. Kenen and R.W. Jones, (eds.), *Handbook of International Economics*, Chapter 17. Amsterdam: North-Holland.

Smith, G.W. and R.T. Smith (1990), 'Stochastic process switching and the return to gold, 1925', *Economic Journal* **100**, 164–75.

The Commercial and Financial Chronicle (1925), vol. 119, part 2 and vol. 120, parts 1 and 2. Washington: William B. Dana Company.

PART IV

LIMITED RESERVES AND SUSTAINABILITY

8 Speculative attacks on target zones

PAUL KRUGMAN and JULIO ROTEMBERG

There are two extensive theoretical literatures that emphasize the interaction between shifts between fixed and floating exchange rates, on one hand, and expectations, on the other. The speculative attack literature, in which the seminal insight of Salant and Henderson (1978) was applied by Krugman (1979), Flood and Garber (1984), and many others to exchange rates, focussed on the collapse of fixed rate systems; the stochastic target zone literature, building on the initial contribution of Krugman (forthcoming), focusses on the behaviour of floating rates subject to limits. There are evident affinities between these two literatures, already noted by Flood and Garber (1989); the purpose of this paper is to build an explicit bridge.

To do this, we consider a model in which the monetary authority uses unsterilized intervention to attempt to keep the exchange rate within a target zone, but has limited reserves. Because these reserves are limited, the target zone may be unsustainable. A potentially unsustainable target zone, not surprisingly, has different implications for exchange rate behaviour than a fully credible one.

The paper is in five sections. Section 1 lays out the basic exchange rate model, and derives its behaviour under a pure exchange rate float. Section 2 considers the effect of a one-sided exchange rate target in a situation in which the monetary authority has 'small' reserves (in a sense that will become apparent). This analysis turns out not to yield the 'smooth-pasting' result of the now-standard target zone model, but instead to yield a result closer to that found in the earlier speculative attack literature. Section 3 then examines how the result changes as the monetary authority's reserves get larger, and shows how there is a transition to the smooth-pasting equilibrium. Sections 4 and 5 apply the analysis to the case of an occasionally collapsing gold standard, which we show can usefully be regarded as the boundary between two one-sided target zones.

1 The basic model

We consider a basic log-linear monetary model of the exchange rate. The exchange rate at any point in time is determined by

$$s = m + v + \gamma E[ds]/dt \tag{1}$$

where s is the log of the price of foreign exchange, m the log of the money supply, v a money demand shock term (incorporating shifts in real income, velocity, etc.), and the last term captures the effect of expected depreciation.

Money demand is assumed to follow a random walk with drift:

$$dv = \mu\, dt + \sigma\, dz \tag{2}$$

As Miller and Weller (1989) have shown, more complex processes, notably autoregressive ones, can be incorporated into the analysis without changing the qualitative results. We stick with this process for simplicity.

The general solution to the model defined by (1) and (2) for a fixed money supply has by now become familiar (see for example Froot and Obstfeld, 1989). It takes the form

$$s = m + v + \gamma\mu + Ae^{a_1 v} + Be^{a_2 v} \tag{3}$$

where a_1, a_2 are parameters that will be determined in a moment, and A and B are free parameters that need to be tied down by the economics of the situation.

To determine a_1 and a_2, we first note that by applying Ito's Lemma we have

$$E[ds]/dt = \mu + \mu[a_1 Ae^{a_1 v} + a_2 Be^{a_2 v}] + \frac{\sigma^2}{2}[a_1^2 Ae^{a_1 v} + a_2^2 Be^{a_2 v}] \tag{4}$$

Substituting (4) back into (1), and comparing it with (3), we find that the roots are

$$a_1 = \frac{-\gamma\mu + \sqrt{\gamma^2\mu^2 + 2\gamma\sigma^2}}{\gamma\sigma^2} > 0$$
$$a_2 = \frac{-\gamma\mu - \sqrt{\gamma^2\mu^2 + 2\gamma\sigma^2}}{\gamma\sigma^2} < 0 \tag{5}$$

We can now turn to the economic interpretation of (3). The first three terms in (3) evidently represent a sort of 'fundamental' exchange rate: they reflect the combination of money supply, money demand, and the known drift in money demand. The other terms represent a deviation of the exchange rate from this fundamental value.

Suppose that the money supply were expected to remain unchanged at its initial level forever. Notice that v can take on any value. It seems reasonable to exclude solutions for the exchange rate that deviate arbitrarily far from the fundamental level when v takes on large positive or negative values. Thus under a pure float, in which the monetary authority is expected to remain passive whatever the exchange rate may do, we may assume $A = B = 0$. The exchange rate equation under a pure float is therefore

$$s = m + v + \gamma\mu \tag{6}$$

2 An exchange rate target with 'small' reserves

Now let us suppose that the monetary authority, instead of being passive, attempts to place an upper limit on the price of foreign exchange. Specifically, the monetary authority is willing to buy foreign exchange in an unsterilized intervention, up to the limit of its reserves, when the exchange rate goes above some level s_{max}.

Provided that these reserves are small enough (we will calculate the critical size below), this attempt will lead to a speculative attack in which the whole of the reserves are suddenly exhausted when the exchange rate reaches s_{max}.

We start by defining the initial money supply as the sum of reserves and domestic credit:

$$m = ln(D + R) \tag{7}$$

Following the speculative attack, the money supply will fall to

$$m' = ln(D) \tag{8}$$

Figure 8.1 illustrates the equilibrium before and after the speculative attack. After the attack, the exchange rate will be freely floating, with money supply m'; so the post-attack exchange rate equation is

$$s = m' + v + \gamma\mu \tag{9}$$

shown in Figure 8.1 as the locus $F'F'$.

The attack will occur when v reaches the level at which the reduction in the money supply that results from the attack validates itself, by leading to the exchange rate s_{max}; this is shown in Figure 8.1 as point C, and corresponds to the level of v, v', such that

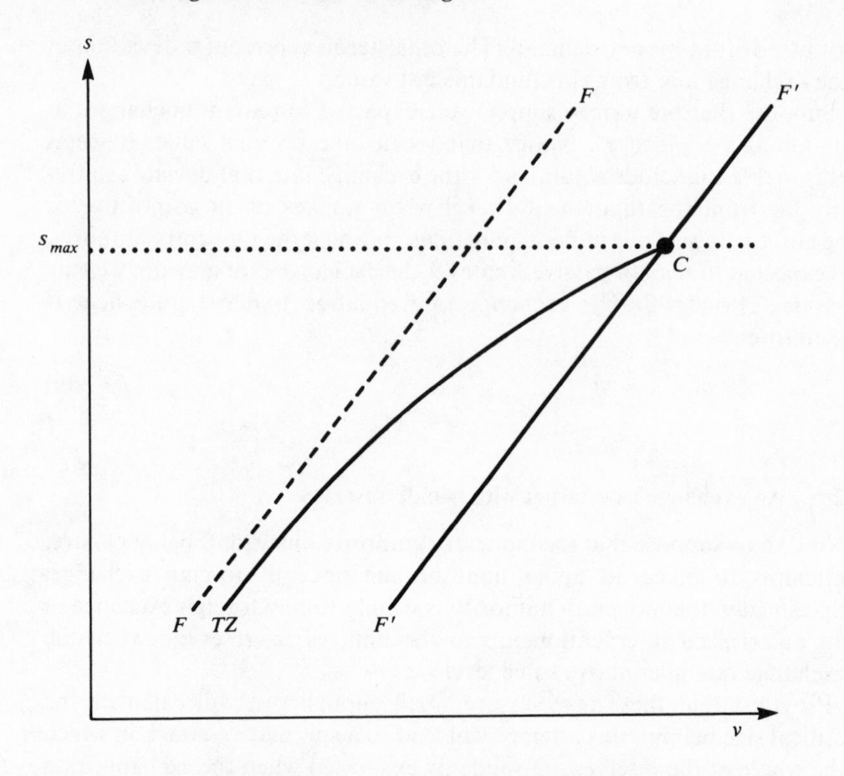

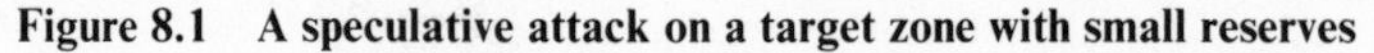

Figure 8.1 A speculative attack on a target zone with small reserves

$$s_{max} = m' + v' + \gamma\mu \tag{10}$$

What about the exchange rate before the speculative attack? First, we note that since a regime change will be triggered if v goes above a certain level, we can no longer use a no-bubbles argument to require $A = 0$ in equation (3). (Since this exchange rate target is one-sided, there is no lower limit on v, so we still must have $B = 0$). The pre-attack exchange rate equation is therefore

$$s = m + v + \gamma\mu + Ae^{a_1 v} \tag{11}$$

To tie down A, we use the standard speculative attack argument: there must be no foreseeable jump in the exchange rate, so we must choose A so that $s = s_{max}$ when $v = v'$. It is apparent from Figure 7.1 that this requires $A < 0$. The result is therefore that up until the attack the knowledge that the monetary authority will attempt to defend the currency will tend to hold down the price of foreign exchange. This may be seen in Figure 8.1 from the fact that the actual relationship TZ between v and s before the attack lies everywhere below the free float relationship *FF* corresponding to the initial money supply m.

When reserves are small, then, the monetary authority fails in its effort to enforce an exchange rate target. The knowledge that it will try supports the currency; but eventually the target is overrun by a speculative attack. Notice that 'smooth pasting' nowhere makes its appearance in this analysis. Indeed, the pre-attack schedule in Figure 8.1 is not tangent to the exchange rate target.

Our next step is to enlarge the monetary authority's reserves, and show that if these reserves are sufficiently large, a 'smooth-pasting' solution emerges.

3 A target zone with large reserves

A variety of alternative potential speculative attack scenarios can be generated by varying the parameter A in equation (11). In Figure 8.2 we show the curves traced out by increasingly negative values of A. A small absolute value of A corresponds to a speculative attack at C_1. A larger absolute value of A would produce an attack somewhere to the right of C_1, and this attack would consume more reserves because the implied fall in the money supply – measured as the horizontal distance from the attack point to the free float locus – would be larger.

It is immediately apparent, however, that one cannot in this way generate arbitrarily large speculative attacks. The reason is that the family of curves corresponding to different (negative) values of A all turn downward at some point, and for a sufficiently negative A the maximum of the curve lies below s_{max}. But it is not possible for the exchange rate pre-attack to lie on a locus that passes above s_{max} before the attack takes place, since that would trigger the central bank's intervention.

The upshot is that the analysis of the previous section is valid only if the size of reserves is not too large; specifically, if the free float locus corresponding to the money supply that would follow elimination of all reserves does not lie to the right of the point C_2 in Figure 8.2.

If reserves are larger than this level, what must happen is that the pre-attack exchange rate equation is precisely that which leads to C_2. That is, A must be chosen so that the exchange rate locus is tangent to the target. Smooth pasting therefore emerges, not as the general solution of this model, but as its solution when the central bank's reserves are sufficiently large.

We can derive the critical level of reserves as follows. First, the exchange rate locus must be flat at v':

$$ds/dv = 1 + a A e^{a_1 v'} = 0 \tag{12}$$

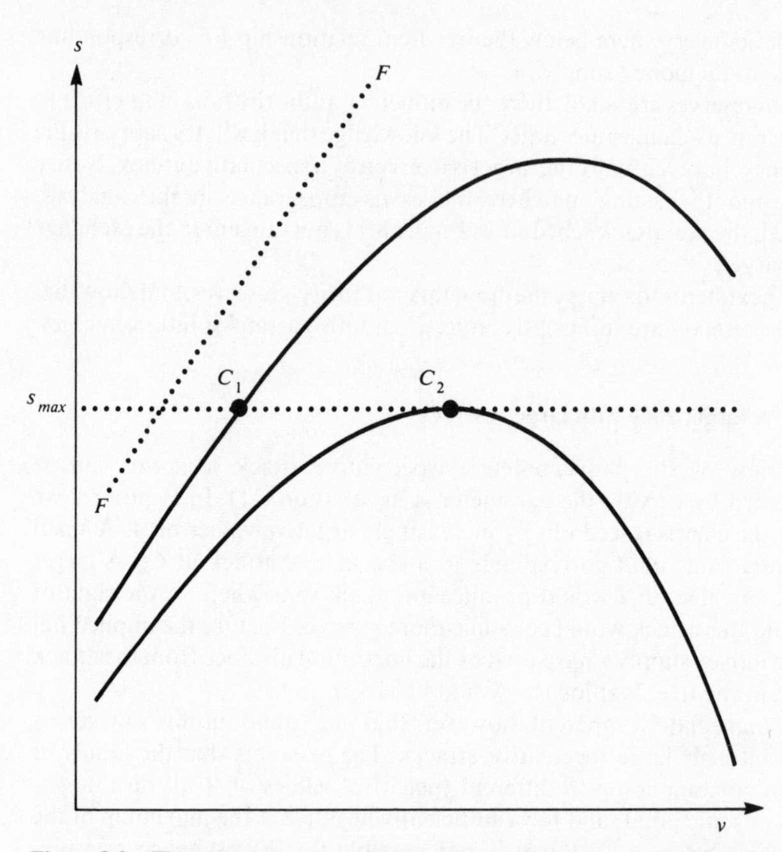

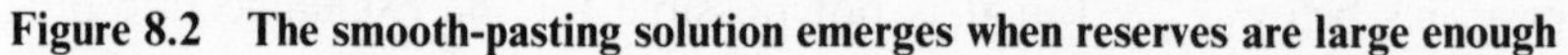

Figure 8.2 The smooth-pasting solution emerges when reserves are large enough

It must also be true that the actual exchange rate at v' is precisely the target rate s_{max}:

$$s_{max} = m + v' + \gamma\mu + Ae^{a_1 v'} \tag{13}$$

Substituting (12) into (13), we find

$$s_{max} = m + v' + \gamma\mu - \frac{1}{a_1} \tag{14}$$

But now notice that immediately following a speculative attack, the exchange rate must also be s_{max}:

$$s_{max} = m' + v' + \gamma\mu \tag{15}$$

From (14) and (15) we can therefore determine the change in the money supply that occurs at the maximum size speculative attack:

$$m' - m = -\frac{\mu}{a_1} \tag{16}$$

But the change in the money supply in a speculative attack depends on the ratio of reserves to domestic credit:

$$m' - m = -ln\left(\frac{D+R}{D}\right) = -ln\left(1 + \frac{R}{D}\right) \tag{17}$$

So the nature of the equilibrium changes from speculative attack to smooth pasting when

$$\frac{R}{D} > e^{\frac{\mu}{a_1}} - 1 \tag{18}$$

When this criterion is met, the central bank is able to hold the line at s_{max} with an infinitesimal intervention that slightly reduces the money supply, shifting the relationship between v and s down. If v then falls again, the exchange rate retreats down this new schedule; if v rises, another intervention must take place. These successive interventions would gradually shift the exchange rate schedule to the right. As long as the reserves remain sufficiently large, s_{max} will act as a reflecting barrier for the exchange rate, which will sometimes rise to s_{max}, sometimes fall below it.

It is immediately apparent, however, that this process cannot go on indefinitely. When v is high, the monetary authority loses reserves; when v falls again, it does not regain them. So there is a gradual loss of reserves, which will gradually shift the exchange rate schedule to the right. Eventually the level of reserves will fall to the critical level where a speculative attack becomes possible; at that point, the next time that the exchange rate drifts up to the level s_{max} there will be a full-scale speculative attack that eliminates all remaining reserves. In other words, a country that starts with large reserves will go through a 'smooth-pasting' phase where small interventions succeed in holding the line on the exchange rate; but there will be a gradual (albeit intermittent) drain on reserves, and as in conventional speculative attack models there will eventually be a crisis once reserves have dropped to a critical level.

This is not a very complicated analysis. Nonetheless, it makes several points that have been obscured in some of the recent literature on the subject.

First, it is clear from this model that looking at the case of bounded fundamentals is not equivalent to looking at the case of an exchange rate target. If we were to use the bounded fundamentals technique on this model, we would replace the idea of a target on s with that of an upper limit on $m + v$. This would correctly capture the notion of what happens as long as reserves are sufficiently large to achieve the smooth-pasting solution; but it would miss both the case where initial reserves are small, and the logic of eventual crisis.

Second, in a related point, smooth pasting is not a general result of this model, the way it appears to be in the bounded fundamentals formulation. On the contrary, it is a special case that obtains when reserves are sufficiently large; otherwise the logic is that of speculative attack: the present exchange rate is tied down by the requirement that there be no foreseeable jumps in the future exchange rate.

Third, this model helps settle a controversy about the justification for the smooth-pasting result. Some economists approaching the problem from the perspective of optimization models have questioned the use of the smooth-pasting condition in *ad hoc* monetary models of this kind, arguing that a condition that arises from optimization is hard to justify when optimizing behaviour is at best implicit. Those of us doing the *ad hoc* models have argued on the contrary that the condition can equally be seen as being implied by arbitrage.[1] In this model we see smooth pasting emerge as the limit of the 'no foreseeable jumps' condition of a speculative attack model – essentially an arbitrage condition – when reserves are sufficiently large.

4 A gold standard model

In the remainder of this paper we make use of the type of analysis developed in earlier sections to attack a particular problem that has been the subject of several recent papers, that of the role of speculative attacks under a gold standard system.

Several papers, notably Buiter (1989) and Grilli (1989), have analysed the problem of speculative attack in a gold standard model. Grilli implements the model empirically as well. However, as we will show shortly, straightforward application of the standard speculative attack model to the problem of a gold standard runs into serious problems. The standard model, in its simplest version, seems to suggest that there will in fact be no speculative attacks on a gold standard, that such a regime will end with a whimper rather than a bang; this runs counter to both intuition and experience. Worse yet, with a little elaboration one runs into a serious conceptual paradox that undermines the logic of the analysis. What we will do in this part of the paper is show how an economically reasonable model of speculative attacks on a gold standard can be created by treating such a standard as a boundary between two imperfectly sustainable target zones.

The basic gold standard model may be presented as a two-country version of the model at the beginning of this paper. The exchange rate depends on the ratio of two countries' money supplies, a demand shock term, and the expected rate of depreciation:

$$s = m - m^* + v + \gamma \frac{E[ds]}{dt} \tag{19}$$

Each country's money supply consists of domestic credit plus reserves:

$$\begin{aligned} m &= ln(D + R) \\ m^* &= ln(D^* + R^*) \end{aligned} \tag{20}$$

Reserves, however, are now taken to consist of gold, which is in fixed world supply:

$$R + R^* = G \tag{21}$$

As before, we need to specify a process for the money demand term. We will initially suppose that it is a simple random walk without drift – i.e., $\mu = 0$. The implications of more complex stochastic processes are discussed below.

We suppose that the monetary authorities of the two countries stand ready to buy or sell gold to maintain fixed prices of their currencies in terms of gold, and hence in terms of each other; the implied exchange rate is s_{par}. This regime will continue until one country or the other runs out of gold.

The seemingly obvious assumptions are that as long as the regime is in effect, there will be no expected change in exchange rates; and that when the regime collapses, the exchange rate reverts to a free float. It turns out, however, that this combination of assumptions yields the economically implausible result that there are no speculative attacks.

To see why, first ask how reserves would appear to evolve if we in fact assume $E[ds]/dt = 0$. Then when v rises, gold will flow from the first country to the second; when it falls, it will flow in the other direction. Ignoring the possibility of speculative attack, this process could continue until the ratio of money supplies reaches either a maximum or minimum value. The maximum value of $m - m^*$ occurs when all gold has flowed out of the first country; at that point we have

$$m = ln(D) \tag{22}$$

and

$$m^* = ln(D + G) \tag{23}$$

Similarly, $m - m^*$ reaches a minimum when all the gold has flowed to the first country, so that

$$m = ln(D + G) \tag{24}$$

and

$$m^* = ln(D) \tag{25}$$

In the conventional speculative attack literature, we show the necessity of a speculative attack by noticing that if agents were naive, and did not anticipate the possibility of regime collapse, there would be a foreseeble capital gain or loss at the moment of transition. Suppose, then, that agents were naive, and did not realize that a regime change was in prospect. Would they be missing a profit opportunity? Under the assumption of naivete, the gold standard would last until reserves of one country or another run out. Let us suppose that it is the first country that runs out of gold; it would run out at a level of v, v_1, determined by the condition

$$s_{par} = m - m^* + v_1 \tag{26}$$

If the exhaustion of the country's gold is followed by a transition to pure floating, the exchange rate following the transition would be determined by

$$s = m - m^* + v \tag{27}$$

But by comparing (26) and (27) we find that

$$s = s_{par} \tag{28}$$

That is, there is no jump in the exchange rate. This implies that there need not be any speculative attack.

This is an economically implausible conclusion. Matters become even worse if the process determining v is not a simple random walk – if it has drift, or autoregression. In that case one arrives not simply at an implausible result but at a paradox: under some conditions a country may run out of reserves under a fixed rate *before* it meets the usual criterion for a speculative attack. This 'gold standard paradox' has been the subject of several recent papers (Krugman and Rotemberg, 1990; Buiter and Grilli, 1989). However, in this paper we focus only on the case of a random walk, in which there is not strictly speaking a paradox, simply an implausible result.

What we show next is that a much more satisfactory result emerges if we view a gold standard not as a one-time regime that is gone when once it has collapsed, but instead as a regime that is reinstated when feasible. In this case, as we will see, the gold parity becomes a boundary between two target zones.

5 Gold parity as a boundary[2]

The analysis of speculative attacks on a gold standard can be made much more plausible if we make one assumption that is slightly different from the usual speculative attack setup.

The necessary assumption is the following: *central banks do not give up when they run out of gold.* Instead, they remain willing to buy gold at the par value, and thus to reinstate a gold standard if the opportunity arises.

An example may convey the essence of this assumption. Suppose that our two countries are America and Britain, and that they have established par values of gold of $35 and £7 per ounce. If both countries have positive gold reserves, this will peg the dollar–pound exchange rate at 5. Suppose, however, that America has run out of gold. Then the exchange rate may float above this level – say, at $7 per pound. The price of gold will be set by the willingness of the British central bank to sell it, at £7 per ounce.

What we will assume is that even though America has run out of gold, its central bank still remains willing to buy gold if the price falls to 35 dollars. (It would be willing to sell gold at that price also, but it doesn't have any to sell). With an exchange rate of 7, of course, the price of gold is $49, so there will be no current sales; but if the exchange rate falls (the dollar appreciates) to 5, gold purchases will commence.

Conversely, if Britain has run out of gold, the exchange rate will float at a level below 5; but if it rises to 5, Britain's central bank will again buy gold.

Consider what this implies. If the exchange rate is above 5, then everyone knows that if it falls to 5 America will buy gold and Britain sell it – which means that America will increase its money supply and Britain reduce its money supply. This means that when America is out of gold, and the exchange rate is floating, the float is *not* free. Instead, there is in effect a one-sided target zone, in which there is a *de facto* commitment to support the pound with unsterilized intervention if the dollar strengthens too much.

The reverse is also true: when Britain has run out of gold, the float is in effect a target zone with a commitment to support the dollar with unsterilized intervention if the pound strengthens to its par value.

This tells us that the par value implied by the prices at which each currency is pegged to gold may be regarded as a boundary between two one-sided target zones. In the lower zone, in which America has all the gold – which we will call the A-zone – the dollar–pound exchange rate is held below its free-float locus by the prospect of US gold sales and British

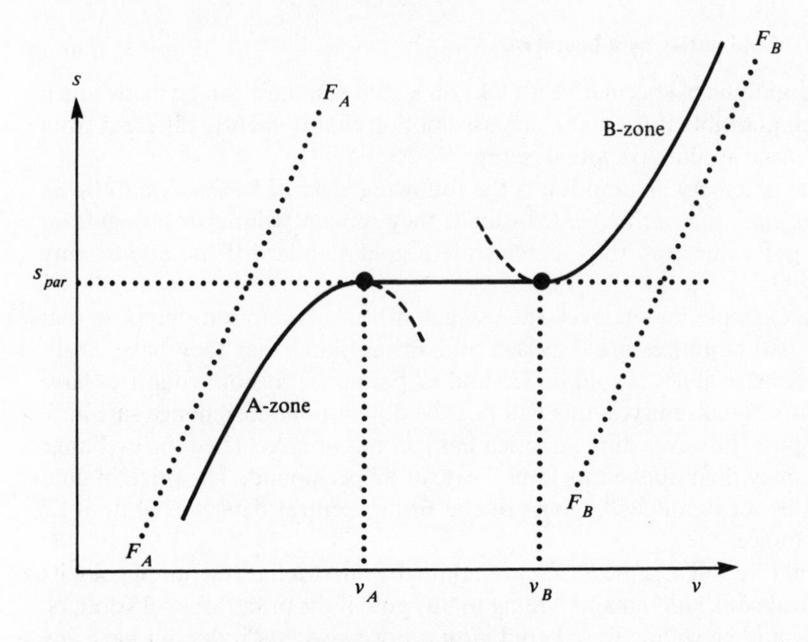

Figure 8.3 A gold standard with large reserves

gold purchases if the pound rises too much. In the B-zone, where Britain has all the gold, the rate is correspondingly held above its free-float locus.

If the world's gold stock is large enough, the picture looks like Figure 8.3, which plots the exchange rate against v. (We will describe the case with insufficient gold backing for the world's currencies below). The lines F_AF_A and F_BF_B represents the free-float loci – that is, F_AF_A represents how s would vary with v if America had all the gold and there was no prospect of future intervention, and F_BF_B the corresponding case with all gold in British hands. The actual relationship in the A-zone, however, is that which we have already seen for a one-sided target zone with large reserves: a curve that lies below the free-float locus and is tangent to the par value line at some value v_A. Similarly, in the B-zone the relationship between v and s lies above the free-float locus and is tangent to the par value line at v_B.

The relationship between v and s is therefore indicated by the curve on the left up to v_A; the par value is sustained between v_A and v_B; and s follows the curve on the right for v greater than v_B. Outside the range where the par value is sustained, the prospect of a return to the gold standard either supports or depresses the exchange rate.

What happens if v starts within the range where the par value can be sustained, then drifts out of that range, say to v_B? The answer is that as long as we are on the 'flat', there will be a gradual American loss of gold. When v_B is reached, however, there will be a speculative attack that leads to a discrete American loss of its remaining gold. The reason is that the post-attack $v - s$ relationship is convex, so that the variance term makes $E[ds]/dt$ positive. That is, when the gold standard collapses the expected rate of dollar depreciation immediately goes from zero to some positive number, reducing relative American money demand – even if v is expected to fall. Similarly, if v drops to the bottom of the range there will be a speculative attack that leads to a discrete British loss of its remaining gold.

The reason why the currency of the country that runs out of gold is expected to depreciate immediately following the gold exhaustion is somewhat ironic: it is the result of the expectation that the country will try to buy gold if its currency should subsequently appreciate to the par value, which therefore depresses its value under the float.

What happens if America has no gold, and v drifts back into the range in which the par value is enforced? The answer is that there is a speculative run *into* the dollar, leading to a discrete gain in reserves at British expense.

It may be useful to illustrate this model of the gold standard more explicitly, retaining the assumption that v follows a random walk (although Figure 8.3 remains valid even when v follows more complex processes; see Krugman and Rotemberg, 1990).

We begin by noting that when v follows a random walk with no drift, the two roots in the solution sum to zero. Thus the basic exchange rate equation may be written

$$s = m - m^* + v + Ae^{av} + Be^{-av} \tag{29}$$

where a may be calculated using the methods of Section 1.

There are now two *de facto* target zones: the 'A-zone' in which America has all the gold, and the 'B-zone' in which Britain has all the gold. The relative money supplies in these zones are therefore as follows: in the A-zone,

$$m - m^* = ln\left(\frac{D + G}{D^*}\right) \tag{30}$$

while in the B-zone

$$m - m^* = ln\left(\frac{D}{D^* + G}\right) \tag{31}$$

To calculate v_A, we first note that since in the A-zone v is unbounded below, we must have $B = 0$, and must choose a value of A such that the exchange rate reaches its par value at v_A:

$$s_{par} = ln\left(\frac{D+G}{D^*}\right) + v_A + Ae^{av_A} \tag{32}$$

Also, the curve must be flat at v_A:

$$\frac{ds}{dt} = 1 + aAe^{av_A} = 0 \tag{33}$$

Putting these together, we find that

$$v_A = s_{par} - ln\left(\frac{D+G}{D^*}\right) + \frac{1}{a} \tag{34}$$

A similar calculation shows that

$$v_B = s_{par} - ln\left(\frac{D}{D^*+G}\right) - \frac{1}{a} \tag{35}$$

What is the significance of the term $1/a$? It is the horizontal distance from each end of the gold standard range to the corresponding free float locus. It therefore measures the extent to which the target zone aspect of the exchange regime when one country has run out of gold leads to a collapse of the gold standard *before* the gold would have run out under a perfectly credible system. And $1/a$ also measures the change in the log of the ratio of national money supplies that occurs when there is a speculative attack.

This example illustrates how a gold standard with limited gold reserves may be modelled as a boundary between two target zones. However, the example also reveals a problem. As drawn in Figure 8.3, we show $v_B > v_A$, so that there is a range in which the par value can be maintained. But there is no guarantee that this is true. We note that

$$v_B - v_A = ln\left(\frac{D^*+G}{D}\right) + ln\left(\frac{D+G}{D^*}\right) - \frac{2}{a} \tag{36}$$

This will be positive only if gold reserves G are large enough relative to the world money supply. When gold reserves *are* sufficient, we get the story illustrated in Figure 8.3. But what if they are not sufficient?

On reflection, the story is apparent: it is illustrated in Figure 8.4. The par exchange rate s_{par} still represents the boundary between two target zone regimes, but the loci in each regime no longer 'smooth paste' to the par value. Instead, they smooth paste to each other at some critical value of v. Whenever v crosses that value, there is a speculative attack that transfers

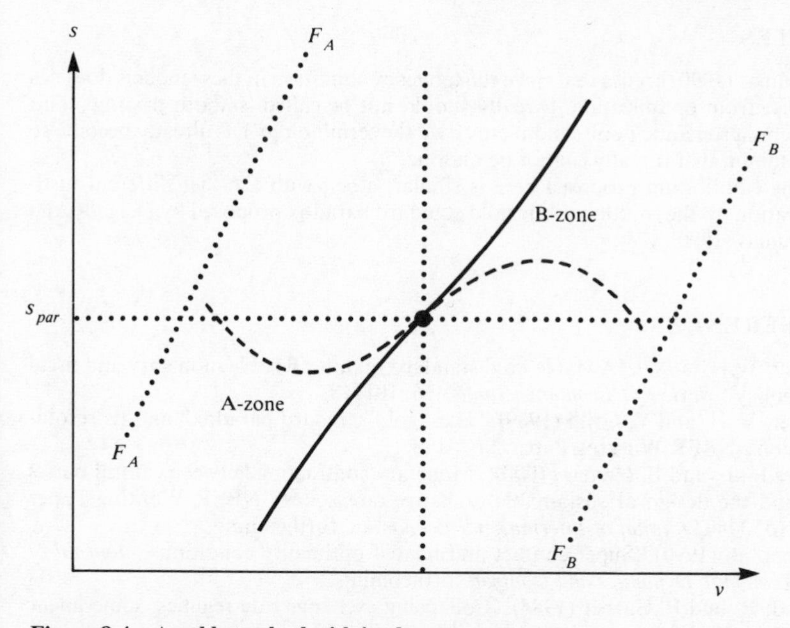

Figure 8.4 A gold standard with inadequate reserves

all of the gold from America to Britain or vice versa. The central banks are trying to enforce a gold parity, but one or the other is always failing.

6 Conclusions

The literature on deterministic speculative attacks and the more recent literature on target zones share the insight that to understand how an exchange regime works, one must also understand how it ends. Capital flows under fixed rates depend critically on expectations of abandonment of parities. Exchange rates under floating may depend equally critically on expectations of future efforts to peg. These literatures therefore are closely related in spirit, and one would like to tie them together.

This paper offers one way to link the two views. Speculative attacks on target zones emerge in much the same way as speculative attacks on fixed rates, but the stochastic aspect of the model makes the analysis richer and, one hopes, adds insight. In particular, a target zone approach allows a much more satisfying analysis of speculation under a gold standard than is possible using the previous standard models.

NOTES

1 Dumas (1990) argues that since the tangency condition in these models does not arise from optimization, it really should not be called 'smooth pasting'. This seems a semantic point, and in any case the terminology has already become so common that it really cannot be undone.
2 The equilibrium proposed here is similar, albeit with a rather different justification, to the solution to the gold standard paradox proposed by Delgado and Dumas (1990).

REFERENCES

Buiter, W.H. (1989), 'A viable gold standard requires flexible monetary and fiscal policy', *Review of Economic Studies* **56**, 101–18.

Buiter, W.H. and V. Grilli (1989), 'The "gold standard paradox" and its resolution', NBER Working Paper No. 3178.

Delgado, F. and B. Dumas (1990), 'Monetary contracting between central banks and the design of sustainable exchange-rate zones', NBER Working Paper No. 3440, *Journal of International Economics*, forthcoming.

Dumas, B. (1990), 'Super contact and related optimality conditions', *Journal of Economic Dynamics and Control*, forthcoming.

Flood, R. and P. Garber (1984), 'Collapsing exchange rate regimes: some linear examples', *Journal of International Economics* **17**, 1–13.

(1989), 'The linkage between speculative attack and target zone models of exchange rates', NBER Working Paper No. 2918, and see their chapter in this volume.

Froot, K. and M. Obstfeld (1989), 'Stochastic process switching: some simple solutions', NBER Working Paper No. 2998, this volume, and *Econometrica* forthcoming.

Grilli, V. (1989), 'Managing exchange rate crises: evidence from the 1890s', *Journal of International Money and Finance*, forthcoming.

Krugman, P. (1979), 'A model of balance of payments crises', *Journal of Money, Credit and Banking* **11**, 311–25.

(1991), 'Target zones and exchange rate dynamics', *Quarterly Journal of Economics* **106**, forthcoming.

Krugman, P. and J. Rotemberg (1990), 'Target zones with limited reserves', NBER Working Paper No. 3418.

Salant, S. and D. Henderson (1978), 'Market anticipation of government policy and the price of gold', *Journal of Political Economy* **86**, 627–48.

Discussion

BERNARD DUMAS

In earlier work, Krugman and Rotemberg (1990) have examined the possibility of stockouts of reserves in target zone models. They have been led to a remarkable synthesis of the speculative-attacks and target-zone bodies of literature. In the course of this endeavour they have identified a so-called 'gold standard paradox': there exist exchange rate arrangements between two central banks A and B in which bank B running out of reserves triggers an attack against currency A, not currency B.

In the specific paper under discussion Krugman and Rotemberg (KR) give birth to a baby brother of the famous paradox. The traditional analysis of speculative attacks would say that, in the absence of a trend in the fundamental, a fixed-rate system would collapse into a free float without any speculative attack. They consider this to be an 'unreasonable result' and proceed to explain and modify it in the same way that they have earlier explained the paradox.

My remarks deal with four issues: the scope of the paradox, its proposed solutions, the specification of the burden-of-intervention rule and the concept of a gold standard.

1 The scope of the 'gold standard paradox'

The paradox first pointed out in 1989 by Paul Krugman is not specific to the gold standard or even to fixed-exchange rate systems. Indeed, in Delgado and Dumas (1990) it is shown that the same paradox arises in a target-zone situation provided that the target zone is 'narrow enough',[1] and provided that, in case of crisis, the anticipated scenario is a transition to a free float.

One condition which is needed for the paradox to arise in its original form is that the process for the stochastic disturbance and, therefore, the process for the fundamental should have non-zero drift. It can be a constant non-zero drift in which case, as Buiter and Grilli (1989) showed, the paradox arises only on the side of one of the two currencies party to the monetary arrangement. Or it can be a variable drift, as in models of mean-reversion. In that case, the paradox can arise on both sides.

Nonetheless, KR, in the paper under discussion, choose to examine the case of zero drift. They claim that, while it does not lead to a paradox, it does lead to an 'unreasonable result'.

2 *Solutions in the case of a fixed-rate regime*

In the case of a fixed-rate system, the paradox may in some ways be considered solved. In fact, in that case, there is not much of a paradox in the first place. What was considered surprising is that America running out of reserves might in some cases trigger an attack against the pound, not the dollar. Upon reflection, however, that is not surprising since this occurs when the dollar is undervalued *relative to its pre-attack free-float value* and if the transition is from a fixed-rate regime directly to free float (see Delgado and Dumas, 1990). Both central banks are intervening so that it is physically possible for the attack to take place against either one of them. That is the solution.

The milder 'unreasonable result' exhibited by KR is that, in the absence of drift in the fundamental, there would be no attack whatsoever, whether America or Britain first ran out of reserves. This result is not terribly suspect; in fact, the result makes sense considering that, in that case, the value of the fixed exchange rate is exactly equal to its pre-attack free-float value. Whether the result is unreasonable or not is only a matter of taste. There is no blatant failure of the theory.

The interesting contribution of the present paper is the scenario which KR put forth as a replacement for the transition to free float in case of insufficient reserves. They propose a crisis scenario which produces an attack going 'in the right direction', i.e., against the dollar when America runs out of reserves. This new crisis scenario is almost identical to what Delgado and Dumas (1990) (DD) have proposed earlier: instead of a direct switch to free float, in case of crisis, the transition is to the same one-sided zone in the DD and KR renditions. The only difference between the DD one-sided arrangement and the KR one is that DD have Britain enforcing it and pursuing its policy of support for the pound, after America has run out of reserves, while KR have America performing that job, opportunistically selling the dollar and regaining some reserves when by chance the dollar has risen enough. The goal of America's intervention is the return to the earlier fixed rate when, after some time, enough reserves will have been accumulated.

Under a fixed rate arrangement, the new crisis scenario, although it no doubt leads to an interesting behavioural representation, is not strictly needed since the failings of the original theory of speculative attacks are not blatant.

3 *Solutions in case of a target zone*

The paradox is much more severe and remains unsolved in the case of a target zone and non-zero drift in the fundamental. There seems to be no way to work out the transition from the intervention point, at which, say, America runs out of reserves, directly to the free-float locus. There cannot be a sudden upvaluation of the dollar and there also cannot be a drop in the fundamental $m - m^* + v$. Indeed, a drop in the fundamental would imply a drop in Britain's reserves. But that is not just unreasonable; it is an impossibility. When America runs out of reserves, America is intervening in support of the dollar. Britain at that point is not involved in an intervention in support of the pound and so cannot possibly be the victim of an attack.

A change in the crisis scenario, à la DD or KR, would get us out of the paradox but would not literally solve the paradox in the original setting in which the crisis scenario is a direct transition to free float. Buiter and Grilli's (1989) intervention of outside agents who lend reserves to America should also be viewed as a modification of the setup rather than a solution within the context of the original formulation of the paradox.

In my view, in order to get a solution of the paradox within the original setup, one must envisage a preemptive attack against the pound occurring some time *before* America has effectively run out of reserves, on the occasion of a British intervention. When that attack of a new kind would occur is altogether unclear at this point.

4 *The burden of intervention*

To be complete an exchange rate agreement must fully specify which central bank does what and when. Central to the contract between banks is the clause which specifies how the burden of intervention is to be shared when intervention is called for. For instance, Delgado and Dumas (1990, 1991) consider exclusively the case in which intervention occurs at the margins and each central bank intervenes to support its own currency when it is weak. In the DD setting, a central bank does not intervene when its currency is strong, in support of the other currency. Each central bank fights for itself.

The EMS agreements called for a target zone – rather than a fixed-rate system – and called for most of the intervention to take place at the margin, precisely in order that the market exchange rate could serve as an unequivocal indicator of divergence. Intramarginal intervention equivocates the signal of strength or weakness of a currency. Similarly a fixed exchange rate system leaves no room to determine unequivocally which currency is weak and which is strong.

Why did the founders of the EMS want one to be able to observe the weakness or strength of a currency? The answer, I believe, is: in order that one may be able to assign the burden of intervention mostly to the weak currency. The rationale for that asymmetry is the fight against inflation.[2]

A general target-zone agreement would perhaps specify the burden of intervention by means of two numbers a and β:

- when the foreign currency is weak, the foreign central bank performs a fraction a and the domestic central bank a fraction $1 - a$ of the intervention which is called for;
- when the domestic currency is weak, the domestic central bank performs a fraction β and the foreign central bank a fraction $1 - \beta$ of the intervention which is called for.

The special case of a unilateral target zone examined by Svensson (1989) corresponds to: $[a = 0; \beta = 1]$: the domestic central bank does all the work on both sides of the exchange rate band. The DD case corresponds to: $[a = 1; \beta = 1]$. The intriguing case of the 'gold-exchange-standard target zone' would be: $a = \beta = 1/2$, the only parameter combination which guarantees that reserves are trapped in central bank coffers and shuttle between central banks exclusively.

Returning now to the paradox, it may seem surprising that the 'solution' which I suggested in Section 2 above applies to the fixed-rate regime and not to target zones. After all, the fixed-rate regime is nothing but an extremely narrow target zone, obtained as one takes the width of the exchange rate band to zero.[3] That is true as far as exchange rate behaviour is concerned. But one must apply care in taking the intervention-sharing rule to the limit, as I now demonstrate.

In a fixed-rate system, an investor no longer willing to hold pounds goes to the Bank of England window and receives in exchange gold (gold standard) or dollars (gold exchange standard) or generally some financial asset. The reverse is true for an investor wishing to purchase pounds: the Bank of England is at the same time willing to buy or sell pounds at the fixed rate. Symmetrically an investor no longer willing to hold dollars goes to the Federal Reserve foreign exchange window. Hence the burden of intervention is not a function of the weakness or strength of a currency but is partly determined by the market (in a somewhat arbitrary way as long as we do not indicate for what reason the investor is no longer willing to hold pounds or dollars). That is why I found it reasonable indifferently to envisage an attack against the pound or the dollar, whether Britain or America runs out of reserves. That is why also, on a separate matter, KR are able to propose a post-collapse scenario in which America keeps its window open, selling the dollar to regain gold.[4]

In summary, the 'solution' proposed above for the case of fixed exchange rate, as well as the post-crisis scenario of KR, is permissible because the sharing of the burden of intervention is not set *a priori* and banks instead are willing to respond to the requests of customers in either direction (buying or selling).

In the case of a target zone, however, such a specification is hard to conceive of. The two banks cannot both keep windows open which stand ready indifferently to buy or sell at two different exchange rates. Instead, the intervention, whether of the open-market or window type, must be prescribed as a function of the position of the exchange rate in the band. The degree of (non-sterilized) intervention carried out by the two central banks on the foreign-exchange (or money) market is an active decision made by them in one direction only, in application of some more or less explicit contract. A bank currently selling an item is not at the same time willing to buy the same item.

Hence, as far as the intervention sharing rule and the collapse scenarios are concerned, the fixed rate system may not be identical to the limiting narrow target zone. If we looked at a fixed-rate system as the limit of a target-zone system, incorporating some 'α, β' rule, the 'solution' of Section 2 would no longer be one.

5 *What is a gold standard, anyway?*

KR model a fixed-exchange rate gold standard as a system in which there exists a total world stock of gold and this gold only shuttles between the two central banks, never leaving their coffers ($R + R^* = G$, their equation (21)), because there is no private demand for gold. Further, gold is the only reserve asset. This is in line with the work of Buiter (1989) but Buiter himself quotes Barro (1979), Eichengreen (1984, 1985a, b), Barsky and Summers (1988) and Bordo and Schwartz (1984) to underscore the limits of his model as a representation of historical events. The existence of a world stock of monetized gold plays an important role in the KR formulation, in that an insufficient stock leads to some form of nonviability (see the very end of their Section 5). This is an interesting answer to a question of great operational relevance: how much reserves must be available as backing for an exchange rate system?

I have trouble, however, figuring out exactly how this system operates and how the monetized gold is kept in the hands of the central banks. I see two possibilities. The first possibility is that interventions take the form of a foreign exchange window. As mentioned earlier, in that case, an investor wishing to sell pounds goes to the Bank of England. In the KR formulation this investor does not receive gold in exchange for his pounds as this would mean that some gold would escape central bank circulation. It must be that the Bank the England gives dollars to the investor, or some financial asset other than gold; the system should really be referred to as a gold *exchange* standard.[5]

More important than the semantics is the observation that the dollar, or the other financial asset, in that case is a reserve asset for the Bank of England. Gold is not the only reserve asset. What could then be the operational significance of the world stock of gold as a crucial determinant of the viability of the system?

The other possibility is that the intervention takes the form of active open market operations according to some contractual or negotiated agreement such as the 'a, β' rule described in Section 4. This assumes that the two banks are capable of determining at each instant whether a currency is weak or strong. They would be capable of so doing, for instance, if the exchange rate is not literally fixed but bracketed within a very narrow band.

In that case, as mentioned, the only way in which the gold can remain trapped in the hands of central banks and remain the only reserve asset is by setting: $a = \beta = 1/2$. Suppose then that the dollar is weak and America runs out of reserves. If the Fed suspends its intervention in support of the dollar (selling gold, buying the dollar), the Bank of England must also suspend its intervention in support of the pound value of the dollar (selling pounds, buying gold), as otherwise some gold would escape. Because both interventions cease at the same time, there is indeed a transition to a one-sided band.

But consider next the later circumstance in which the dollar having strengthened hits the fixed parity again. There is no sense in which we can consider then, as KR do, that America alone intervenes to buy gold and enforces a one-sided band. Since it cannot buy gold from the public, it must be buying it from the British authorities. So, Britain is also selling gold at the same time. When $a = \beta$, all interventions are necessarily synchronized.

If, on the contrary $a \neq \beta$, some gold escapes and one must explicitly treat the world stock of gold as being partly in the hands of the banks and partly in the hands of the public. The world stock of gold must be kept track of; it is not a fixed stock of reserves in the hands of central banks. Furthermore, KR consider only two extreme regimes in which, for lack of reserves, a one-sided zone is in force. In the A regime, America has all the gold and Britain none. In the B regime, Britain has all the gold and America none. If some gold is in the hands of the public, there would also exist a regime in which the public has all the gold and the authorities none.

There would be some benefit in specifying in greater detail the operational mechanism envisaged by KR in the various circumstances.

NOTES

1 In that paper we specify what 'narrow enough' means.
2 One must recognize that the articles of agreement also specified theoretically that the various central banks would share the burden of intervention when intervention is needed. But, in practice, the asymmetry mentioned in the text has been the rule. The weak currencies have been on their own in their policy of intervention and the strong ones have set the slow pace of monetary growth. Another cooperative disposition, the 'Very Short Term Facility', has practically never been used (see Micossi, 1985).
3 See Svensson (1989), Delgado and Dumas (1991).
4 But see Section 6 below. DD look at the fixed-rate system as a limit of a target zone with $\alpha = \beta = 1$; that is why they only consider the possibility of Britain supporting the pound in the post-collapse scenario.
5 A model cannot be a model of the gold standard (as opposed to the gold exchange standard) without including some private speculative demand for gold.

REFERENCES

Barro, R.J. (1979), 'Money and the price level under the gold standard', *Economic Journal* **89**, 13–33.
Barsky, R.B. and L.H. Summers (1988), 'Gibson's paradox and the gold standard', *Journal of Political Economy* **96**, 528–50.
Bordo, M.J. and A.J. Schwarz, eds. (1984), *A Retrospective on the Classical Gold Standard, 1821–1931*, Chicago: University of Chicago Press.
Buiter, W.H. (1989), 'A viable gold standard requires flexible monetary and fiscal policy', *Review of Economic Studies* **56**, 101–18.
Buiter, W.H. and V. Grilli (1989), 'The "Gold Standard Paradox" and its resolution', working paper, Yale University.
Delgado, F. and B. Dumas (1990), 'Monetary contracting between central banks and the design of sustainable exchange rate zones', NBER working paper No. 3440.
(1991), 'Target zones, broad and narrow', this volume.
Eichengreen, B. (1984), 'Central bank cooperation under the inter-war gold standard', *Exploration in Economic History* **21**, 64–87.
(1985a), 'International policy coordination in historical perspective: a view from the interwar years', in W.H. Buiter and R.C. Marston, (eds.) *International Economic Policy Coordination*, Cambridge: Cambridge University Press, 139–78.
(1985b), *The Gold Standard in Theory and History*, New York: Methuen.
Krugman, P. and J. Rotemberg (1990), 'Target zones with limited reserves', NBER Working Paper No. 3418.
Micossi, S. (1985), 'The intervention and financing mechanisms of the EMS and the role of the ECU', *Banca Nazionale del Lavoro Quarterly Review*, 327–45.
Svensson, L.E.O. (1989), 'Target zones and interest rate variability: where does the variability go, and is a fixed exchange rate regime the limit of a narrow target zone?' Mimeo, Institute for International Economic Studies, University of Stockholm.

9 Anomalous speculative attacks on fixed exchange rate regimes: possible resolutions of the 'gold standard paradox'

WILLEM H. BUITER and
VITTORIO U. GRILLI

1 Introduction

In a recent paper Paul Krugman (1989) (revised as Krugman and Rotemberg, 1990), has shown that in the standard model of speculative attacks on the international reserves on a country participating in a fixed exchange rate regime, perverse or anomalous speculative attacks can occur. This 'gold standard paradox' (a paradox pertaining to all fixed or managed exchange rate regimes when international financial markets are efficient and stocks of reserves are finite) can be characterized as follows. Reasonable specifications of the processes governing the fundamentals that drive the shadow floating exchange rate and the stock of international reserves result in anomalous behaviour: a speculative attack can occur only *after* the country has already run out of reserves without a speculative attack i.e. without a sudden run on its currency that strips the monetary authority of its remaining international reserves in instantaneous 'stock-shift' fashion. Such a 'natural' collapse will be associated with a jump – (discontinuous) *appreciation* of its currency and the expectation of gradual (or smooth) *appreciation* of its currency immediately following the attack and jump-appreciation.

In Krugman's words, the gold standard paradox is that '. . . it is not possible for the public actually to expect zero change in the exchange rate while it is fixed' (Krugman, 1989, p. 18). In addition 'when a country runs out of gold (as a result of a "natural" collapse), its currency appreciates' (Krugman, 1989, p. 20). Finally '. . . a speculative attack, if it occurs will happen only after the country would have run out of gold in the absence of a speculative attack' (Krugman, 1989, p. 21).

In this paper we show first that Krugman's paradox is a phenomenon that is much more general than his paper suggests. It is in particular not dependent on the presence of mean reversion in the fundamentals process. To rule it out requires either that the fundamental and the shadow exchange rate follow a random walk without drift or that they be weakly monotonic over time i.e. either strictly nondecreasing or strictly nonincreasing. What must be ruled out is a kind of mean-reversion in the exchange rate process: we must exclude the possibility that a high value of the shadow exchange rate (a weak currency) be associated with an expectation of future exchange rate appreciation (a strengthening of the currency) and that a low value of the shadow exchange rate be associated with expected future depreciation.

A slightly generalized version of Krugman's model is developed in Section 2.

After demonstrating the full thrust of Krugman's critique of the speculative attack literature in Section 3 for the continuous time case and in Section 4 for the discrete time case, we offer our proposals for a resolution of the paradox in Section 5.

2 The model

The model is given in equations (1) to (6).

$$s(t) = m(t) - m^*(t) + v(t) + \gamma E_t \dot{s}(t) \qquad \gamma > 0 \tag{1}$$

$$m = ln(D + R) \tag{2}$$

$$m^* = ln(D^* + R^*) \tag{3}$$

$$R + R^* = G \tag{4}$$

$$R > \underline{R} \tag{5a}$$

$$R^* > \underline{R}^* \tag{5b}$$

$$G > \underline{R} + \underline{R}^* \tag{6}$$

s is the logarithm of the spot exchange rate, the price of foreign currency in terms of domestic currency. m is the logarithm of the domestic nominal money stock and m^* the logarithm of the foreign nominal money stock. $v(t)$ measures the logarithm of foreign money demand (at a given foreign price level) relative to domestic money demand (at a given domestic price level). v is assumed to be governed by a stationary first-order Markov process. In the continuous time version of the model the sample paths of v will also be assumed to be continuous functions of time. E_t is the expectation operator conditional on information at period t. D is the nominal stock of home country domestic credit and D^* the exogenous and constant nominal stock of foreign domestic credit, both assumed to be exogenous and constant.[1] R is the home country stock of reserves and R^* the foreign stock of reserves.[2] The total world stock of reserves G is constant. Equations (5a, b) define the values of R and R^* for which the fixed exchange rate regime is viable. Each country establishes a constant reserve floor ($\underline{R}$ for the home country and $\underline{R}^*$ for the foreign country). When reserves fall below these floors the fixed exchange rate regime collapses, and a permanent free float begins. Equation (6) states that global gold reserves are sufficient to satisfy the minimal requirements for reserves of both countries simultaneously. Without loss of generality we set $\underline{R} = \underline{R}^* = 0$, so (6) becomes

$$G > 0 \tag{6'}$$

We present two different structural two-country models that yield the quasi-reduced form of equation (1). The first is a model with two monies, domestic and foreign, held by private agents, and gold, which is held only by the two national monetary authorities. There is imperfect (direct) currency substitution in this model. The second model adds two fixed nominal market value, variable interest rate bonds, one denominated in a home country currency and the other in foreign currency. The two bonds are perfect substitutes in private portfolios, but imperfect direct currency substitution between the two currencies is maintained. The two-monies-and-gold model is summarized in equations (7) to (9).

$$m(t) - p(t) = -\tfrac{1}{2}\gamma E_t\dot{s}(t) + ky(t) \qquad \gamma > 0, k > 0 \tag{7}$$

$$m^*(t) - p^*(t) = \tfrac{1}{2}\gamma E_t\dot{s}(t) + ky^*(t) \tag{8}$$

$$p(t) = p^*(t) + s(t) \tag{9}$$

p and p^* are the logarithms of the domestic and foreign price levels respectively, and y and y^* domestic and foreign output. Equations (7) and (8) are standard money demand functions. Equation (9) is the condition for purchasing power parity (PPP). Equations (7) to (9) yield (1) with $v = k(y^*, -y)$.

The two-monies-two-bonds-and-gold model is given by equations (10) through (12) and (9), repeated here for ease of reference.

$$m(t) - p(t) = -\gamma i(t) + ky(t) \qquad \gamma > 0, k > 0 \tag{10}$$

$$m^*(t) - p^*(t) = -\gamma i^*(t) + ky^*(t) \tag{11}$$

$$i(t) = i^*(t) + E_t\dot{s}(t) \tag{12}$$

$$p(t) = p^*(t) + s(t) \tag{9}$$

i and i^* are the domestic and foreign instantaneous nominal rates of interest. Equation (12) is the condition for uncovered interest parity (UIP).

Solving equation (1) forward in time and choosing the unique, continuously convergent solution we get

$$s(t) = \frac{1}{\gamma}\int_t^\infty e^{-\frac{1}{\gamma}(s-t)} E_t[m(s) - m^*(s) + v(s)]\,ds$$

The *dual* shadow floating exchange rate at t that will describe the economy if the home country were to run out of reserves at time t, $\hat{s}(t)$, is defined by:

$$\hat{s}(t) = ln\,D - ln(D^* + G) + \frac{1}{\gamma}\int_t^\infty e^{-\frac{1}{\gamma}(s-t)} E_t v(s)\,ds \tag{13}$$

The *dual* shadow floating exchange rate at time t that will prevail if the foreign country were to run out of reserves at time t, $\hat{s}^*(t)$, is defined by:

$$\hat{s}^*(t) = ln(D + G) - ln\,D^* + \frac{1}{\gamma}\int_t^\infty e^{-\frac{1}{\gamma}(s-t)} E_t v(s)\,ds \tag{14}$$

Note that

$$\hat{s}^*(t) = \hat{s}(t) + K \tag{15a}$$

where

$$K = ln(D + G) + ln(D^* + G) - ln\,D - ln\,D^* > 0 \tag{15b}$$

The world starts at $t = 0$. If at $t = t_1 \geq 0$ a successful speculative attack is launched against the home country's currency, it must be true that

$$\hat{s}(t_1) = s_0 \tag{16a}$$

and

$$\hat{s}(t) < s_0 \qquad \text{for all } t < t_1 \tag{16b}$$

If at $t = t_2 \geq 0$ a successful speculative attack is launched against the foreign currency, it must be true that

$$\hat{s}(t_2) = s_0 \tag{17a}$$

and

$$\hat{s}(t) > s_0 \qquad \text{for all } t < t_2 \tag{17b}$$

The range of values of the shadow floating exchange rate for which there is no risk of a speculative attack on either currency can be expressed as follows in terms of these two shadow floating exchange rates:

$$\hat{s}(t) < s_0 \tag{18a}$$

$$\hat{s}^*(t) = \hat{s}(t) + K > s_0 \tag{18b}$$

or

$$s_0 - K < \hat{s}(t) < s_0$$

We call (18a, b) the condition for S-viability (i.e. for speculative viability) or the *dual* survival criterion.

Let $\hat{v}$ denote the value of v for which $\hat{s} = s_0$. Similarly let $\hat{v}^*$ be the value of v for which $\hat{s}^* = s_0$. Note that $\hat{v}$ and $\hat{v}^*$ will depend on the nature of the stochastic process governing v.

The criterion for S-viability given in equations (18a, b) can be rewritten in terms of the fundamental v as in (19).

$$\hat{v}^* < v < \hat{v} \qquad \text{(S-viability)} \tag{19}$$

We next define $\tilde{v}$ as the minimum value for v for which home country reserves are zero, conditional on the fixed exchange rate regime having survived. As long as the fixed exchange rate regime survives, the behaviour of R is governed by

$$s_0 = ln(D + R(t)) - ln(D^* + G - R(t)) + v(t) + \gamma E_t\dot{s}(t) \tag{20}$$

With continuous time and continuous sample paths for $s(t)$, it will be true that $E_t\dot{s} = 0$ as long as the fixed rate regime survives. $\tilde{v}$ is therefore given by

$$\tilde{v} = s_0(ln\,D - ln(D^* + G)) \tag{21a}$$

Similarly, for the foreign country we define $\tilde{v}^*$ as the maximal value of v for which foreign reserves are zero, conditional on the fixed exchange rate regime having survived. It follows that

$$\tilde{v}^* = s_0 - (ln(D + G) - ln\,D^*) \tag{21b}$$

The fixed exchange rate system will not suffer a natural collapse (will exhibit R-viability) as long as the *primal* criterion given in equation (22) is satisfied:

$$\tilde{v}^* < v < \tilde{v} \qquad \text{(R-viability)} \tag{22}$$

For expository purposes it is convenient to define the two primal shadow fixed exchange rates $\tilde{s}$ and $\tilde{s}^*$ as follows

$$\tilde{s}(t) = ln\,D - ln(D^* + G) + v(t) \tag{23a}$$

$$\tilde{s}^*(t) = ln(D + G) - ln\,D^* + v(t) \tag{23b}$$

$\tilde{s}$ can be interpreted as the lowest value of s that can be established at time t as a viable fixed exchange rate given the actual values of D, D^*, G and v. $\tilde{s}^*$ is the highest value of s that can be established at time t as a viable fixed exchange rate given the actual values of D, D^*, G and v. Therefore $\tilde{s}(t)$ is supported by $R(t) = 0$ and $\tilde{s}^*(t)$ is supported by $R(t) = G$. In the continuous time case, an alternative interpretation of $\tilde{s}$ and $\tilde{s}^*$ is to view them as the dual shadow floating exchange rates that would prevail under static expectations.

Note that just as the equality of the dual shadow floating exchange rates and s_0 define $\hat{v}$ and $\hat{v}^*$, so the equality of the primal shadow fixed exchange rates and s_0 define $\tilde{v}$ and $\tilde{v}^*$. Note also that

$$\tilde{s}^* = \tilde{s} + K$$

The R-viability criterion can be restated as

$$\tilde{s} < s_0 < \tilde{s}^*$$

or

$$\tilde{s} < s_0 < \tilde{s} + K$$

The combined criteria for the system not to suffer either speculative or natural attacks is therefore given by

$$max(\tilde{v}^*, \hat{v}^*) < v < min(\hat{v}, \tilde{v}) \qquad \text{(S \& R-viability)} \qquad (24)$$

While the fixed exchange rate regime endures, i.e. right up to the instant at which either a natural collapse occurs or a successful speculative attack is launched, the expected rate depreciation of the exchange rate is zero. This is so because v, the exogenous forcing variable, is assumed have continuous sample paths (such as the sample paths generated by Brownian motion). If the stock of reserves exceeds by any finite amount, however small, the larger of zero and the value of the reserve stock that would be withdrawn in speculative stock-shift fashion in the cases of a successful speculative attack, then the instantaneous probability of a collapse is zero and the exchange rate is expected to remain constant this instant.

A 'correct' speculative attack is a speculative attack in the right direction. A correct speculative attack against the home currency when $\hat{s} = s_0$ for the first time requires that the expected rate of depreciation of the exchange rate at the moment of the attack should increase from zero (which is the rational expectation while the fixed exchange rate regime prevails) to some positive value. Only then will there be the stock-shift reduction in the relative demand for home country money that, with D and D^* given, achieves the stock-shift reduction in home country reserves to its critical threshold (zero in our model). If the (rationally) expected rate of depreciation remains zero after the collapse, there is no (stock-shift) speculative attack: natural and speculative attacks coincide.

Analogously a correct speculative attack against the foreign currency requires that at the moment of the attack and collapse the expected proportional rate of depreciation of the home currency falls from zero to some negative value. Again, if the (rationally) expected rate of depreciation remains at zero, there is no (stock-shift) speculative attack.

A moment's reflection will confirm that the speculative attack at the upper bound of the S & R viable range will be correct (i.e. involve a speculative run against the home currency which strips the home country monetary authorities of their remaining reserves) if and only if

$$\hat{v} \leq \tilde{v} \qquad \text{(correct attack at upper boundary)} \tag{25a}$$

The speculative attack at the upper boundary should occur at a value of v no greater than the value of v at which a natural attack occurs. Loosely speaking this can be rephrased as the speculative attack should occur before the natural collapse.

Similarly the criterion for a correct speculative attack at the lower boundary (a speculative run stripping the foreign monetary authority of its remaining reserves) is

$$\tilde{v}^* \leq \hat{v}^* \qquad \text{(correct attack at lower boundary)} \tag{25b}$$

The relative money demand term $v(t)$ is assumed to be governed by the following stochastic process:

$$dv = \mu\, dt - \rho(v - v_0)\, dt + \sigma\, dz \qquad \sigma \geq 0 \tag{26}$$

$z(t)$ is standardized Brownian motion i.e. the increments dz are identically, independently, and normally distributed with zero mean and unit variance. Equation (26) is a slight generalization of Krugman's equation because a drift or trend term μ is included. Values of $\rho > 0$ indicate mean-reversion in the autoregressive component of (26); $\rho < 0$ indicates non-stationary behaviour of the autoregressive component of (26).

Given (1) and assuming $1 + \gamma\rho > 0$ which is required for convergence of the integrals in equations (13) and (14) when v is governed by (26), the two shadow floating exchange rates and the two shadow fixed exchange rates are given by:

$$\hat{s} = \ln D - \ln(D^* + G) + \frac{\gamma}{1 + \gamma\rho}(\rho v_0 + \mu) + \frac{1}{1 + \gamma\rho} v_t \tag{27a}$$

with

$$E_t d\hat{s}(t) = \frac{1}{1 + \gamma\rho}[\mu - \rho(v(t) - v_0)]\, dt \tag{27b}$$

$$\hat{s}^* = \ln(D + G) - \ln D^* + \frac{\gamma}{1 + \gamma\rho}(\rho v_0 + \mu) + \frac{1}{1 + \gamma\rho} v_t \tag{28a}$$

with

$$E_t d\hat{s}^*(t) = \frac{1}{1+\gamma\rho}[\mu - \rho(v(t) - v_0)]dt \tag{28b}$$

$$\tilde{s}(t) = ln\,D - ln(D^* + G) + v(t) \tag{29}$$

$$\tilde{s}^*(t) = ln(D + G) - ln\,D^* + v(t) \tag{30}$$

We now have the information to determine $\hat{v}$ and $\hat{v}^*$. ($\tilde{v}$ and $\tilde{v}^*$ are always given by (21a, b)).

$$\hat{v} = [1+\gamma\rho][s_0 - (ln\,D - ln(D^* + G))] - \gamma\rho\left(v_0 + \frac{\mu}{\rho}\right) \tag{31a}$$

$$\hat{v}^* = [1+\gamma\rho][s_0 - (ln(D + G) - ln\,D^*)] - \gamma\rho\left(v_0 + \frac{\mu}{\rho}\right) \tag{31b}$$

Note from (31a, b), (21a, b) and (15b) that

$$\hat{v} = \hat{v}^* + [1+\gamma\rho]K$$

$$\tilde{v} = \tilde{v}^* + K$$

Therefore we have, since $[1+\gamma\rho] > 0$ and $K > 0$,

$$\hat{v} > \hat{v}^*$$

$$\tilde{v} > \tilde{v}^*$$

The criterion for a correct speculative attack at $\hat{v}$, the upper boundary of the S-viable range, can be restated for this particular v process as:

$$E_t\dot{s}\Big|_{v=\hat{v}} = (1+\gamma\rho)^{-1}[\mu - \rho(\hat{v} - v_0)] \geq 0 \tag{32a}$$

The criterion for a correct speculative attack at $\hat{v}^*$, the lower boundary of the S-viable range can be restated as:

$$E_t\dot{s}\Big|_{v=\hat{v}^*} = (1+\gamma\rho)^{-1}[\mu - \rho(\hat{v}^* - v_0)] \leq 0 \tag{32b}$$

In Table 9.1 we summarize the various viability and correctness conditions. When an economy has a non-zero S & R viable range of v values and when the speculative attacks at the upper and lower bounds are in the correct directions, the economy has achieved Viability as defined in equation (33).

$$\tilde{v}^* \leq \hat{v}^* < v < \hat{v} \leq \tilde{v} \qquad \text{(Viability)} \tag{33}$$

Table 9.1. *Summary of viability and correctness criteria*

S-viability:

$$\hat{v}^* < v < \hat{v} \tag{21}$$

R-viability:

$$\tilde{v}^* < v < \tilde{v} \tag{23}$$

(S & R-viability):

$$\max(\tilde{v}^*, \hat{v}^*) < v < \min(\hat{v}, \tilde{v}) \tag{24}$$

Correct attack at upper boundary:

$$\hat{v} \leq \tilde{v} \tag{25a}$$

or

$$E_t \dot{s}(\hat{v}) = (1 + \gamma\rho)^{-1}[\mu - \rho(\hat{v} - v_0)] \geq 0 \tag{32a}$$

Correct attack at lower boundary:

$$\tilde{v}^* \leq \hat{v}^* \tag{25b}$$

or

$$E_t \dot{s}(\hat{v}^*) = (1 + \gamma\rho)^{-1}[\mu - \rho(\hat{v}^* - v_0)] \leq 0 \tag{32b}$$

Viability: (S & R viability and correct speculative attacks at both boundaries):

$$\tilde{v}^* \leq \hat{v}^* < v < \hat{v} \leq \tilde{v} \tag{33}$$

3 The paradox stated and illustrated

3.1 v is a random walk without drift

Consider the case when $\mu = \rho = 0$. In this case the fundamental v, the shadow floating exchange rates $\hat{s}$ and $\hat{s}^*$ and the shadow fixed exchange rates $\tilde{s}$ and $\tilde{s}^*$ all will be (continuous time) random walks without drift.

$$\hat{s} = \tilde{s} = ln\,D - ln(D^* + G) + v \tag{34}$$

$$\hat{s}^* = \tilde{s}^* = ln(D + G) - ln\,D^* + v \tag{35}$$

Also,

$$\hat{v} = \tilde{v} = s_0 - (ln\,D - ln(D^* + G)) \tag{36}$$

and

$$\hat{v}^* = \tilde{v}^* = s_0 - (ln(D + G) - ln\,D^*) \tag{37}$$

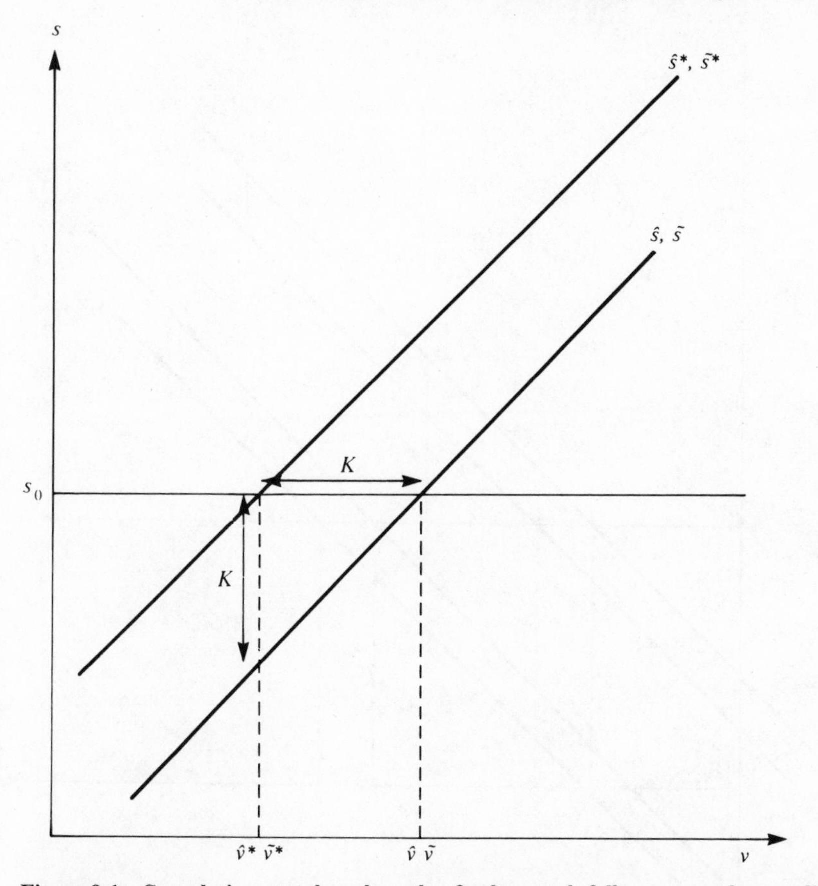

Figure 9.1 Speculative attacks when the fundamental follows a random walk without drift: $\rho = \mu = 0$

Figure 9.1 shows the characterization of this economy when v follows a random walk without drift. $\hat{s}$ and $\tilde{s}$ coincide as do $\hat{s}^*$ and $\tilde{s}^*$, $\hat{v}$ and $\tilde{v}$ as well as $\hat{v}^*$ and $\tilde{v}^*$. The S & R-viable range of v is between $\hat{v}^*$ ($= \tilde{v}^*$) and $\hat{v}$ ($= \tilde{v}$). It has length K and is independent of s_0. As $\hat{v}$ is approached from below, the fixed exchange rate regime collapses as the home country runs out of reserves. Since the postcollapse expected rate of exchange rate depreciation is zero (see (32a)), there is no stock-shift loss of reserves when the collapse occurs. Speculative and natural collapses coincide.

As $\hat{v}^*$ is approached from above, the foreign country runs out of reserves, again without a stock-shift speculative attack. Note that the S & R-viability criterion is satisfied (equation (24)) as well as the two criteria for correct attacks at the upper and lower boundaries.

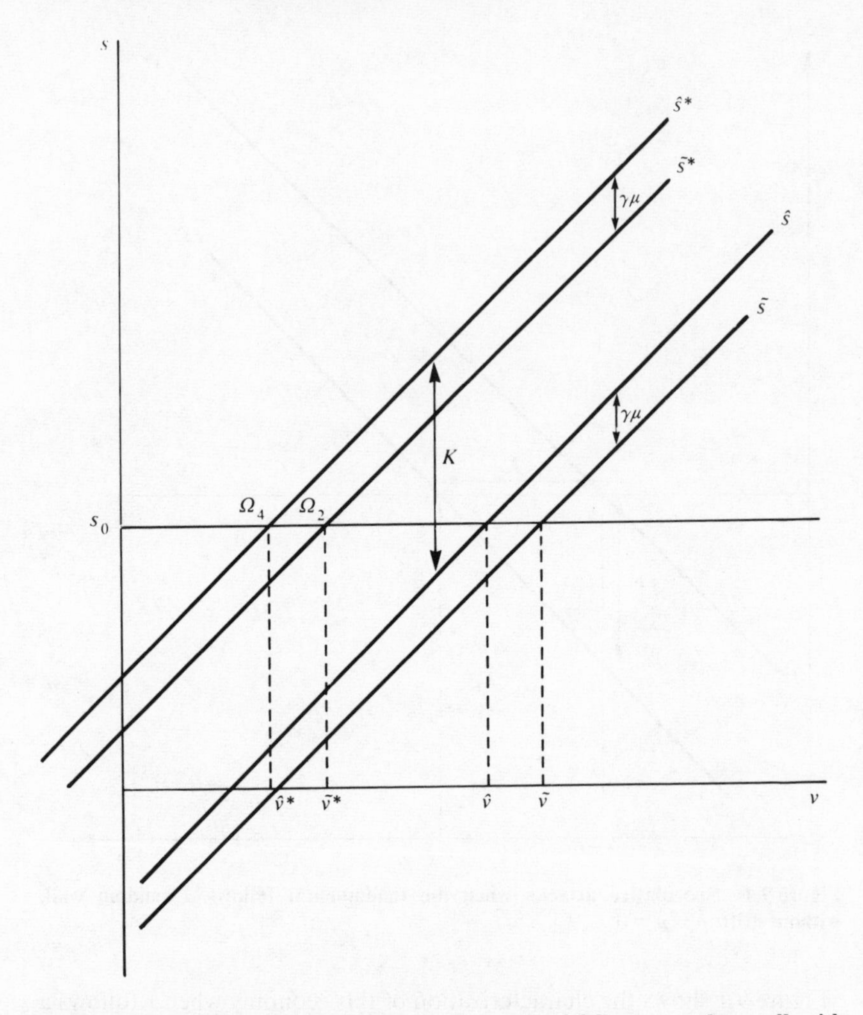

Figure 9.2 Speculative attacks when the fundamental follows a random walk with positive drift: $\rho = 0$, $\mu > 0$

3.2 v is a random walk with drift

Now consider the case where $\rho = 0$, and $\mu > 0$[3] shown in Figure 9.2. In this case we have

$$\hat{s} = ln\,D - ln(D^* + G) + v + \gamma\mu \tag{38}$$

$$\hat{s}^* = ln(D + G) - ln\,D^* + v + \gamma\mu \tag{39}$$

$$E_t\dot{s}(\hat{v}) = \mu \tag{40}$$

$$E_t\dot{s}(\hat{v}^*) = \mu \tag{41}$$

$\tilde{s}$ and $\tilde{s}^*$ are always as in (29) and (30).

Note that the S-viable range of v between $\hat{v}^*$ and $\hat{v}$ has length K. The S & R viable range is between $\tilde{v}^*$ and $\hat{v}$, and has length $K - \gamma\mu$. Clearly μ can be so large that $K < \gamma\mu$. In that case there is no S & R viable range since $\tilde{v}^* > \hat{v}$. In what follows we assume $K - \gamma\mu > 0$. The criterion for a correct speculative attack at the upper boundary is satisfied: $\hat{v} < \tilde{v}$ or $E_t\dot{s}(\hat{v}) = \mu > 0$. This speculative attack will involve a stock-shift loss of reserves for the home country. The criterion for a correct speculative attack at the lower boundary fails, however: $\hat{v}^* < \tilde{v}^*$ or $E_t\dot{s}(\hat{v}^*) = \mu > 0$. It does not make sense to launch a speculative attack against the foreign country currency through a stock-shift increase in relative demand for foreign money and consequently a stock-shift inflow of reserves into the foreign country.

Note that the failure of the fixed exchange rate regime to make sense at the lower boundary has nothing to do with mean-reversion in the process governing the fundamental. The relative money demand process is non-stationary in our example.

If the v process is deterministic ($\sigma = 0$), any v process starting above $\tilde{v}^*$ (and below $\hat{v}$) would result in a finite life for the fixed exchange rate regime and a correct collapse at the upper boundary. If the v process had nonnegative increments, there also would be no risk of running into the incorrect attack problem at the lower boundary even if the increments were stochastic (e.g. exponentially distributed).

With $\sigma > 0$ however, there is a positive probability that, with v governed by Brownian motion (i.e. normal, identically distributed independent increments), any process starting off at v' with $\tilde{v}^* < v' < \hat{v}$ will reach $\tilde{v}^*$ in finite time. (Note that since $\mu > 0$, the probability that v will reach any lower bound in finite time is strictly less than 1).

What happens when v falls to $\tilde{v}^*$? If agents are myopic and have static expectations after the natural collapse (that is they continue to expect $E_t\dot{s} = 0$, even for $v \leq \tilde{v}^*$), the economy will move along the shadow fixed exchange rate curve $\tilde{s}^*$ after v reaches $\tilde{v}^*$ for the first time. There is no speculative attack. Private agents are singularly uninformed but satisfied with their money holdings.

Suppose instead that, when v reaches $\tilde{v}^*$ from above, private agents correctly realize that following the collapse (for whatever reason) of the fixed exchange rate regime there will be a free float with a positive expected rate of depreciation of the home country's currency. In this case there will, when $v = \tilde{v}^*$, be a stock-shift increase in the demand for foreign money and a stock-shift reduction in the demand for home country money. There would be a stock-shift rush of reserves into the foreign country. Another way to look at this is that for $\hat{v}^* < v \leq \tilde{v}^*$ in Figure 9.2, $\hat{s}^* > s_0$. The post-natural collapse exchange rate represents a finite jump depreciation of the home country's exchange rate. This makes foreign currency a great investment, so reserves rush into the foreign country. This 'collapse scenario' therefore make no sense. No equilibrium exists at $\tilde{v}^*$.

3.3 v is a nonstationary first-order autoregression without drift

When $\mu = 0$ but $\rho \neq 0$, v follows what is sometimes called the 'Ornstein–Uhlenbeck (OU)' process. With $\rho < 0$, the process is nonstationary. We have

$$\hat{s} = ln\, D - ln(D^* + G) + v_0 + \frac{1}{1 + \gamma\rho}(v - v_0) \tag{42}$$

$$E_t\dot{s}\Big|_{v = \hat{v}} = \frac{-\rho}{1 + \gamma\rho}(\hat{v} - v_0) \tag{43}$$

$$\hat{s}^* = ln(D + G) - ln\, D^* + v_0 + \frac{1}{1 + \gamma\rho}(v - v_0) \tag{44}$$

$$E_t\dot{s}\Big|_{v = \hat{v}^*} = \frac{-\rho}{1 + \gamma\rho}(\hat{v}^* - v_0) \tag{45}$$

$\tilde{s}$ and $\tilde{s}^*$ are given in (29) and (30).

With $\rho < 0$ but $1/(1 + \gamma\rho) > 0$, the $\hat{s}$ schedule and $\hat{s}^*$ schedule have a common slope in v, s space $[1/(1 + \gamma\rho)]$ which exceeds the unitary slopes of the $\tilde{s}$ and $\tilde{s}^*$ curves. The $\hat{s}$ and $\tilde{s}$ curves intersect at $v = v_0$. So too do the $\hat{s}^*$ and the $\tilde{s}^*$ curves. As always, the $\hat{s}^*$ curve lies a vertical distance K above the $\hat{s}$ curve, and the $\tilde{s}^*$ curve lies a vertical distance K above the $\tilde{s}$ curve.

The configuration drawn in Figure 9.3 exhibits Viability. There is a finite S & R viable range $(\hat{v}^*, \hat{v})$, and $\tilde{v}^* < \hat{v}^*$ while $\hat{v} < \tilde{v}$.

While this case is in some ways rather like that of a random walk with positive drift, the difference here is that there is a correct speculative attack at the lower boundary. Since $v_0 > \hat{v}^*$, at the lower boundary $\hat{v}^*$ the informed speculator, knowing that $Edv = -\rho(v - v_0)$, expects v to fall further (the model is unstable). The expected rate of change of s at $\hat{v}^*$ is therefore negative, and a speculative attack is launched against the foreign currency at $\hat{v}^*$.

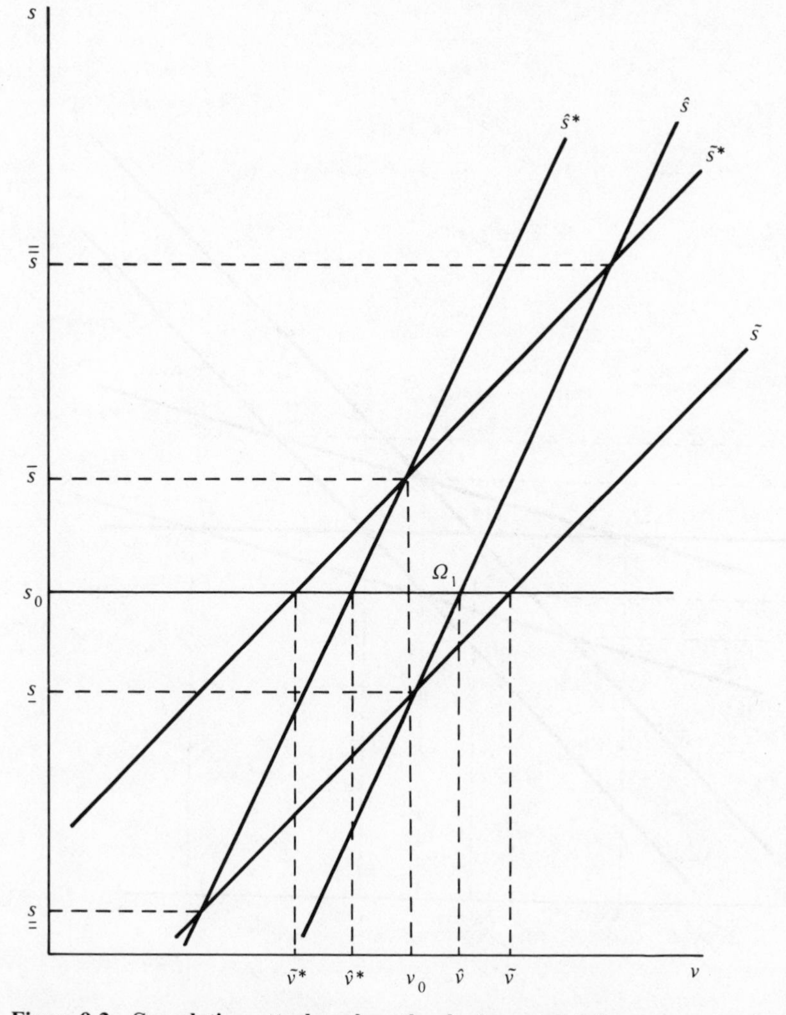

Figure 9.3 Speculative attacks when the fundamental follows a nonstationary first-order autoregressive process: $\mu = 0$, $\rho < 0$

There are however many other configurations. They can be characterized graphically by moving the fixed exchange rate s_0 up or down. When s_0 is above $\bar{s}$ (the value of s at which the $\hat{s}^*$ and $\tilde{s}^*$ curves intersect), we lose the correct speculative attack at the lower boundary: $\hat{v}^* < \tilde{v}^*$, and $v_0 < \hat{v}^*$. When s_0 rises to or above $\bar{\bar{s}}$ (the value of s at which the $\hat{s}$ and $\tilde{s}^*$ curves intersect) the S & R viable range vanishes altogether.

When s_0 is below $\underline{s}$ (the value of s at which the $\hat{s}$ and $\tilde{s}$ curves intersect),

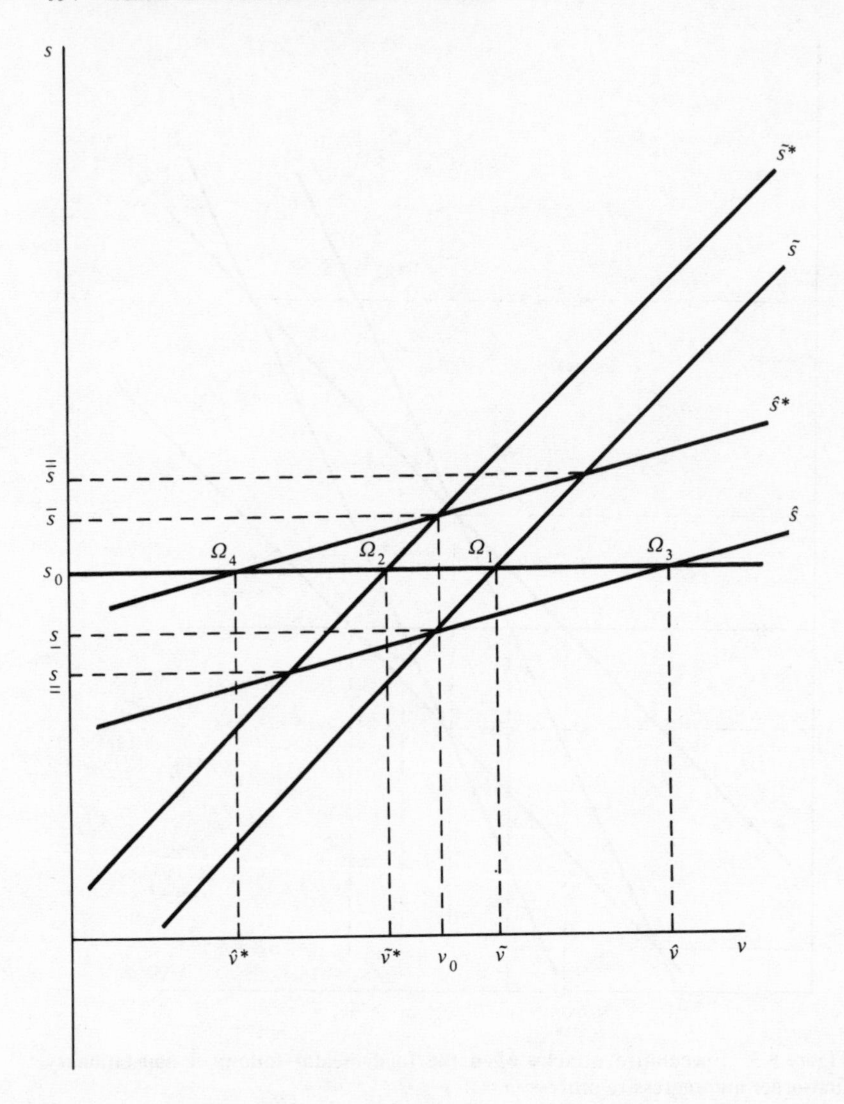

Figure 9.4 Speculative attacks when the fundamental follows a stationary first-order autoregressive process: $\mu = 0, \rho > 0$

we lose the correct speculative attack at the upper boundary. When s_0 is at or below $\underline{\underline{s}}$ (the value of s at which the $\hat{s}^*$ and the $\tilde{s}$ curves intersect), the S & R viable range again vanishes altogether.

3.4 v is a stationary first-order autoregression without drift

The case $\mu = 0$, $\rho > 0$ is the stationary (or mean-reverting) first-order AR process for the fundamental analyzed by Krugman. The equations for $\hat{s}$, $\hat{s}^*$, $E_t\dot{s}(\hat{v})$ and $E_t\dot{s}(\hat{v}^*)$ are as in equations (42)–(45). With $\rho > 0$, the $\tilde{s}^*$ and $\hat{s}$ curves have less than unitary slopes. The configuration analysed by Krugman is shown in Figure 9.4. While there is a finite S & R viable range $(\tilde{v}^*, \tilde{v})$, we have incorrect speculative attacks both at the upper and at the lower boundary: $\hat{v} > \tilde{v}$, and $\hat{v}^* < \tilde{v}^*$. With $\hat{v}^* < \tilde{v}^* < v_0 < \tilde{v} < \hat{v}$, the expected rate of change of s is negative at $\tilde{v}$ (and a fortiori at $\hat{v}$) and positive at $\tilde{v}^*$ (and a fortiori at $\hat{v}^*$). When v is large private agents expect it to decline towards v_0, and when s is high private agents expect it to fall. When v is low, private agents expect it to rise towards v_0. And when s is low, private agents expect it to rise. Thus mean-reversion in the endogenous variable, the exchange rate, at the boundaries of the S & R-viable zone implies anomalous speculative attacks. This does not, however, require mean-reverting behaviour of the exogenous fundamental process, v.

Raising s_0 above $\bar{s}$, the value of s at which the $\tilde{s}^*$ and $\hat{s}^*$ curves intersect, eliminates the anomalous attack at the lower boundary. We now have $v_0 < \tilde{v}^* < \hat{v}$. Raising s_0 further above $\bar{\bar{s}}$, the value of s at which the $\hat{s}^*$ and $\tilde{s}$ curves intersect, causes the S & R viable range to vanish.

Lowering s_0 below $\underline{s}$, the value of s at which the $\hat{s}$ and $\tilde{s}$ curves intersect, eliminates the anomalous speculative attack at the upper boundary with $\hat{v} < \tilde{v} < v_0$. Reversion to v_0 now means that when v is large (but still less than v_0) private economic agents expect a further rise. When s is high private economic agents expect a further increase. The speculative attack at the upper bound of the S & R viable range $(\hat{v})$ is correct: a stock-shift loss of reserves for the home country.

When s_0 is at or below $\underline{\underline{s}}$, the value of s at which the $\tilde{s}^*$ and $\hat{s}$ curves intersect, the S & R viable range again vanishes. With $\rho > 0$, there is therefore no value of s_0 for which Viability prevails.

4 The gold standard paradox in a discrete time model

In order to confirm that the paradox is not an artifact of continuous time models driven by Brownian motion, we reformulate in equations (46) through (50) the model of equations (1) through (6) as a discrete time model. This will also facilitate the interpretation of our resolution of the paradox in Section 5.

$$s_t = m_t - m_t^* + v_t + \gamma E_t(s_{t+1} - s_t) \qquad \gamma > 0 \tag{46}$$

$$v_t = \mu + \rho v_0 + (1 - \rho) v_{t-1} + z_t \tag{47a}$$

$$\begin{aligned} Ez_t &= 0 \\ Ez_t z_s &= 0 \qquad \text{if } t \neq s \\ &= \sigma^2 \geq 0 \text{ if } t = s \end{aligned} \tag{47b}$$

$$m_t = ln(D + R_t) \tag{48a}$$

$$m_t^* = ln(D^* + R_t^*) \tag{48b}$$

$$R_t + R_t^* = G \tag{49a}$$

$$G > 0 \tag{49b}$$

$$R_t > 0 \tag{50a}$$

$$R_t^* > 0 \tag{50b}$$

The last two equations again define the conditions under which the fixed exchange rate regime will survive.

We define the following variables:

$$\Delta = ln D - ln(D^* + G)$$

$$\Delta^* = ln(D + G) + ln D^*$$

Note that

$$K = \Delta^* - \Delta$$

The two 'dual' shadow floating exchange rates $\hat{s}$ and $\hat{s}^*$ are given by

$$\hat{s}_t = \Delta + \frac{\gamma}{1 + \gamma\rho}(\rho v_0 + \mu) + \frac{1}{1 + \gamma\rho} v_t \tag{51a}$$

$$\hat{s}_t^* = \Delta^* + \frac{\gamma}{1 + \gamma\rho}(\rho v_0 + \mu) + \frac{1}{1 + \gamma\rho} v_t \tag{51b}$$

Also

$$E_t s_{t+1} - s_t = \frac{1}{1 + \gamma\rho}(\rho v_0 + \mu) - \frac{\rho}{1 + \gamma\rho} v_t \tag{51c}$$

Just as in the continuous time case, $\hat{s}_t$ is the exchange rate that prevails in period t if the gold standard collapses that period because the home country runs out of reserves. $\hat{s}_t^*$ is the exchange rate that prevails in period t if the gold standard collapses in that period because the foreign authority runs out of reserves. During a period in which a collapse occurs, reserves can be bought and sold at two potentially distinct prices, s_0 and $\hat{s}_t$, or s_0 and $\hat{s}_t^*$. Thus for a collapse to occur through the home country authority running out of reserves it is necessary and sufficient that $\hat{s}_t \geq s_0$.

If $\hat{s}_t < s_0$ and the home authorities nevertheless were about to run out of reserves for 'natural' (that is non-speculative) reasons (say through a sequence of increasing values of v), private agents pursuing pure arbitrage profits would sell reserves to the domestic authority in exchange for home currency at s_0 and would instantaneously sell the home currency thus acquired at the postcollapse price of foreign exchange $\hat{s}_0$. Any private agent with access to gold or foreign currency could engage in this profitable set of riskless transactions, say by buying gold from the foreign authority in exchange for foreign currency and presenting the gold thus obtained to the home authority in exchange for domestic currency at the fixed rate s_0.

Any incipient exhaustion of the home currency stock of reserves if $\hat{s}_t < s_0$ would therefore be reversed *before it could materialize* through arbitrage-induced private portfolio transactions. Home country reserves would be replenished instantaneously and the collapse would be avoided. The same holds *mutatis mutandis* for incipient 'natural' reserve exhaustion in the foreign country when $\hat{s}^*_t > s_0$.

As before we define $\hat{v}$ as the minimal value of v consistent with $\hat{s} \geq s_0$. Similarly, $\hat{v}^*$ is defined as the maximal value of v consistent with $\hat{s}^* \leq s_0$. Therefore we have

$$\hat{v} = (1 + \gamma\rho)(s_0 - \Delta) - \gamma(\rho v_0 + \mu) \qquad (52a)$$

$$\hat{v}^* = (1 + \gamma\rho)(s_0 - \Delta^*) - \gamma(\rho v_0 + \mu) \qquad (52b)$$

Note that

$$\hat{s}^* = \hat{s} + K$$

and

$$\hat{v} = \hat{v}^* + (1 + \gamma\rho)K$$

In order to have convergent solutions we require $1 + \gamma\rho > 0$.

Speculative attack viability or S-viability again requires that

$$\hat{v}^* < v < \hat{v} \qquad \text{(S-viability)} \qquad (53)$$

While the fixed exchange rate regime survives the behaviour of reserves is governed by

$$s_0 = ln(D + R_t) - ln(D^* + G - R_t) + v_t + \gamma E_t(s_{t+1} - s_0)$$

In order to have $R_t > 0$ it is therefore necessary and sufficient that

$$v_t < -\Delta + s_0 - \gamma E_t(s_{t+1} - s_0)$$

In order to have $R^*_t > 0$ it is necessary and sufficient that

$$v_t > -\Delta^* + s_0 - \gamma E_t(s_{t+1} - s_0)$$

The minimal value of v_t for which $R_t = 0$ is given by

$$\tilde{v}_t = s_0 - \Delta - \gamma E_t(s_{t+1} - s_0) \tag{54a}$$

The maximal value of v_t for which $R_t^* = 0$ is given by

$$\tilde{v}_t^* = s_0 - \Delta^* - \gamma E_t(s_{t+1} - s_0) \tag{54b}$$

Reserve viability or R-viability therefore requires

$$\tilde{v}^* < v < \tilde{v} \qquad \text{(R-viability)} \tag{55}$$

Note that as before

$$\tilde{v} = \tilde{v}^* + K$$

$$\text{Let} \quad \pi_t \equiv \text{Probability}(\hat{s}_{t+1} \geq s_0 \,|\, \hat{s}_t < s_0);$$

$$\pi_t^* \equiv \text{Probability}(\hat{s}_{t+1}^* \leq s_0 \,|\, \hat{s}_t^* > s_0)$$

$$E_t \hat{s}_{t+1} \equiv E_t(\hat{s}_{t+1} \,|\, \hat{s}_{t+1} \geq s_0, \hat{s}_t < s_0)$$

and

$$E_t \hat{s}_{t+1}^* \equiv E_t(\hat{s}_{t+1}^* \,|\, \hat{s}_{t+1}^* \leq s_0, \hat{s}_t^* > s_0)$$

It follows that the *unconditional* future expected exchange rate, $E_t s_{t+1}$ is given by

$$E_t s_{t+1} = \pi_t E_t \hat{s}_{t+1} + \pi_t^* E_t \hat{s}_{t+1}^* + (1 - \pi_t - \pi_t^*) s_0 \tag{56}$$

We now specialize the stochastic process z_t given in (47b) as follows:

$$\begin{aligned} z_{t+1} &= \delta \quad \text{with probability } 0.5 \\ &= -\delta \quad \text{with probability } 0.5 \\ \delta &\geq 0 \end{aligned} \tag{57}$$

The variance of z, σ^2 in (47b), is δ^2 in this case.
We define

$$\eta_t = (1 + \gamma\rho)(s_0 - \Delta) - (1 + \gamma)(\rho v_0 + \mu) - (1 - \rho) v_t \tag{58a}$$

$$\eta_t^* = (1 + \gamma\rho)(s_0 - \Delta^*) - (1 + \gamma)(\rho v_0 + \mu) - (1 - \rho) v_t \tag{58b}$$

Note that

$$\eta = \eta^* + (1 + \gamma\rho) K \tag{59}$$

By inspection of (51a), (47a) and (58a) (and of (51b), (47a) and (58b)) it follows that $\pi_t = \text{Probability}(z_{t+1} \geq \eta_t)$ and $\pi_t^* = \text{Probability}(z_{t+1} \leq \eta_t^*)$. We therefore can establish the following:

$$\pi_t = 0 \quad \text{if } \eta_t > \delta \tag{60a}$$

$$\pi_t = 0.5 \quad \text{if } -\delta < \eta_t \leq \delta \tag{60b}$$

$$\pi_t = 1 \quad \text{if } \eta_t < -\delta \tag{60c}$$

$$\pi_t^* = 0 \quad \text{if } \eta_t^* < -\delta \quad \text{i.e.} \quad \text{if } \eta_t < -\delta + (1+\gamma\rho)K \tag{60d}$$

$$\pi_t^* = 0.5 \quad \text{if } -\delta \leq \eta_t^* < \delta \tag{60e}$$
$$\text{i.e.} \quad \text{if } -\delta + (1+\gamma\rho)K \leq \eta_t < \delta + (1+\gamma\rho)K$$

$$\pi_t^* = 1 \quad \text{if } \eta_t^* \geq \delta \quad \text{i.e.} \quad \text{if } \eta_t \geq \delta + (1+\gamma\rho)K \tag{60f}$$

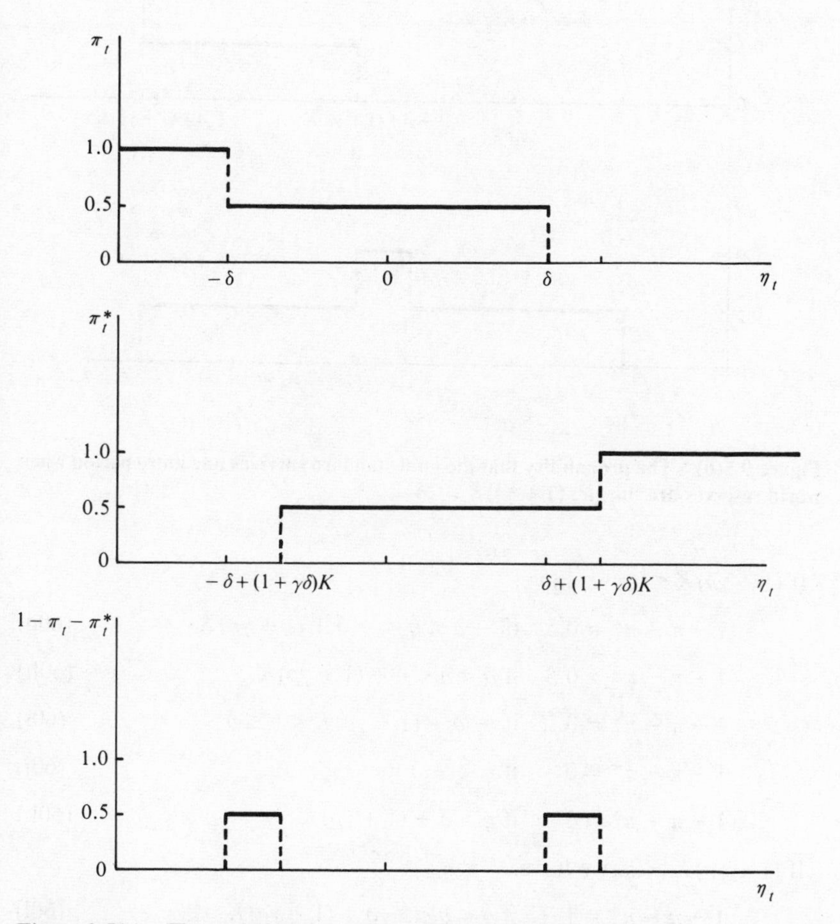

Figure 9.5(a) The probability that the gold standard survives one more period when world reserves are 'small': $(1 + \gamma\delta)K < 2\delta$

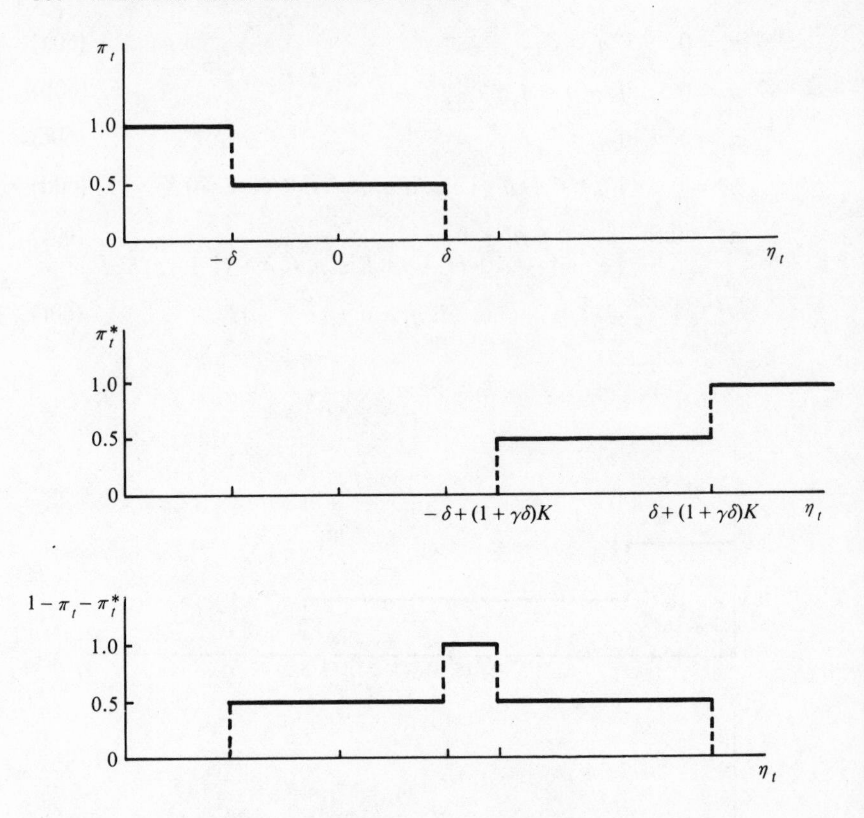

Figure 9.5(b) The probability that the gold standard survives one more period when world reserves are 'large': $(1 + \gamma\delta) K > 2\delta$

If $(1 + \gamma\rho) K \leq 2\delta$ we have:

$$1 - \pi - \pi^* = 0.5 \quad \text{if } -\delta < \eta < -\delta + (1 + \gamma\rho) K \tag{60g}$$

$$1 - \pi - \pi^* = 0.5 \quad \text{if } \delta < \eta < \delta + (1 + \gamma\rho) K \tag{60h}$$

$$1 - \pi - \pi^* = 0 \quad \text{if } -\delta + (1 + \gamma\rho) K < \eta \leq \delta \tag{60i}$$

$$1 - \pi - \pi^* = 0 \quad \text{if } \eta < -\delta \tag{60j}$$

$$1 - \pi - \pi^* = 0 \quad \text{if } \eta > \delta + (1 + \gamma\rho) K \tag{60k}$$

If $(1 + \gamma\rho) K > 2\delta$ we have:

$$1 - \pi - \pi^* = 1 \quad \text{if } \delta < \eta < -\delta + (1 + \gamma\rho) K \tag{60l}$$

$$1 - \pi - \pi^* = 0.5 \quad \text{if } -\delta < \eta < \delta \tag{60m}$$

$$1 - \pi - \pi^* = 0.5 \quad \text{if } -\delta + (1+\gamma\rho)K < \eta < \delta + (1+\gamma\rho)K \tag{60n}$$

$$1 - \pi - \pi^* = 0 \quad \text{if } \eta < -\delta \tag{60o}$$

$$1 - \pi - \pi^* = 0 \quad \text{if } \eta > \delta + (1+\gamma\rho)K \tag{60p}$$

Figure 9.5 illustrates these probabilities. Note that there is no range of values of η_t for which the survival until the next period of the fixed exchange rate regime is certain if the world stock of reserves isn't large enough ($(1+\gamma\rho)K \leq 2\delta$). This case is drawn in Figure 9.5(a). Figure 9.5(b) has a range of η_t values ($\delta < \eta_t < -\delta + (1+\gamma\rho)K$) for which the gold standard is certain to survive until the next period. This requires $(1+\gamma\rho)K > 2\delta$.

Note that, unless $\eta_t \leq -\delta$, only a positive realization ($+\delta$) can push z_{t+1} beyond η_t for the first time and that, unless $\eta_t^* \geq \delta$ (that is unless $\eta_t \geq \delta + (1+\gamma\rho)K$), only a negative ($-\delta$) realization can push z below η^* for the first time. We therefore have:

$$\begin{aligned} E_t\hat{s}_{t+1} &= \Delta + (1+\gamma\rho)^{-1}[(1+\gamma)(\rho v_0 + \mu) + (1-\rho)v_t + \delta] \\ &\quad \text{if } \eta_t > -\delta \\ &= \Delta + (1+\gamma\rho)^{-1}[(1+\gamma)(\rho v_0 + \mu) + (1-\rho)v_t] \\ &\quad \text{if } \eta_t \leq -\delta \end{aligned} \tag{61a}$$

and

$$\begin{aligned} E_t\hat{s}^*_{t+1} &= \Delta^* + (1+\gamma\rho)^{-1}[(1+\gamma)(\rho v_0 + \mu) + (1-\rho)v_t - \delta] \\ &\quad \text{if } \eta_t^* < \delta \\ &= \Delta^* + (1+\gamma\rho)^{-1}[(1+\gamma)(\rho v_0 + \mu) + (1-\rho)v_t] \\ &\quad \text{if } \eta_t^* \geq \delta \end{aligned} \tag{61b}$$

From (56), (60) and (61) we finally obtain $E_t s_{t+1}$. First consider the case illustrated in Figure 9.5(a) where $(1+\gamma\rho)K \leq 2\delta$.

$$\begin{aligned} E_t s_{t+1} &= 0.5 s_0 + 0.5\{\Delta + (1+\gamma\rho)^{-1}[(1+\gamma)(\rho v_0 + \mu) + (1-\rho)v_t + \delta]\} \\ &\quad \text{if } -\delta < \eta_t < -\delta + (1+\gamma\rho)K. \end{aligned} \tag{62a}$$

In this case there is a fifty percent chance of a collapse of the home currency in the next period.

$$\begin{aligned} E_t s_{t+1} &= 0.5 s_0 + 0.5\{\Delta^* + (1+\gamma\rho)^{-1}[(1+\gamma)(\rho v_0 + \mu) + (1-\rho)v_t - \delta]\} \\ &\quad \text{if } \delta < \eta_t < \delta + (1+\gamma\rho)K. \end{aligned} \tag{62b}$$

In this case there is a fifty percent chance of a collapse of the foreign currency in the next period.

$$\begin{aligned} E_t s_{t+1} &= 0.5\{\Delta + (1+\gamma\rho)^{-1}[(1+\gamma)(\rho v_0 + \mu) + (1-\rho)v_t + \delta]\} + \\ &\quad 0.5\{\Delta^* + (1+\gamma\rho)^{-1}[(1+\gamma)(\rho v_0 + \mu) + (1-\rho)v_t - \delta]\} \end{aligned} \tag{62c}$$

$$\text{if } -\delta + (1+\gamma\rho)K < \eta_t < \delta.$$

In this case a collapse in the next period is certain and it is equally likely to be a collapse of the home currency as a collapse of the foreign currency.

$$E_t s_{t+1} = \Delta + (1+\gamma\rho)^{-1}[(1+\gamma)(\rho v_0 + \mu) + (1-\rho)v_t] \quad \text{if } \eta_t \leq -\delta. \tag{62d}$$

In this case there is a certain collapse of the home country currency in the next period.

$$E_t s_{t+1} = \Delta^* + (1+\gamma\rho)^{-1}[(1+\gamma)(\rho v_0 + \mu) + (1-\rho)v_t] \quad \text{if } \eta_t \geq \delta + (1+\gamma\rho)K. \tag{62e}$$

In this case there is a certain collapse in the next period of the foreign currency.

Next consider the case illustrated in Figure 9.5(b) where $(1+\gamma\rho)K > 2\delta$.

$$E_t s_{t+1} = s_0 \quad \text{if } \delta < \eta_t < -\delta + (1+\gamma\rho)K. \tag{63a}$$

In this case the fixed exchange rate regime is certain to survive until the next period.

$$E_t s_{t+1} = 0.5 s_0 + 0.5\{\Delta + (1+\gamma\rho)^{-1}[(1+\gamma)(\rho v_0 + \mu) + (1-\rho)v_t + \delta]\} \quad \text{if } -\delta < \eta_t < \delta. \tag{63b}$$

There is a fifty percent chance of a collapse of the home currency during the next period.

$$E_t s_{t+1} = 0.5 s_0 + 0.5\{\Delta^* + (1+\gamma\rho)^{-1}[(1+\gamma)(\rho v_0 + \mu) + (1-\rho)v_t - \delta]\} \quad \text{if } -\delta + (1+\gamma\rho)K < \eta_t < \delta + (1+\gamma\rho)K. \tag{63c}$$

There is a fifty percent chance of a collapse of the foreign currency next period.

$$E_t s_{t+1} = \Delta + (1+\gamma\rho)^{-1}[(1+\gamma)(\rho v_0 + \mu) + (1-\rho)v_t] \quad \text{if } \eta_t \leq -\delta. \tag{63d}$$

There is a certain collapse of the home currency in the next period.

$$E_t s_{t+1} = \Delta^* + (1+\gamma\rho)^{-1}[(1+\gamma)(\rho v_0 + \mu) + (1-\rho)v_t] \quad \text{if } \eta_t \geq \delta + (1+\gamma\rho)K. \tag{63e}$$

There is a certain collapse of the foreign currency in the next period.

Now that we know $E_t s_{t+1}$ from equations (62) and (63) we can calculate $\tilde{v}_t$ and $\tilde{v}_t$ from equations (54a, b). With $\hat{v}$ and $\hat{v}^*$ given in equations (52a, b) we can establish whether the gold standard paradox arises in this model.

There is a paradox if $\tilde{v} < \hat{v}$ or if $\tilde{v}^* > \hat{v}^*$. In that case a country will 'run out of reserves' without a speculative attack even though the economy possesses a speculative collapse point. For brevity's sake we focus on $\tilde{v} < \hat{v}$. The $\tilde{v}^* > \hat{v}^*$ case is symmetric.

The easiest example that proves that the paradox can occur is the special case of the discrete time model in which it replicates exactly the key features of the continuous time model of Section 3. This is the case where the survival of the gold standard into the next period is guaranteed, i.e. the case with $E_t s_{t+1} = s_0$ given in equation (63a). It requires $(1 + \gamma\rho)K > 2\delta$ and $\delta < \eta_t < -\delta + (1 + \gamma\rho)K$. In this case $\tilde{v} = s_0 - \Delta$ and since we always have $\hat{v} = (1 + \gamma\rho)(s_0 - \Delta) - \gamma(\rho v_0 + \mu)$ the analysis of Section 3 is directly transferable.

For instance, we have $\tilde{v} < \hat{v}$ if $\rho = 0$ and $\mu < 0$. If v follows a random walk with negative drift there will be a natural collapse at the upper boundary (the home country runs out of reserves) before a speculative attack occurs. Alternatively, if $\mu = 0$ and $0 < 1 + \rho < 1$ (v is a first order stationary autoregression without drift) then $\tilde{v} < \hat{v}$ if $s_0 > v_0 + \Delta$.

The occurrence of the paradox is not dependent on the special feature of the previous examples that $E_t s_{t+1} = s_0$. One further illustration should suffice to make this point. Consider the case where there is a fifty percent chance of a collapse of the foreign currency in the next period and no chance at all of a home currency collapse. We choose $(1 + \gamma\rho)K < 2\delta$ so the relevant equation for $E_t s_{t+1}$ is (62b) with $\delta < \eta_t < \delta + (1 + \gamma\rho)K$. For simplicity consider the case where v follows a random walk with drift ($\rho = 0$). In this case $\hat{v} = s_0 - \Delta - \gamma\mu$ and $\tilde{v}$ is solved from equations (62b) and (54a). This yields

$$\tilde{v} = s_0 - (1 + 0.5\gamma)^{-1}\{\Delta + 0.5\gamma[\Delta^* + (1 + \gamma)\mu - \delta]\}$$

It follows that

$$\hat{v} - \tilde{v} = 0.5\gamma(1 + 0.5\gamma)^{-1}[K - (\mu + \delta)] > 0 \quad \text{if } K > \mu + \delta \qquad (64)$$

Apart from demonstrating the analytical advantages of working with continuous time models, Section 4 proves that the gold standard paradox is not an artifact of the special class of continuous time processes studied by Krugman and in Sections 2 and 3 of this paper. It also supplies the convenience of a finite length unit period which may facilitate the interpretation of some of the resolutions of the paradox we propose in Section 5.

5 The paradox resolved

5.1 The scope of the paradox

The reason for the occurrence of the paradox should by now be clear: if a low value of the currency is associated with expectations of appreciation (a high value of $\hat{s}$ is associated with $E_t\dot{s}(t) < 0$ following the collapse in the continuous time model or a high value of $\hat{s}$ is associated with a lower value of $E_t(s_{t+1} - s_t)$ following the collapse in the discrete time model), there will be an anomalous speculative attack at the upper boundary of the S & R viable zone. If a high value of the currency is associated with expectations of depreciation (a low value of $\hat{s}$ is associated with $E_t\dot{s}(t) > 0$ following the collapse or a low value of $\hat{s}$ is associated with a higher value of $E_t(s_{t+1} - s_t)$ following the collapse), there will be an anomalous speculative attack at the lower boundary of the S & R viable zone. This means there will never be any trouble when the shadow exchange rates are weakly monotonic over time. In that case the movement of the actual shadow exchange rate is always in the same direction as the change in the expected rate of change of the exchange rate at the moment a collapse occurs: if the actual and expected shadow exchange rate always rise or remain constant (fall or remain constant), there will always be a correct speculative attack at the upper (lower) boundary of the S & R viable zone. If we start above (below) the lower (upper) boundary, the system will never descend (rise) towards it.

Deterministic models with a constant rate of change of the fundamental ($\rho = 0$, $\sigma = 0$) therefore never present any problems. If the drift is zero ($\mu = 0$), the fixed exchange rate regime will survive forever provided the initial value of v is in the interior of the S & R viable zone. With $\sigma = 0$, positive drift ($\mu > 0$) means a certain collapse at the upper boundary (a selling attack against the home country currency). Negative drift means a certain collapse at the lower boundary (a selling attack against the foreign currency). Such models were considered in Krugman (1979), Flood and Garber (1984) and Buiter (1987).

Stochastic models in which the increments in v are always positive (say because they are drawings from an exponential distribution) will also display a monotonically nondecreasing shadow exchange rate over time. The only possible collapse is a correct collapse at the upper boundary. Such models were considered by Flood and Garber (1984), and Buiter (1987).

The random walk without drift ($\mu = \rho = 0$) is trouble free not because its actual movement over time is monotonic but because for every value of $v(t)$, $E_t dv(t) = 0$, and for every value of $s(t)$, $E_t ds(t) = 0$. There are never any (stock-shift) speculative attacks in that model.

For all other models in the class of v processes given in (26) there are parameter configurations with anomalous attacks at the lower boundary and/or at the upper boundary. Examples are Grilli (1986), Obstfeld (1986b) and Buiter (1989). An S & R viable range may also fail to exist when $\mu \neq 0$ and/or $\rho \neq 0$, but that poses no paradox. The paradox is the existence of an S & R feasible range with anomalous attacks at one or both boundaries. In other words, the paradox is the failure of a well-defined equilibrium to exist for some range of values of the fundamentals.[4]

Krugman proposes to resolve the paradox by concluding that, except in the special cases just referred to, there can be no nonparadoxical fixed exchange rate regime or gold standard. In Krugman and Rotemberg (1990) it is proposed that the 'two-sided' fixed exchange rate regime be abandoned, and replaced with the analysis of an exchange rate target zone in which limited reserves are used to 'regulate' the fundamental at the edges or boundaries of the target zone. These interventions stop the exchange rate from rising above the upper boundary and from falling below the lower boundary, as long as the reserves exceed their exogenously given threshold levels. Changes in the unregulated fundamental that move the exchange rate from either of its boundaries back into the interior of the target zone are not counteracted. A fixed exchange rate is approximated when the upper and lower boundaries of the target zones are brought very close together.

This approach is logically coherent and interesting, and ties in neatly with the by now vast literature on exchange rate target zones (see e.g. Dixit, 1988; Krugman, 1987, 1988, 1989; Miller and Weller, 1988a, b, 1989; Flood and Garber, 1989; Froot and Obstfeld, 1989a, b; and Dumas, 1989).

We believe, however, that interest continues to attach to the analysis of the traditional two-sided fixed exchange rate regime under perfect capital mobility, and therefore do not wish to throw the fixed exchange rate regime baby with the anomalous speculative attack bath water. The argument that even the historical gold standard was not a truly fixed exchange rate regime but rather a (very narrow) target zone because of the existence of the 'gold points' misses the point. The gold points wedge reflected the real cost of shipping gold (mainly between the US and Britain) and does not represent distinct floor and ceiling prices, net of transportation costs, of foreign exchange. These transportation and transactions costs are anyway surely negligible today. Charles de Gaulle may have insisted on physical shipment of gold from Fort Knox to Paris, but efficient business practice today means the (virtually costless) exchange of paper ownership claims to gold rather than physical transshipment. Most foreign exchange reserves today are paper claims rather than heavy physical objects in any case. Reserve gains and losses are bookkeeping entries that can be effected virtually instantaneously and at negligible cost.

Clearly a truly fixed exchange rate regime is an abstraction that very closely approximates some historical international monetary arrangements as well as some prospective future arrangements (e.g. those that are emerging for the EC). In the next two subsections we present alternative ways of guaranteeing the existence of an equilibrium without abandoning the assumption of a fixed exchange rate regime.

5.2 *The missing equation and the missing money holdings of arbitrageurs in the two-monies-and-gold model*

Unlike the exposition of the gold standard paradox in the previous two Sections, its resolution is a brief affair. It is implicit in our discussion at the beginning of Section 4 of what happens during the period in which (at the instant at which) a country runs out of official reserves and a floating exchange rate is adopted. During that period, currencies can be sold in exchange for reserves and repurchased instantaneously at two potentially distinct prices: s_0 and $\hat{s}$ in the case of a collapse of the home currency; s_0 and $\hat{s}^*$ in the case of a collapse of the foreign currency. This possibility of risk-free arbitrage profits, or rather the market response that eliminates this possibility, is not part of the formal structure of either the continuous time model (equations (1) through (6)) or the discrete time model (equations (46) through (50)). Inclusion of this missing equation (given as equation (66a, b) below) and inclusion of the missing economic agents (currency arbitrageurs) dissolves the paradox and confirms the validity of the formal analyses of the conventional approach.

Without loss of generality we focus in what follows on a threatening home currency collapse in period t with $\tilde{v}_t < \hat{v}_t$. If $\tilde{v}_t < \hat{v}_t$ it follows that when $v_t = \hat{v}_t$ we have $\hat{s}_t < s_0$.

The money demand functions represented in equations (1) and (46) only represent the demands for home and foreign currency *excluding* any demand reflecting international currency arbitrage. Let m and m^* denote, as before, the stocks of home and foreign currency. Money holdings of international currency arbitrageurs are denoted m^a and m^{*a}. The monetary equilibrium condition including the money holdings of arbitrageurs is, in discrete time

$$s_t = m_t - m_t^* - (m_t^a - m_t^{*a}) + v_t + \gamma E_t(s(t+1) - s(t)) \qquad (65a)$$

The nonarbitrage demand for home currency (relative to foreign currency), $m^n - m^{*n}$ is of course given by

$$m_t^n - m_t^{*n} - s_t = -v_t - \gamma E_t(s(t+1) - s(t)) \tag{65b}$$

The presence of efficient arbitrageurs ready to avail themselves of opportunities for riskless profit means that we can impose the 'no arbitrage profits' assumption given in equations (66a, b).

Assumption 1: no arbitrage

$$\hat{s}_t - s_0 \geq 0 \quad \text{iff } R_t = 0 \tag{66a}$$

and

$$\hat{s}_t^* - s_0 \leq 0 \quad \text{iff } R_t^* = 0 \tag{66b}$$

To remove a major indeterminacy from the model we assume that if there are no pure arbitrage profits to be earned, arbitrageurs will reduce $m^a - m^{*a}$, their relative holdings of home currency to foreign currency (henceforth to be referred to as relative currency holdings) to zero. The problem of determining the *gross* asset holdings of arbitrageurs (private agents ready to exploit risk-free opportunities for pure profit by constructing zero net worth portfolios that will yield a strictly positive return in at least one state of nature and non-negative returns in all states of nature) when there are no pure profit opportunities to be had, is a general one.

Assumption 2: minimum efficient size arbitrage portfolios

$$\begin{aligned} &\text{If } m_t^a - m_t^{*a} = 0 \text{ implies } R(t) > 0 \text{ and } R^*(t) > 0 \\ &\quad \text{then } m_t^a - m_t^{*a} = 0 \end{aligned} \tag{67}$$

$$\text{If } R_t = 0 \text{ and } \hat{s}_t \geq s_0 \text{ then } m_t^a - m_t^{*a} = 0$$
$$\text{If } R_t^* = 0 \text{ and } \hat{s}_t^* \leq s_0 \text{ then } m_t^a - m_t^{*a} = 0$$

Second order costs of managing any portfolio other than $m^a - m^{*a} = 0$ could be used to rationalize (67).

While it would be interesting to consider a model in which arbitrageurs hold gold as well as home and foreign currency, we wish to modify the standard model in as few ways as possible. We therefore assume that gold is only used by arbitrageurs to switch between home and foreign currency and that their gold holdings are zero. Equations (4) and (49a) are therefore maintained.

There will be pure arbitrage profit opportunities whenever $R_t = 0$ (the home country abandons the fixed exchange rate standard) and $\hat{s}_t < s_0$. By using reserves to purchase home currency at s_0 and instantaneously reselling that home currency at $\hat{s}$, arbitrageurs can earn riskless positive profits. The same holds when the foreign country abandons the fixed exchange rate regime ($R_t^* = 0$) and $\hat{s}_t^* > s_0$.

When $R_t = 0$ and $\hat{s}_t < s_0$, the opportunity cost variable governing non-arbitrage relative money demands $m_t^n - m_t^{*n} - s_t$ is still the *intertemporal* *relative price* $-E_t ds(t)$ (or $-E_t(s_{t+1}-s_0)$ in the discrete time case). The relevant opportunity cost variable governing relative arbitrage demand for money $m^a - m^*_a$ is the *instantaneous or static relative price* $-(s_t - s_0)$ and the sensitivity of relative arbitrage demand for money to this opportunity cost variable is infinite. Since the market cannot eliminate this pure arbitrage profit opportunity once the contingency triggering it has occurred (i.e. once $R_t = 0$) and the home country abandons the fixed exchange rate regime with $s_t = \hat{s}_t$, the market instead prevents the contingency that triggers the pure arbitrage opportunity from occurring: it removes the threat of a home country collapse with $\hat{s} < s_0$ by ensuring that home country official reserves stay above the critical threshold level of zero as long as $\hat{s} < s_0$. The mechanism that brings this about is that arbitrageurs replenish home country official reserves when $v \geq \tilde{v}$ (and $v < \hat{v}$), or equivalently that for $\tilde{v} \leq v < \hat{v}$, as changes in v are absorbed into equivalent changes in relative money holdings of arbitrageurs.

What this means is that when $\tilde{v} \leq v < \hat{v}$, the stock of international reserves R is no longer governed by v. Reserves are kept just above the minimal threshold level by the missing actors in the account of the Gold Standard paradox: the international currency arbitrageurs.

It is important to note that the arbitrageurs' reverse flow of gold to the home country authorities (their absorption of relative home currency) is never more nor less than the amount required to restore reserves to a positive level. That it is never less follows from equations (66a, b). That it is never more follows from equation (67). In the continuous time case where dz is an infinitesimal, the arbitrageurs' response at each instant will have the same infinitesimal magnitude. As soon as $R_t > 0$, the arbitrageurs' incentive to sell reserves in exchange for home country currency vanishes as the probability of an immediate collapse with $\hat{s} < s_0$ disappears. If, however, equation (67) did not hold, then arbitrageurs, indifferent between holding home and foreign currency when $R > 0$ and $R^* > 0$ could arbitrarily set reserves at any level by choosing arbitrary values of $m^a - m^{*a}$.

Recapitulating, if $R_t = 0$ and $\hat{s}_t < s_0$, arbitrageurs would buy up the entire domestic money stock at the fixed exchange rate s_0 in order to get rid of it again that same instant (in the same period) at $\hat{s}$. The fact that if $\hat{s}_t < s_0$ a large (stock-shift) inflow of reserves, driven by arbitrage, would take place bounds R_t away from (above) zero. This will occur for as long as $\hat{s} < s_0$. What this means is that for values of v such that $\tilde{v} \leq v < \hat{v}$, arbitrageurs will increase or reduce their money holdings according to $d(m^a - m^{*a}) = dv$. This will preserve money market equilibrium at the fixed exchange rate since with $s = s_0$ and $E_t ds(t) = 0$ (in the continuous time case; the discrete time case is slightly more complex) we have $d(m^n - m^{*n}) = -dv$.

Thus, in Figure 9.4, when $\tilde{v} \leq v < \hat{v}$, as v increases from $\tilde{v}$ we move horizontally to the right along the s_0 schedule from Ω_1 to Ω_3. At Ω_3 there is a collapse of the home currency with $R = 0$, but since $s_0 = \hat{s}$ this creates no problem for the conventional analysis. As the fixed exchange rate regime collapses at Ω_3 because $R = 0$, the expected rate of depreciation becomes negative (after being equal to zero in the continuous time model; after being equal to some higher (possibly non-zero) rate in the discrete time model). There is a stock-shift *increase* in the relative non-arbitrage demand for home currency.

Where does the money come from that satisfies the increased (relative) non-arbitrage demand for home currency when the expected rate of depreciation falls following a collapse? Not out of domestic credit: by assumption D and D^* are constant. Not out of the official reserves of the home country, which are given at zero. It comes out of money balances released by arbitrageurs who (by equation (67)), since $R = 0$ and $s_0 \geq \hat{s}$) now reduce their relative money demand to zero. The (relative) home country currency accumulated by arbitrageurs at $\hat{v}$ (at Ω_3) in Figure 9.4 is $m^a - m^{*a} = \hat{v} - \tilde{v}$. This will be shown to also be equal to the stock-shift increase in the relative demand for home currency by non-arbitrageurs at $\hat{v}$.

In the continuous time model, for any v satisfying $\tilde{v} \leq v < \hat{v}$, the relative demand for home currency by non-arbitrageurs is given by

$$m^n - m^{*n} = s_0 - v \tag{68a}$$

For the same range of values of v, the relative holdings of home currency by arbitrageurs are given by

$$m^a - m^{*a} = v - \tilde{v} \tag{68b}$$

When $v = \hat{v}$ the relative demand for home currency by arbitrageurs falls to zero, i.e. is reduced by $\hat{v} - \tilde{v}$. The relative demand for home currency by non-arbitrageurs increases by $-\gamma E_t \dot{s}|_{v=\hat{v}}$. From equations (31a), (21a) and (27a, b) it follows that:

$$\hat{v} - \tilde{v} = -\gamma E_t \dot{s}\Big|_{v=\hat{v}} = \gamma\rho\left[s_0 - (ln D - ln(D^* + G)) - \left(v_0 + \frac{\mu}{\rho}\right)\right] \tag{69}$$

Thus the increase in the relative demand for home country currency by non-arbitrageurs at $\hat{v}$ can be met and is met exactly out of the money holdings released by arbitrageurs who no longer have any riskless profit motive for holding on to home currency.

The gold standard therefore collapses in Figure 9.4 at Ω_3, as the traditional analysis asserted. Unlike what was suggested by the traditional analysis, however, there is no speculative attack on the remaining home country reserves at Ω_3. Instead the increased non-arbitrage demand for relative home country currency associated with the fall in the expected depreciation rate at Ω_3 is met out of the accumulated money balances of arbitrageurs who maintained the gold standard between Ω_1 and Ω_3.

In a similar manner, in Figure 9.4 to the left of Ω_2 (for $\hat{v}^* < v \leq \tilde{v}^*$) arbitrageurs will be building up relative holdings of foreign currency, thus preventing foreign reserves R^* from falling to zero. At Ω_4 where $v = \hat{v}^*$ there is a collapse of the gold standard as R^* falls to zero (after being infinitesimally above zero for all v between $\hat{v}^*$ and $\tilde{v}^*$). There is a stock-shift increase in the relative non-arbitrage demand for foreign currency at $\hat{v}^*$, which is associated with the increase in the expected rate of depreciation of the home currency. This increase in the relative non-arbitrage demand for foreign currency is met out of the now redundant holdings of relative foreign currency by arbitrageurs. From Ω_2 to Ω_4 the exchange rate stays at s_0. Once Ω_4 is reached, $\hat{s}^*$ takes over. Exactly the same story can be told about the behaviour of the economy between Ω_2 and Ω_4 in Figure 9.2.

5.3 *The resolution of the gold standard paradox when bond arbitrage occurs*

In the case where arbitrage is conducted through interest-bearing bonds denominated in different currencies, the argument of Section 5.2 is applicable only if it can be shown that this bond arbitrage spills over into the monetary equilibrium condition. That is, it must affect either the relative money demands or the relative stocks of domestic credit.

The reason why the introduction of interest-bearing capital-value-certain assets with positive nominal interest rates threatens the existence of a proper speculative attack equilibrium is the following.

Consider the case where the nominal interest rates on the two bonds are positive (and equal, because of UIP) while the fixed exchange rate regime survives ($R > 0$ and $R^* > 0$). Arbitrageurs will prefer holding bonds to holding money in this case. Therefore, at a point like Ω_1 in Figure 9.4, where the price of domestic currency is about to undergo a discontinuous increase, there are only would-be sellers of foreign-currency-denominated debt in the private sector. Every arbitrageur will be attempting to be short in (borrow by issuing) foreign-currency-denominated debt instruments and to be long in (lend by purchasing) domestic-currency-denominated debt instruments. With D and D^* exogenous, there also are no public sector purchasers of foreign currency denominated debt or sellers of domestic currency denominated debt. If would-be bond arbitrageurs can find no takers for their offers to sell foreign currency denominated debt, one might think they would have no choice but to switch their arbitrage operations to the other foreign currency denominated asset (non-interest-bearing foreign currency itself) for which there is a public sector taker at the fixed rate of exchange. Thus the frustrated would-be bond arbitrage spills over into the currency markets, home country official foreign exchange reserves are replenished and the threats to the fixed exchange rate regime to the bond market are simultaneously canceled.

The problem with this argument is that, as soon as domestic currency reserves are restored above their minimal threshold level and the threat of a discrete appreciation of the home country currency is thereby eliminated, arbitrageurs will once again wish to switch out of home country currency into bonds with a positive nominal rate of interest. Home country reserves are threatened again. No equilibrium exists in this case.

While an exhaustive analysis of the two monies, two bonds and gold model remains to be done, we can point to a number of instances in which a well-defined equilibrium can exist even in this case.

(1) *There is no equilibrium with interest-bearing assets.*

In two-period overlapping generations (OLG) models of a closed economy with each generation consisting of identical individuals and without firms whose 'life span' exceeds that of individuals, there can be no private lending or borrowing. If in addition there is no interest-bearing public debt outstanding and there are no real assets, but there is a noninterest-bearing 'outside' stock of money, we have a single country money-only model. There are no equilibria with debt of any kind. In a two-country version of this model, further restrictions on the international uses of national currencies would have to be imposed to obtain limited substitutability between domestic and foreign currency and a determinate exchange rate (see Kareken and Wallace, 1981).

(2) *Interest is paid on currency.*

If interest is paid on currency and if the currency interest rates mimic the bond interest rates, we again would have direct currency arbitrage.

(3) *Money demand and bond demand are segmented.*

A subset of private agents may be constrained not to hold bonds but can hold the two currencies. The single-country version of such a model can be found in Sargent and Wallace's 'Unpleasant Monetarist Arithmetic' OLG model (Sargent and Wallace, 1981). Small bills-type arguments and the assumption that the poor cannot pool resources to invest in interest-bearing assets that can be acquired only in large denominations lead to an equilibrium in which the poor hold only money and (if the nominal interest rate is positive) the rich only hold bonds. An obvious two-country extension results in one set of agents (the poor) holding only the two currencies while the rich hold the two bonds. The poor would supply the direct currency arbitrage that would make the argument of the previous subsection applicable. To obtain limited direct currency substitution in the non-arbitrage demands for the two currencies, some further restrictions on the uses of the national currencies would have to be imposed.

(4) *Saving the bond market.*

Where the previous three arguments had the bond arbitrageurs' demand spill over directly into the relative demands for currency, our final argument assumes an impact of bond arbitrage on the stocks of domestic credit, D and D^*.

Assume that v reaches $\tilde{v} < \hat{v}$ from the left, at a point such as Ω_1 in Figure 9.4, and that a natural collapse of the home currency occurs. In that case there would, with D and D^* constant, be a collapse of the foreign currency denominated bond market: every arbitrageur would try to sell foreign currency denominated debt (and indeed go short in it) and buy home currency denominated debt. If the authorities respond to this threatened collapse of the foreign bond market by undertaking the minimal open-market operations required to prevent a bond market collapse, they would choose D and D^* such that

$$(D^* + G)^{-1} dD - D^{-1} dD = dv \tag{70}$$

If $dv > 0$, this could involve the foreign country's government switching from borrowing from the private sector to borrowing from its central bank. In addition (or instead) the home government could move in the opposite direction and engage in an open-market sale. If the assumption of exogenous domestic credit were replaced by (70) when $\tilde{v} \leq v < \hat{v}$, then the two governments would effectively take over from the private currency arbitrageurs described in the previous subsection. The prevention of a collapse of the fixed exchange rate regime would be a by-product of policies aimed at preventing a bond market collapse. At $\hat{v}$ there would be a stock-shift reversal of the cumulative flow open market operations that brought the economy from $\tilde{v}$ to $\hat{v}$. There would be an open market purchase by the home government and/or an open market sale by the foreign government to provide private agents with the relatively larger stocks of home money demanded at the negative post-collapse expected rate of depreciation of the exchange rate.

This argument can be clarified with the help of Figure 9.4. Consider e.g. the central banks' behaviour at the upper end of the S & R viable range. The policy rule has two parts:

(I) Any time there is a transition to a floating exchange rate, the stocks of domestic credit will revert to the original levels of D and D^*, that is the values of the stocks of domestic credit that prevailed when v first reached $\tilde{v}$ from the left. This fixes the $\hat{s}$ and $\hat{s}^*$ schedules (which depend on the post-attack stocks of domestic credit) in the same positions that they had when domestic credit was assumed to be exogenous throughout.

(II) In order to prevent the natural collapse, for values of v such that $\tilde{v} \leq v < \hat{v}$, the authorities engage in the minimal size open market operations required to keep home country reserves positive. Since the $\tilde{s}$ and $\tilde{s}^*$ schedules are defined for the actual current stocks of domestic credit, they will shift with the actual values of v (keeping the same slopes) between $\tilde{v}$ and $\hat{v}$. When v reaches $\hat{v}$, $\tilde{s}$ and $\hat{s}$ intersect at Ω_3 where $\tilde{s} = \hat{s} = s_0$, and the natural and speculative collapses coincide.

It is hardly surprising that (relative) domestic credit expansion policies can be used to stabilize reserves in the face of exogenous relative money demand shifts. It is nevertheless interesting that such a policy can be rationalized as a response to a threatened bond market collapse. If government debt is denominated in the national currency, a forward-looking foreign government may well have a strong incentive to prevent a collapse in the market for its debt.

The 'discretionary' behaviour of the authorities when v is between $\tilde{v}$ and $\hat{v}$, characterized above, can be made automatic if we extend the governments' exchange rate commitment to include sales or purchases at the official parity of all their nominal assets, that is both currency and interest-bearing debt. This would restore the private (bond) arbitrageur to the position of the only active agent, with the authorities merely accommodating incipient private excess demand and supply at the fixed parity. Historical evidence exists that is consistent with our interpretation – for example the US gold standard crisis during the 1890s. As analysed in Grilli (1990), between 1893 and 1896 there was a widespread fear that the US Treasury would run out of gold reserves and that the US would have to abandon the gold standard. During this period the financial markets were very unstable, and this instability reached a peak with the panic of 1893. To ensure the viability of the gold standard, on four occasions the US Treasury issued bonds. These operations were exactly of the kind illustrated above: a swap of gold for domestic bonds. In one instance (the issue of February 1895), in addition to issuing bonds the Treasury also 'subsidized' speculators (the Belmont–Morgan syndicate) in order for them to hold domestic currency. In this way they transformed money into an interest-bearing asset – a measure which would also provide a remedy to the crisis, as illustrated in Section 5.2 above.

(5) *Other approaches to direct currency arbitrage in the presence of debt with positive nominal interest rates.*

In all of Section 5, and especially in Section 5.3, the importance has become apparent of the details of the specification of the choice problem that generates the demands for the pecuniary rate of return dominated assets home and foreign currency. Without explicit microfoundations of the demands for the two national currencies, the case for and against direct currency arbitrage in the presence of assets (capital-certain bonds with positive nominal interest rates) that dominate currency in rate of return cannot be resolved conclusively. It seems likely, however, that it will be possible to generate plausible conditions under which private agents who hold various national currencies for transactions or precautionary motives can be induced to depart from their normal cash holdings in response to opportunities for pure arbitrage profits.

6 Conclusions

The gold standard paradox turns out not to be a gold standard contradiction or inconsistency. Krugman's critical probing of the speculative attack literature has brought out serious weaknesses in the way in which these models were interpreted and described, but not in the formal analyses of when and under what circumstances fixed exchange rate regimes collapse or of how the post-collapse exchange rate behaves.

The explicit recognition in speculative attack models of the role of arbitrageurs faced with the prospect of an imminent collapse of the fixed exchange rate regime and the associated possibility of riskless profits permits us to rule out the possibility of a natural collapse occurring before the speculative attack takes place. Speculative collapses occur where and when the traditional literature says they will.

The (stock-shift) changes in non-arbitrage money demand associated with collapses are however in the paradoxical cases identified by Krugman not accommodated by (stock-shift) changes in official international reserves but instead come out of the accumulated money balances of arbitrageurs who release them when a conventional collapse (which eliminates their opportunity for riskless profits) occurs. Between a paradoxical natural collapse point and the proper speculative collapse point private arbitrageurs keep the government whose reserves are about to be exhausted supplied with the minimal amount of reserves required for the survival of the fixed exchange rate regime. If the fundamentals drive the shadow exchange rate to the conventional speculative attack point, the arbitrageurs release the money holdings they had accumulated while they kept the threatened government supplied with reserves and thus satisfy the increased non-arbitrage demand for money. A conventional transition to a free float (or to some other post-collapse regime not analyzed in this paper) then takes place.

NOTES

We would like to thank Chris Sims and the participants at the Warwick Summer Research Workshop on 'Exchange Rates and Financial Markets', 9–27 July 1990 for helpful comments on an earlier version of this paper.

1 A nonconstant but exogenous $D(t)$ or $D^*(t)$ can be subsumed under $v(t)$.
2 The purist will note some untidiness as regards the composition of the stock of reserves. If reserves are gold, let p^G be the domestic currency price of gold and p^{*G} the foreign currency price of gold. Then $m = ln(D + p^G R)$ and $m^* = ln(D^* + p^{*G} R^*)$. The exchange rate $S \equiv e^s = (p^G / p^{*G})$. Without loss of generality we can choose units such that $p^G = p^{*G} = 1$, but in that case we must also set $s_0 = 1$.
3 The case $\mu < 0$ is conceptually identical.
4 Note that if we consider arbitrary (nonlinear) v processes the shadow exchange rate curves may intersect the s_0 line more than once, and we could get several S & R viable ranges with different combinations of correct and incorrect speculative attacks at the boundaries!

REFERENCES

Buiter, W.H. (1987), 'Borrowing to defend the exchange rate and the timing and magnitude of speculative attacks', *Journal of International Economics* **23**, 221–39.
(1989), 'A viable gold standard requires flexible monetary and fiscal policy', *Review of Economic Studies* **56**, 101–18.
Dixit, A. (1988), 'A simplified exposition of some results concerning regulated Brownian motion', Princeton University Working Paper.
Dumas, B. (1989), 'Super contact and related optimality conditions: a supplement to Avinash Dixit's: "A simplified exposition of some results concerning regulated Brownian motion"', NBER Technical Working Paper No. 77.
Flood, R. and P. Garber (1984), 'Collapsing exchange rate regimes; some linear examples', *Journal of International Economics* **17**, 1–13.
(1989), 'The linkage between speculative attack and target zone models of exchange rates', NBER Working Paper No. 2918, see also this volume.
Froot, K.A. and M. Obstfeld (1989a), 'Exchange rate dynamics under stochastic regime shifts: a unified approach', NBER Working Paper No. 2835.
(1989b), 'Stochastic process switching: some simple solutions', NBER Working Paper No. 2998, see also this volume.
Grilli, V.U. (1986), 'Buying and selling attacks on fixed exchange rate systems', *Journal of International Economics* **20**, 143–56.
(1990), 'Managing exchange rate crises: evidence from the 1890's', *Journal of International Money and Finance*.
Kareken, J.H. and N. Wallace (1981), 'On the Indeterminacy of equilibrium exchange rates', *Quarterly Journal of Economics* **96**, 207–22.

Krugman, P. (1979), 'A model of balance of payments crises', *Journal of Money, Credit and Banking* **11**, 311–25.
(1987), 'Trigger strategies and price dynamics in equity and foreign exchange markets', NBER Working Paper No. 2459.
(1988). 'Target zones and exchange rate dynamics', NBER Working Paper No. 2481, forthcoming in the *Quarterly Journal of Economics*.
(1989), 'Target zones with limited reserves', mimeo.
Krugman, P. and J. Rotemberg (1990), 'Target zones with limited reserves', mimeo, July.
Miller, M. and P. Weller (1988a), 'Target zones, currency options and monetary policy', mimeo, see also this volume.
(1988b), 'Exchange rate bands and realignments in a stationary stochastic setting', mimeo.
(1989), 'Solving stochastic saddlepoint systems: a qualitative treatment with economic applications', CEPR Discussion Paper No. 308.
Obstfeld, M. (1986a), 'Rational and self-fulfilling balance of payments crises', *American Economic Review* **76**, 72–81.
(1986b), 'Speculative attacks and the external constraint in a maximizing model of the balance of payments', *Canadian Journal of Economics* **19**, 1–22.
Sargent, T.J. and N. Wallace (1981), 'Some unpleasant monetarist arithmetic', *Federal Reserve Bank of Minneapolis Quarterly Review*, Autumn, reprinted in T.J. Sargent, *Rational Expectations and Inflation*, New York, Harper and Row, 1986, Chapter 5, pp. 158–90.

Discussion

MAURICE OBSTFELD

Can a country be forced off a fixed exchange rate if speculators expect its currency to *appreciate* on the date of the collapse? Willem Buiter and Vittorio Grilli use a two-country gold standard model for a careful analysis of conditions in which this 'gold standard paradox' seems to arise.

The authors then turn to two broad approaches to eliminating the paradox. The first is to introduce new agents into the model: currency arbitrageurs who disregard interest rates and base their relative demands for national monies on expected exchange rate changes only. The second is to assume different government policies, and thus to alter the asset markets' supply side rather than their demand side.

I will make three main points in this discussion.

(1) The gold standard paradox is a situation in which *equilibrium simply cannot exist*. Buiter and Grilli assert this fact, but in my opinion do not emphasize it sufficiently or demonstrate how devastating the problem is. Indeed, an implication of the gold standard paradox and of similar paradoxes is that a fixed exchange rate cannot equal the present discounted value of its fundamental determinants.

(2) This nonexistence of equilibrium is a direct result of inconsistent government policy rules – rules that are inconsistent in the sense that they are inherently self-contradicting. A corollary of this observation is that the gold standard paradox is not some peculiar failing of the speculative-attack literature. The paradox is most apparent there because of some unfortunate assumptions researchers (including myself) have tended to make in analysing attacks. But it is easy to devise related 'Catch-22' policy rules in other contexts.

(3) More sensible and realistic rules for deciding when to abandon a fixed exchange rate result in a unique, well-behaved equilibrium.

These conclusions determine my attitude toward the two approaches to resolving the paradox that Buiter and Grilli explore. Let me state that attitude right away. While it is intriguing to study exchange-rate behaviour under alternative assumptions about money demand, the introduction of additional market agents with *ad hoc* objectives can only obscure the fundamental role of government policy antinomies in destroying equilibrium. (After all, our standard, representative-agent models require no additional actors to rule out anticipated exchange rate jumps.[1]) As a result, I am more sympathetic to the authors' second approach, which focuses on the rationality of official policies.

An illustration of the problem

A flexible-price monetary setting simpler than the one Buiter and Grilli analyse serves to illustrate the basic nature of the gold standard paradox. Think of a small country that pegs its currency to that of a foreign reserve currency, and thus takes the foreign-currency price level, $p^*(t)$, and nominal interest rate, $i^*(t)$ as given.[2] Using the Buiter-Grilli notation, and assuming (noncovered) interest parity, purchasing power parity, and the portfolio-balance condition $m(t) - p(t) = ky(t) - \gamma i(t)$, I can represent equilibrium by the requirement that

$$s(t) = m(t) + \omega(t) + \gamma E_t(ds(t))/dt \tag{1}$$

where the money supply is the sum of domestic credit and the home-currency value of past foreign reserves acquisitions,

$$m(t) = ln\left(D(t) + \int_{-\infty}^{t} S(v)\,dR(v)\right) \tag{2}$$

and where $\omega(t) \equiv \gamma i^*(t) - (p^*(t) + ky(t))$. For notational convenience I assume $\omega(t) = 0$, for all t, so that (1) becomes

$$s(t) = m(t) + \gamma E_t(ds(t))/dt \tag{3}$$

Imagine that at time $t = 0$, the exchange rate has always been pegged at S_0 while domestic credit has always been constant at the level $D_0 < S_0$. Thus, (log) private currency balances at $t = 0$ are $m(0) = ln(D_0 + S_0 R(0))$. The authorities suddenly announce, however, that at time $T_1 > 0$ domestic credit will rise to the level $D_1 > S_0$; moreover, at time $T_2 > T_1$, domestic credit will be reduced below its starting level, to $D_2 < D_0$.

In Figure 9A.1, the lower panel shows the path of domestic credit (in log terms) as the step function $d(t)$. Because $d_0 < s_0$, an exchange rate fixed at s_0 is compatible with a positive level of foreign reserves for $t < T_1$. If the authorities cannot borrow reserves, however (so that negative reserve levels are infeasible), the fixed exchange rate will have to be abandoned at T_1, when domestic credit jumps to $d_1 > s_0$: money-market equilibrium would be possible at $s(T_1) = s_0$ only if a currency appreciation, and not a fixed rate, were expected.

The upper panel of Figure 9A.1 shows the 'shadow' floating exchange rate $\tilde{s}(t)$, defined as the floating rate that would prevail with zero reserves:

$$\tilde{s}(t) \equiv \int_{t}^{\infty} e^{-(v-t)/\gamma} E_t(ln\,D(v)/\gamma)\,dv$$

The path of this variable is at the heart of the gold standard paradox and related problems. Because domestic credit is expected to decline so sharply at T_2, the shadow rate lies *below* the peg s_0 even at T_1. In contrast, if the increase in domestic credit at T_1 were permanent (giving the path $d(t)'$ in the lower panel), the shadow exchange rate would follow $\tilde{s}(t)'$ in the upper panel. In this case a very standard attack would occur at point A, with speculators cleaning out official reserves then and the currency moving to a float without a discrete anticipated jump in its exchange rate.

Under the initial domestic-credit path $d(t)$, however, the fixed exchange rate need not be abandoned until time T_1. The manner in which this is done is crucial to the existence of equilibrium. One possibility is that the authorities make the following announcement: 'We will allow the currency to float at $t = T_1$; but we will defend the currency up to that moment by standing ready to buy and sell foreign exchange at the price s_0.' We can understand the economy's subsequent equilibrium path by recalling that the arbitrage condition $s(T_1) = s_0$ has to hold. An instant before T_1, the authorities therefore will experience a sharp foreign-reserve movement

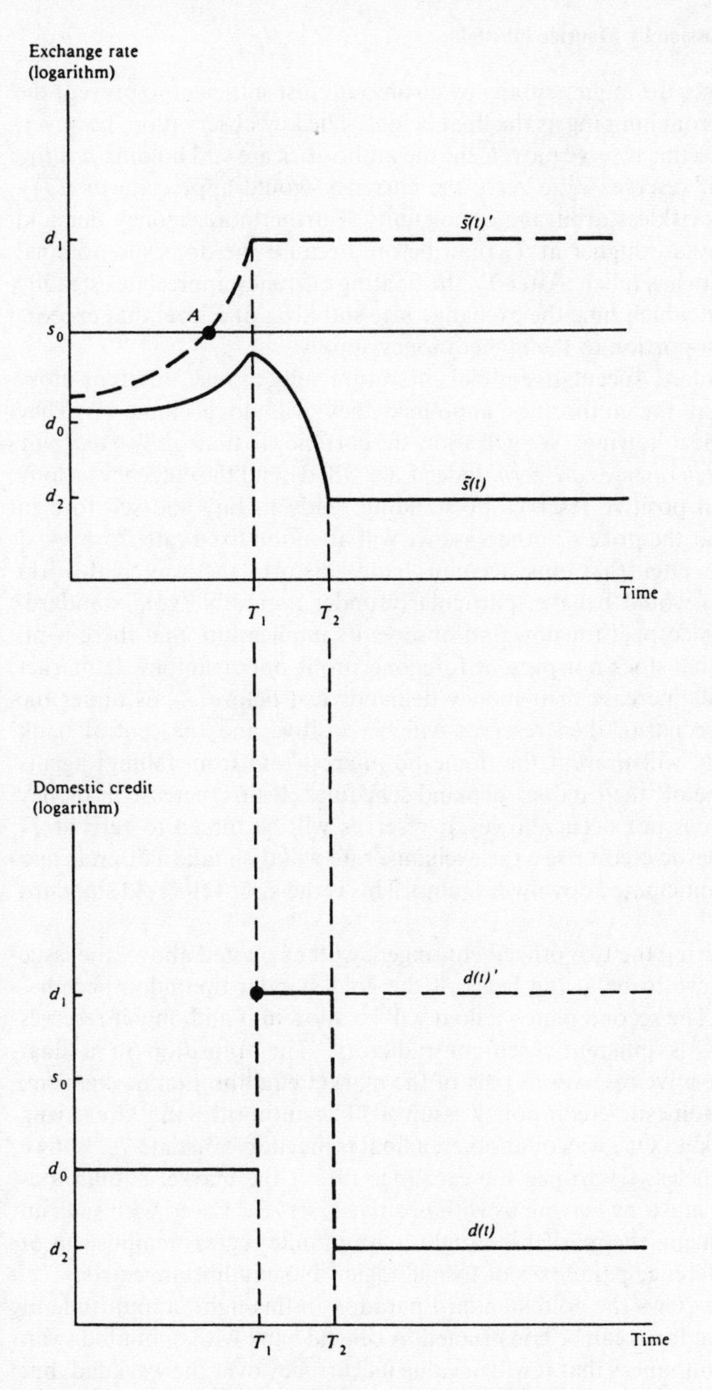

Figure 9A.1 Paradoxical and nonparadoxical collapses

that changes the money supply by an amount just sufficient to prevent the currency from jumping as the float begins. The key observation, however, is that after this reserve movement the authorities are still holding *positive* reserves; if reserves were zero, the currency would appreciate to $\tilde{s}(T_1)$, creating a riskless arbitrage opportunity. Furthermore, money demand and supply are higher at T_1 than before because the domestic nominal interest rate has fallen. After T_1, the floating currency appreciates steadily until T_2, at which time the exchange rate stabilizes at a level that exceeds $\tilde{s}(T_2)$ in proportion to the higher money supply.

The standard speculative-attack literature tells a very different story about what the authorities announce they will do at time T_1. They promise the following: 'We will allow the currency to float at T_1 *if and only if our foreign reserves are zero*. Indeed, we will defend the currency as long as we hold positive reserves by standing ready to buy and sell foreign exchange at the price s_0; otherwise we will abandon fixed rates forever.' I will argue later that this account badly distorts the way real-world authorities would behave, particularly under a credible gold standard. But let us accept it for now and observe its implication, that there is no outcome that does not present foregone profit opportunities. If market participants increase their money demands just before T_1, as under the previous scenario, then reserves will be positive and the central bank accordingly will prevent the domestic interest rate from falling: agents thus will be off their money demand schedules. If this increase in money demand does not occur, however, reserves will be forced to zero at T_1 when domestic credit rises: the exchange rate will then take a discrete and perfectly anticipated downward jump. This is the gist of the gold standard paradox.

In comparing the two official contingency plans quoted above, the issue that I believe to be at the heart of the gold standard paradox becomes apparent. The second plan – a float will be allowed if and only if reserves are zero – is inherently self-contradictory. The transition to a float *requires* positive reserves as part of the market equilibration mechanism, given the domestic-credit policy assumed. The authorities thus are saying to the market: 'One way or another, a float is inevitable on date T_1. But we will nonetheless try to peg the exchange rate if the market equilibrates itself, as it must, by leaving us with positive reserves.' Faced with such an announcement, the market is caught in an infinite regress reminiscent of the self-reference paradoxes of formal logic.[3] No equilibrium exists.

Once one views the gold standard paradox in this light, a multitude of similar paradoxes can be constructed. A central bank with unlimited swap facilities announces that it will devalue its currency over the weekend, but only if no reserves are lost the Friday before. What is the market response? An agent who believes that reserves will fall on Friday, and that consequently no devaluation will occur, will have no reason to buy reserves from the central bank. If all agents hold this belief, all will act in the same way, so reserves will not fall and the currency will be devalued. A belief that reserves will not fall, on the other hand, will lead to massive reserve outflows on Friday. But the central bank can and will intervene *à l'outrance*, even if this means buying back the entire domestic money supply; and on Monday morning the previous parity will still be in force. This is a game without a Nash equilibrium in pure strategies.

The failure of the present-value relation

One way of diagnosing potential nonexistent equilibria is to examine the present-value relation. If the exchange rate is the expected present value of its fundamental determinants, then it must follow a continuous path in expectation. Anticipated jumps in the exchange rate, such as those that occur in the gold standard paradox, therefore imply that the present-value relation doesn't hold.

The standard continuous-time speculative attack model offers a good example of this principle. On any date t at which the exchange rate is still pegged at s_0, there is a random interval of length $\tilde{T}$ over which the fixed rate will survive. The ground rules are, as above, that the forcing function for domestic credit is exogenous, and that a permanent float begins when, and only when, reserves first hit zero. So at time t, the distribution of $\tilde{T}$ depends only on the stochastic process generating domestic credit and its current realization, $D(t)$.[4] The probability distribution function for $\tilde{T}$ is $F(T|D(t)) \equiv \text{Prob}(\tilde{T} \leq T|D(t))$.

Now suppose that the present-value relation holds:

$$s_0 = \int_t^{\infty} e^{-(v-t)/\gamma} E_t(m(v)/\gamma)\,dv \tag{4}$$

In view of (2) and the last paragraph's definitions, this equation can be written as

$$\begin{aligned} s_0 = \int_0^{\infty} \Bigg[\int_t^{t+T} & e^{-(v-t)/\gamma} E_t(ln(D(v) + S_0 R(v))/\gamma \,|\, \tilde{T} = T)\,dv \\ & + \int_{t+T}^{\infty} e^{-(v-t)/\gamma} E_t(ln\, D(v)/\gamma \,|\, \tilde{T} = T)\,dv \Bigg] dF(T|D(t)) \end{aligned} \tag{5}$$

Because the exchange rate is fixed at s_0 until $t + T$, equation (3) implies that for $v < t + T$,

$$E_t(ln(D(v) + S_0 R(v))/\gamma \,|\, \tilde{T} = T) = s_0/\gamma$$

Combining this result with (5) leads, however, to the equality:

$$\int_{t}^{\infty} e^{-T/\gamma}\left[s_0 - \int_{t+T}^{\infty} e^{-[v-(t+T)]/\gamma} E_t(\ln D(v)/\gamma \mid \tilde{T} = T)\, dv\right] dF(T \mid D(t)) = 0 \tag{6}$$

To understand better the implications of (6), define $\bar{D}$ as the unique level of domestic credit at which reserves are first depleted: $\tilde{T} = T$ if and only if $D(t + T) = \bar{D}$. Then for $v \geq t + T$,

$$E_t(\ln D(v)/\gamma \mid \tilde{T} = T) = E(\ln D(v)/\gamma \mid D(t + T) = \bar{D})$$

so (6) becomes:

$$\int_{0}^{\infty} e^{-T/\gamma}\left[s_0 - \int_{t+T}^{\infty} e^{-[v-(t+T)]/\gamma} E(\ln D(v)/\gamma \mid D(t + T) = \bar{D})\, dv\right] dF(T \mid D(t)) = 0$$

Looking at the equation above, we see that the present-value formula (4) will certainly fail to hold if for every time $t + T$ at which collapse can occur,

$$s_0 > \int_{t+T}^{\infty} e^{-[v-(t+T)]/\gamma} E(\ln D(v)/\gamma \mid D(t + T) = \bar{D})\, dv \tag{7}$$

But the right-hand side of (7) is just the shadow floating exchange rate on the date of the collapse, $\tilde{s}(t + T)$. So the condition that

$$s_0 > \tilde{s}(t + T) \tag{8}$$

for all collapse dates $t + T$ – the condition that defines a 'paradoxical' attack – also implies that the pre-attack exchange rate diverges from the present discounted value of fundamentals. Unless we admit the possibility of bubbles, this arbitrage opportunity implies that the fixed exchange rate is unsustainable, even as a temporary equilibrium.

An alternative interpretation of collapsing exchange parities

The standard exchange-rate attack literature assumes that a parity will be abandoned if and only if reserves are at their minimum level. One obvious objection is that there may be no effective minimum reserve level in a world of free capital mobility and liberal inter-government swap facilities. Furthermore, domestic-credit policy is not always paralysed, and to a large degree can substitute for operations in foreign exchange.

There is another serious problem with the literature that becomes particularly apparent once gold-standard paradoxes are contemplated. An exchange authority fixes an exchange rate by agreeing to buy and sell unlimited amounts of foreign currency at that rate. When reserves are depleted, the authority can no longer sell reserves to prevent a depreciation of the domestic currency; but it can certainly *buy* them to prevent an appreciation.

This is exactly the situation arising in a gold standard paradox – reserves hit zero and the currency appreciates – so there clearly is nothing to prevent the exchange authority from continuing to peg. It is still perfectly feasible to buy foreign exchange, even if there is none on hand to sell. Merely observing this fact does not make the gold standard paradox go away; but it suggests an alternative and eminently plausible policy response to collapse that does lead to a well-defined equilibrium.[5]

Suppose now that the authorities promise the following: 'We will stand ready to sell foreign currency for domestic money at the exchange rate s_0 as long as our reserves are positive. Furthermore, we will stand ready *indefinitely* to buy foreign currency with domestic money at the same rate.' While there are cases in which fixed rates were abandoned in favour of a more-or-less open-ended float, there are many more in which some return to a peg was intended. The formulation given above is particularly apt when applied to the gold standard, which is sometimes interpreted as a flexible rule – one that includes an implicit escape clause providing for temporary suspension but an eventual return to the pre-existing parity.[6]

Let's look at this situation in light of the example depicted in Figure 9A.1. If the authorities pledge to rely on market arbitrage to prevent currency appreciation, even when they lack the means to forestall depreciation, they place a floor of s_0 under the shadow floating exchange rate $\tilde{s}(t)$. We can understand the market response to the domestic-credit path $d(t)$ shown in the figure's lower panel by working backward. On date T_2 the currency will be repegged at s_0: if the authorities have no reserves just before that date, their willingness to buy them at price s_0 will ensure a reserve influx. From time T_2 on, reserves will have to equal $R(T_2) = S_0 - D_2$.

Make the tentative assumption that $R(t) = 0$ for $T_1 \leq t < T_2$; we shall see in a moment that this must be the case. The exchange rate on date T_1 is then the shadow floating rate; but in the present scenario with ultimate repegging, its value is

$$\tilde{s}(T_1) = \frac{1}{\gamma}\left[\int_{T_1}^{T_2} e^{-(v-T_1)/\gamma} \ln D_1 \, dv + \int_{T_2}^{\infty} e^{-(v-T_1)/\gamma} \ln M(v) \, dv\right]$$

$$= (1 - e^{-(T_2-T_1)/\gamma}) \ln D_1 + (e^{-(T_2-T_1)/\gamma}) s_0$$

Notice that $\tilde{s}(T_1) > s_0$ because $\ln D_1 > s_0$; there is thus no paradox. To prevent the exchange rate from taking a sharp *upward* jump at time T_1, a classic speculative attack will have to occur at some time T before T_1. Time T is determined by the usual zero-profit condition:

$$s_0 = (1 - e^{-(T_1 - T)/\gamma})\, ln\, D_0 + (e^{-(T_1 - T)/\gamma})\tilde{s}(T_1)$$

Because $ln\, D_0 < s_0$, the foregoing equation determines a unique time $T < T_1$ at which speculators acquire all foreign reserves, leaving the exchange rate free to float gradually upward.

The story we arrive at is decidedly nonparadoxical. Imagine that a brief war breaks out: the financial markets know that government finance will require a temporary increase in domestic-credit growth. Even before the credit expansion occurs, there is an exchange-rate crisis that forces the country off fixed rates. As the war is successfully prosecuted, however, the now-floating currency appreciates in the foreign exchange market toward its previous parity. The latter is reinstated once victory is achieved and financial stability restored.

While this example leads to reasonable conclusions, I think that in general we should avoid trying to proceed too far without a more explicit model of the government's objectives and constraints. Absent a coherent account of what the government is trying to accomplish, and under what conditions, we will often be quite in the dark in assessing the relevance of seemingly paradoxical equilibria.

NOTES

I thank the National Science Foundation for financial support.

1 See Obstfeld (1986), for example.
2 As per the usual notational convention, lower-case letters, other than those standing for interest rates, denote natural logarithms of variables represented by the corresponding upper-case letters.
3 Recall, for example, the Cretan who asserts that all Cretans are liars. Does he speak truthfully?
4 This assertion assumes that $D(t)$ follows a first-order Markov process.
5 Krugman and Rotemberg (1990) take this tack in analysing attacks on a two-country gold standard.
6 See Bordo and Kydland (1990). In arguing that it is always feasible to buy reserves, I am ignoring the kind of situation analysed by Grilli (1986).

REFERENCES

Bordo, M., and F. Kydland (1990), 'The gold standard as a rule', NBER Working Paper No. 3367, May.

Grilli, V. (1986), 'Buying and selling attacks on fixed exchange rate systems', *Journal of International Economics* **20**, 143–56.
Krugman, P., and J. Rotemberg (1990), 'Target zones with limited reserves', NBER Working Paper No. 3418, August.
Obstfeld, M. (1986), 'Speculative attack and the external constraint in a maximizing model of the balance of payments', *Canadian Journal of Economics* **19**, 1–22.

10 Sustainable intervention policies and exchange rate dynamics

GIUSEPPE BERTOLA and
RICARDO J. CABALLERO

1 Introduction

Recent work on stochastic exchange rate models has focused on the nonlinearities induced by intervention aimed at maintaining exchange rates within target zones and by exchange-rate regime shifts. In this literature, the stochastic process followed by the fundamental determinants of exchange rates is modeled as a combination of continuous developments, assumed exogenous, and infrequent shifts (either infinitesimal, as in Krugman, 1991, or of finite size, as in Flood and Garber, 1989) occurring on a measure-zero set of time points (or perhaps at one point in time only, as in some models of Froot and Obstfeld, 1989). Exchange rate determination has typically been modeled in terms of money market equilibrium conditions, and this has led to interpreting the infrequent fundamental shocks as (nonsterilized) intervention in the foreign exchange or money market. Since foreign exchange reserves impose obvious limits on the size of cumulative interventions, some attention has been devoted to the sustainability of such intervention schemes (see Delgado and Dumas, 1989).

This paper discusses these aspects and their relationship to each other. In a stylized probabilistic model of exchange rate fundamentals, we find that if the cumulation of infrequent fundamental movements has bounded support (which is necessary for the intervention policy to be sustainable in the long run), then not only is the long-run relationship between fundamentals and exchange rates the same that would be valid under a free-float exchange rate regime, but also the possibly very pronounced within-band nonlinearities in the exchange rate-fundamentals relationship induced by 'intervention' cancel each other out when weighed by their long-run probabilities.

The paper is organized as follows. Section 2 describes, under simplifying assumptions, the general structure of the class of models we study.

Section 3 interprets the technical assumptions in terms of exchange rates and fundamentals, and notes that sustainability issues arise when cumulative intervention has no role in determining the behaviour of fundamentals. Section 4 addresses those issues by allowing the probability of repeated, stochastic realignments to vary as a function of cumulative intervention; Section 5 characterizes exchange rate behaviour under such an intervention scheme; and Section 6 studies the long-run implications of sustainability for the relationship between exchange rates and their fundamental determinants. Section 7 concludes outlining directions for further research.

2 The probability structure of intervention and realignment models

We denote with $\{x_t\}$ the log-exchange rate process, and we assume the familiar asset-pricing relationship

$$x_t = f_t + \frac{a}{dt} E_t\{dx_t\} \tag{1}$$

where $E_t\{\cdot\}$ denotes the conditional expectation formed on the basis of relevant information available at time t, and $\{f_t\}$ denotes the process followed by the *fundamental* determinants of exchange rates, e.g. the variables appearing in the excess money demand function. Ruling out bubbles, we can integrate equation (1) between t and infinity to obtain

$$x_t = \frac{1}{a}\int_t^{\infty} E_t\{f_\tau\} e^{-(\tau - t)/a} d\tau \tag{2}$$

Without specifying the economic counterpart of f_t, we simply write $f_t = i_t + z_t$: by assumption, the levels of the $\{i_t\}$ and $\{z_t\}$ processes have identical roles in exchange rate determination, but their dynamic behaviour is different. To capture the expectational effects emphasized by the literature on target zones and on intervention, we assume continuous sample paths of infinite variation to the $\{z_t\}$ process, while $\{i_t\}$ is constant almost everywhere on the time line and increases or decreases by finite or infinitesimal amounts on a measure-zero set of time points.

We let the dynamics of $\{z_t\}$ be given by

$$dz_t = \sigma\, dW_t \tag{3}$$

and all movements of $\{i_t\}$ have equal absolute size Δf. If j_t denotes the *net* number of jumps up to an including time t (i.e. the number of positive jumps *minus* that of negative jumps), we then have

$$i_t = j_t \Delta f$$

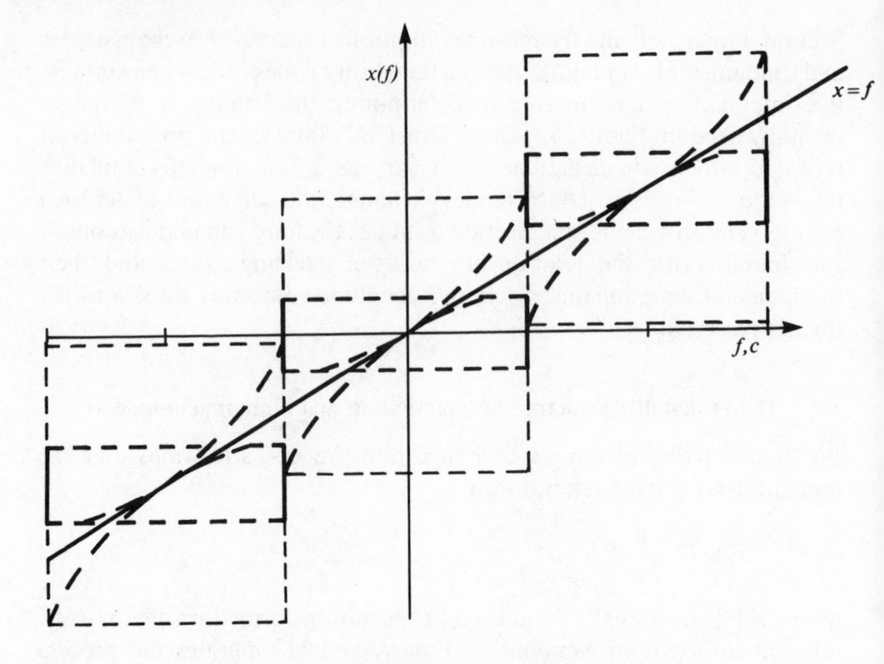

Figure 10.1 Exchange rate and fundamental fluctuation bands

Allowing for non-zero $\{z_t\}$ drift or for jumps of different sizes, while conceptually easy, would considerably complicate the notation and the algebraic derivations.

If $\Delta f = 0$, i.e. if no jumps ever occur in the fundamentals process, then

$$E_t\{f_\tau\} = E_t\{z_\tau\} = z_t = f_t \qquad \forall \tau \geq t$$

which, by equation (2), yields the exchange rate solution $x_t = f_t$ for all t, plotted in Figure 10.1 as the solid diagonal line.

When $\Delta f > 0$, the likelihood of a jump at every point in time has an essential role in determining the relationship between f_t and x_t. We denote with p_t^u the probability of a positive jump at time t, with p_t^d that of a negative jump, and with $1 - p_t^u - p_t^d \geq 0$ the probability of no jump at time t.

If the jump probabilities are *constant* or, more generally, independent of the exchange rate and fundamental processes, the relationship between fundamentals and exchange rates remains linear.[1] To obtain the nonlinear relationships emphasized in the target zone literature, it is necessary to allow the size and/or the probability of jumps to vary over time *in a way that is related to the position of the fundamentals*.

The simplest of the models proposed in our earlier paper (Bertola and

Caballero, 1990), for example, is obtained if the jump probabilities are specifed as

$$p_t^u = \begin{cases} p & \text{if } f_t = c_t + \Delta f \\ (1-p) & \text{if } f_t = c_t - \Delta f \\ 0 & \text{otherwise;} \end{cases} \qquad p_t^d = \begin{cases} (1-p) & \text{if } f_t = c_t + \Delta f \\ p & \text{if } f_t = c_t - \Delta f \\ 0 & \text{otherwise,} \end{cases} \tag{4}$$

where the auxiliary 'central parity' process $\{c_t\}$ jumps up by $2\Delta f$ when $f_t = c_t + \Delta f$ and i_t jumps upwards, down by $2\Delta f$ when $f_t = c_t - \Delta f$ and i_t jumps downwards. This process has no direct effect on exchange rates, but its level does determine the probability of $\{i_t\}$ jumps.

The horizontal axis in Figure 10.1 may then be divided into adjoining segments of length $2\Delta f$ ('fluctuation bands'), each centered at a value of c. In the interior of every band jumps have probability zero and $\{f_t\}$ has the dynamics of $\{z_t\}$ in equation (3). By (2), the exchange rate can, as a conditional expectation, be written as a function of f_t and c_t processes; and the usual stochastic calculus arguments imply that in the interior of regions where c_t and i_t are constant this function should satisfy the differential equation

$$x(f; c) = f + \frac{\alpha\sigma^2}{2} x''(f; c) \tag{5}$$

where $x''(f; c) \equiv \partial^2 x(f; c)/\partial f^2$. It should also be the case that

$$\begin{aligned} (c + 2\Delta f; c + 2\Delta f) + (1-p)x(c; c) &= x(c + \Delta f; c) \\ (c - 2\Delta f; c - 2\Delta f) + (1-p)x(c; c) &= x(c - \Delta f; c) \end{aligned} \qquad \forall c \tag{6}$$

namely that the two possible exchange rates just after a jump be equal, when weighted by their respective probabilities, to the exchange rate prevailing at the instant before the jump. From the economic point of view, these boundary conditions rule out arbitrage opportunities; from the purely technical standpoint, they ensure that equation (1) is satisfied at the instant before a jump: $E_t\{dx_t\}$ would be larger than infinitesimal if (6) did not hold with equality, and no finite exchange rate could satisfy (1), where $E_t\{dx_t\}/dt \to \infty$.

All solutions to the differential equation in (5) have the form

$$x(f; c) = f + A_1(c)e^{\lambda f} + A_2(c)e^{-\lambda f}, \qquad \lambda \equiv \sqrt{\frac{2}{\alpha\sigma^2}} \tag{7}$$

Using (7) in (6), we obtain

$$A_1(c) = -\frac{(1-2p)\Delta f}{e^{\lambda(\Delta f + c)} - e^{-\lambda(\Delta f - c)}} \qquad A_2(c) = -\frac{(1-2p)\Delta f}{e^{\lambda(\Delta f - c)} - e^{-\lambda(\Delta f + c)}}$$

The two $A(\cdot)$ functions have opposite signs for every c, and in the interior of every zone the relationship between exchange rates and fundamentals takes an S-shaped form like those plotted by dashed lines in Figure 10.1.

If $p = \frac{1}{2}$, then $E_t\{f_\tau\} = f_t$ for all $\tau \geq t$, and $x(f; c)$ once again lies on the $x = f$ line. If $p < \frac{1}{2}$, however, $x(f; c) \lesseqgtr f$ according to $f \gtreqless c$: because the jump in fundamentals at the upper (lower) boundary of a zone is expected to be negative (positive), $E_t\{f_\tau\} < f_t$ if f_t is close to $c + \Delta f$, and $E_t\{f_\tau\} > f_t$ if f_t is close to $c - \Delta f$. Symmetrically, if $p > \frac{1}{2}$ then $x(f; c) \lesseqgtr f$ according to $f \lesseqgtr c$.

3 Intervention, reserves and sustainability

Other specifications for the probability and size of i_t jumps may be recast in terms of Section 2's notation along similar lines. The full-credibility model in Krugman (1990) lets the jump component be infinitesimally small (and therefore unrelated to the width of the fundamental fluctuation band, $\bar{f}$), and assumes

$$p_t^u = \begin{cases} 1 & \text{if } f_t = c_t - \bar{f} \\ 0 & \text{otherwise;} \end{cases} \qquad p_t^d = \begin{cases} 1 & \text{if } f_t = c_t + \bar{f} \\ 0 & \text{otherwise,} \end{cases}$$

while Flood and Garber (1989) make similar assumptions on the probabilities and let jumps have finite size. Svensson (1989) considers both infinitesimal and discrete movements in the $\{i_t\}$ component of fundamentals, making assumptions similar to Krugman's on the former and letting the latter have constant probability and size, and Bertola and Svensson (1990) extend the model to allow for stochastic fluctuations in the probability and size of $\{i_t\}$ jumps.

Following these and other authors, this probabilistic framework can be interpreted as a stylized model of (adjustable) exchange rate bands. The Brownian motion component of fundamentals $\{z_t\}$ may be viewed as a money velocity shock, or perhaps as monetization of government deficits beyond the control of the monetary authorities, and the jump component $\{i_t\}$ may be taken to represent nonsterilized intervention in the foreign exchange market.

Intervention, of course, entails a variation in foreign exchange reserves; and if only the infrequent $\{i_t\}$ component is associated with interventions, then the variation of reserves corresponds to the variation in $\{i_t\}$. To illustrate this point and introduce sustainability issues, consider the simple probabilistic assumptions of equation (4), where the size Δf of the $\{i_t\}$ jumps coincides with a half-width of the fundamental fluctuation band, $\bar{f}$. These assumptions correspond to the economic framework of our earlier paper, where authorities *intervene* at prespecified, common knowledge points $c_t - \bar{f}$, $c_t + \bar{f}$: *either* defending the band and bringing f and x

back to the centre of the current band (c_i), *or* realigning the central parity and declaring a new fluctuation band, adjoining the current one, with centre $c_{t+} \equiv c_t + 2\bar{f}$ and unchanged width. By a normalization, set $z_0 = i_0 = 0$ and let reserves be equal to zero at time zero. Starting at zero, z_t takes a random, finite time to reach one of the boundaries and to trigger the first jump. Either boundary can be reached with probability $\frac{1}{2}$ since $\{f_t\}$ follows a driftless Brownian motion. Denoting by $\tau > 0$ the time at which the first jump occurs, we have:

$i_\tau = -\bar{f}$ if $\{z_t\}$ has drifted upwards to $\bar{f}$ and the band has been defended *or* if $\{z_t\}$ has drifted downwards to $-\bar{f}$ and a realignment has taken place: the combined probability of these events is $\frac{1}{2}(1-p) + \frac{1}{2}p = \frac{1}{2}$;

$i_\tau = +\bar{f}$ if $\{z_t\}$ has drifted downwards to $-\bar{f}$ and the band has been defended *or* if $\{z_t\}$ has drifted upwards to $\bar{f}$ and a realignment has taken place: the combined probability of these events is, again, $\frac{1}{2}p + \frac{1}{2}(1-p) = \frac{1}{2}$;

The derivation in Karatzas and Schreve (1988, especially pp. 99–100) can be adapted to show that the time interval between jumps is finite with probability one and has expectation $(\bar{f}/\sigma)^2$; its distribution is independent of the past history of the stochastic processes under study, which enjoy the strong Markov property. Thus, *regardless of the realignment probabilities*, $\{i_t\}$ follows a generalized random walk with variable time steps, constant state steps, and constant transition probabilities under our stylized assumptions; this is true, in particular, when the fluctuation band is fully credible ($p = 0$).[2]

Reserves therefore follow a random walk on a redefined time scale and, over an infinite time horizon, reach arbitrarily large and arbitrarily small levels with probability one, raising obvious issues of *sustainability* of the exchange rate regime.[3] To obtain a (stochastically) bounded reserve process when *intervention* is taken to occur only at the boundaries and is interpreted in terms of purchases/sales of foreign exchange, the probability and size of upwards and downwards jumps should be allowed to depend on reserve levels or, equivalently, on cumulative intervention up to date. For example, the probability structure of interventions might be assumed to be independent of reserves until these reach some prespecified boundary, and to change abruptly at that point, adapting to the problem at hand the assumptions of the literature on exchange rate regime collapses (Krugman, 1979; Flood and Garber, 1984). Delgado and Dumas (1989) analyse the case of infinitesimal interventions at the margin of fluctuation zones along these lines, supposing that exchange rates revert to a one-sided or two-sided float when reserves reach a nonrandom, prespecified limit.

Collapse models, however, have several shortcomings. On the one hand, there is no clear-cut upper or lower limit to cumulative exchange rate intervention in reality, since foreign exchange can in principle be borrowed in any amount (provided, of course, that principal and interest are surely repaid over the relevant, possibly infinite time horizon).[4] On the other hand, the assumption of *permanent* reversion to free float when the reserves limits (however specified) are reached is both unrealistic and formally questionable: no central bank ever operates without exchange rate reserves, thus exchange rates are never truly freely floating; and allowing for the free-float regime to be absorbing prevents any study of the long-run properties of the model. Historically, exchange rate crises have most often resulted in a realignment of central parities or in a redefinition of the exchange rate regime. While these points are not essential to the stylized models of Krugman (1979) and Flood and Garber (1984), the discrete time structure of the empirically oriented model of Blanco and Garber (1986) produces stochastic, recurring balance-of-payments crises.

4 A sustainable probability structure

In what follows, we address sustainability issues in the context of a stylized model of repeated, stochastic realignments (of the type studied in Miller and Weller, 1989 and in our earlier paper). To this end, we allow the probability and/or the size of upward and downward fundamental jumps to depend on accumulated interventions or, equivalently, on the net number j_t of interventions. When reserves are plentiful, downward jumps should be more likely (or larger) than upward ones if reserves are to display a tendency to return to normal levels; symmetrically, when reserves move towards minus infinity upward jumps must become more likely (or larger) than downward ones.

As above, let all jumps have absolute size $\bar{f}$, let jumps only occur when f_t is at the edges of a $(c_t - \bar{f}, c_t + \bar{f})$ band, and let a jump that takes f_t beyond the limits of the current fluctuation band be accompanied by a jump in $\{c_t\}$ of the same sign and twice the absolute size: after every jump, the f_t process is always in the middle of its current fluctuation band. Still assuming jumps to have nonzero probability only when fundamentals are at the boundary of a band, we let the probability of an upwards j jump be decreasing in the size of cumulative intervention to date, capturing the qualitatively realistic idea that devaluations are more likely when reserves are low and, for simplicity, we let the probability of upward or downward jumps be the same at both boundaries of the band:

$$p_t^u = \begin{cases} p(j_t) & \text{if } f_t = c_t + \bar{f} \text{ or } c_t - \bar{f} \\ 0 & \text{otherwise;} \end{cases}$$

$$p_t^d = \begin{cases} 1 - p(j_t) & \text{if } f_t = c_t + \bar{f} \text{ or } c_t - \bar{f} \\ 0 & \text{otherwise,} \end{cases} \tag{8a}$$

where

$$0 < p(j) < 1 \text{ for } \underline{j} < j < \bar{j}$$

$$p(j) = 1 \text{ for } j \leq \underline{j} \tag{8b}$$

$$p(j) = 0 \text{ for } j \geq \bar{j}$$

By these assumptions and the arguments above, $\{j(t)\}$ follows a random walk with variable transition probabilities and random time steps over the $(\underline{j}, \bar{j})$ region; $\underline{j}$ and $\bar{j}$ may be, respectively, minus and plus infinity, in which case we require

$$\lim_{j \to -\infty} p(j) = 1, \qquad \lim_{j \to \infty} p(j) = 0$$

Since $0 < p(j) < 1$ in this range, all $\underline{j} \leq j \leq \bar{j}$ can be reached from each other with positive probability, and the corresponding states of the Markov chain are recurrent.[5] The unconditional distributions of the $\{j_t\}$ process, denoted $\phi(\cdot)$, is non-degenerate under our assumptions and can be computed by the invariance relationship

$$\phi(j) = p(j-1)\,\phi(j-1) + (1 - p(j+1))\,\phi(j+1) \tag{9a}$$

and summing-up constraint

$$\sum_{j=\underline{j}}^{\bar{j}} \phi(j) = 1 \tag{9b}$$

The $\phi(j)$ probability distribution has a simple analytic form for simple $p(\cdot)$ functions, and can be computed numerically for any $p(\cdot)$. Our assumptions guarantee that the probability of the absolute value of j ever exceeding arbitrarily large amounts over an infinite time horizon is zero, or vanishingly small. If the jump component of fundamentals is associated with official intervention in exchange rate markets and j_t corresponds to the cumulative variation of reserves, we can thus proceed to model exchange rate behaviour in a 'sustainable' exchange rate regime.

5 Exchange rate dynamics under sustainable intervention

The $\{f_t, c_t, j_t\}$ processes are jointly Markov under the assumptions in (8): the distribution of f_τ at all future times depends only on their current levels. The exchange rate is then, by equation (2), a function of the three driving processes, and this function must once again satisfy

$$x(f;\, c, j) = f + \frac{a\sigma^2}{2} x''(f;\, c, j) \tag{10}$$

when jumps are ruled out (i.e. in the interior of a fluctuation zone), as well as the no-expected-jump conditions

$$\left.\begin{aligned} x(c+\bar{f};\, c, j) &= p(j)\, x(c+2\bar{f};\, c+2\bar{f}, j+1) \\ &\quad + (1-p(j))\, x(c;\, c, j-1) \\ x(c-\bar{f};\, c, j) &= (1-p(j))\, x(c-2\bar{f};\, c-2\bar{f}, j-1) \\ &\quad + p(j)\, x(c;\, c, j+1) \end{aligned}\right\} \quad \forall c, \forall j$$

at the boundaries between fluctuation zones.

It is notationally convenient to define the transformed variables

$$\tilde{x}_t \equiv \frac{x_t - c_t}{\bar{f}} \qquad \tilde{f}_t \equiv \frac{f_t - c_t}{\bar{f}} \tag{11}$$

The assumptions of our simple model guarantee that $-1 \le \tilde{f} \le 1$, and that $\tilde{f}$ jumps to zero with probability one whenever it reaches one or minus one.

In terms of these normalized processes,(10) can be written

$$\tilde{x}(\tilde{f};\, j) = \tilde{f} + \frac{a}{2} \tilde{x}''(\tilde{f};\, j)(\sigma/\bar{f})^2 \tag{12}$$

and the no-expected-jump conditions are satisfied if

$$\left.\begin{aligned} \tilde{x}(1;\, j) &= p(j)\big(\tilde{x}(0;\, j+1) + 2\big) \\ &\quad + \big(1-p(j)\big)\tilde{x}(0;\, j-1) \\ \tilde{x}(-1;\, j) &= (1-p(j))\big(\tilde{x}(0;\, j-1) - 2\big) \\ &\quad + p(j)\,\tilde{x}(0;\, j+1) \end{aligned}\right\} \quad \forall c, \forall j \tag{13}$$

Subtraction of one condition from the other immediately yields $\tilde{x}(1;\, j) = \tilde{x}(-1;\, j) + 2$, for all j. Thus, the difference between the extremes of exchange rate fluctuation bands is independent of reserves, and the general solution of (10) can be written

$$\tilde{x}(\tilde{f};\, j) = \tilde{f} + A(j)\big(e^{\tilde{\lambda}\tilde{f}} + e^{-\tilde{\lambda}\tilde{f}}\big), \qquad \tilde{\lambda} \equiv \frac{\bar{f}}{\sigma}\sqrt{2/a} \tag{14}$$

Using (14) in (13), we obtain a second-order, variable-coefficients difference equation in $A(\cdot)$:

$$\begin{aligned} &(1-p(j))\, A(j-1) - \delta A(j) + p(j)\, A(j+1) = (\tfrac{1}{2} - p(j)) \\ &\delta \equiv \frac{e^{-\tilde{\lambda}} + e^{\tilde{\lambda}}}{2} \end{aligned} \tag{15}$$

At the upper and lower boundaries of the allowable range of reserves, the no-expected-jump conditions and (15) imply that

$$\begin{aligned} \delta A(j) - A(j+1) &= \tfrac{1}{2} \\ \delta A(\bar{j}) - A(\bar{j}-1) &= -\tfrac{1}{2} \end{aligned} \tag{16}$$

The difference equation (15) and boundary conditions (16) form a system of linear equations, which is easily solved for any $p(j)$ function; simple analytical solutions are available for some $p(\cdot)$ functional forms.

Several $p(j)$ functions, the corresponding $A(j)$ and $\phi(j)$ sequences, and the $\tilde{x}(\tilde{f}; j)$ they imply for a selection of j values are plotted in Figures 10.2–10.4. All the $p(j)$ functions considered in the Figures satisfy the assumptions in (8b) and, in all cases, the probability of reserves ever reaching unbounded levels in either direction is zero or vanishingly small. Thus, the exchange rate regime is 'sustainable'. In the Figures, we set $\tilde{\lambda} = \sqrt{2}$, consistently with, for example, $a = 1$ (unitary semi-elasticity of the exchange rate to its own expected rate of change over a time unit) and $\sigma = \bar{f}$ (fluctuations bands and fundamental volatility are such that the expected time to hit either boundary is one time unit).

In Figures 10.2, 3 and 4 the assumed jump probability function is symmetric around zero (in the sense that $p(j) = 1 - p(-j)$), with $p(0) = \frac{1}{2}$. Then, $A(0) = 0$: when intervention is as likely to be positive as it is to be negative over all forecast horizons the relationship between the (normalized) exchange rate and the (normalized) fundamentals is linear, since $E_t\{f_\tau\} = f_t$ for $\tau > t$. The $p(j)$ function considered in Figure 10.2, which is constant throughout and moves sharply to zero or one when reserves reach their absolute limit, models a reversible collapse model. The $p(j)$ function in Figure 10.5 is asymmetric, in the sense that the probability of upward jumps increases faster as $j \rightarrow \underline{j}$ than it decreases as $j \rightarrow \bar{j}$: this may be taken to represent greater concern for unusually low levels of reserves than for unusually high ones, as might be appropriate for a small country, and yields a skewed long-run distribution of reserves.

The relationship between exchange rates, fundamentals, central parities and reserves can be recovered from the change-of-variable in equation (11). Figure 10.6 plots all possible $x(f; c, j)$ relationships in a three dimensional box, and Figure 10.7 plots the $x(f; c, j)$ relationships implied by the probability function of Figure 10.4 in the neighbourhood of $c = 0$, $j = 0$. When $c = 0$ and $j = 0$, exchange rates and fundamentals are driven by z_t fluctuations along the solid 45° line in Figure 10.7. If the upper boundary of the $(-\bar{f}, \bar{f})$ region is reached at point T^u, a jump is triggered in the fundamental process, in the reserves process, and (possibly) in the central parities process. The relevant $x(f; c, j)$ function is then one of those plotted by long dashes in Figure 10.7. With probability $\frac{1}{2}$, an

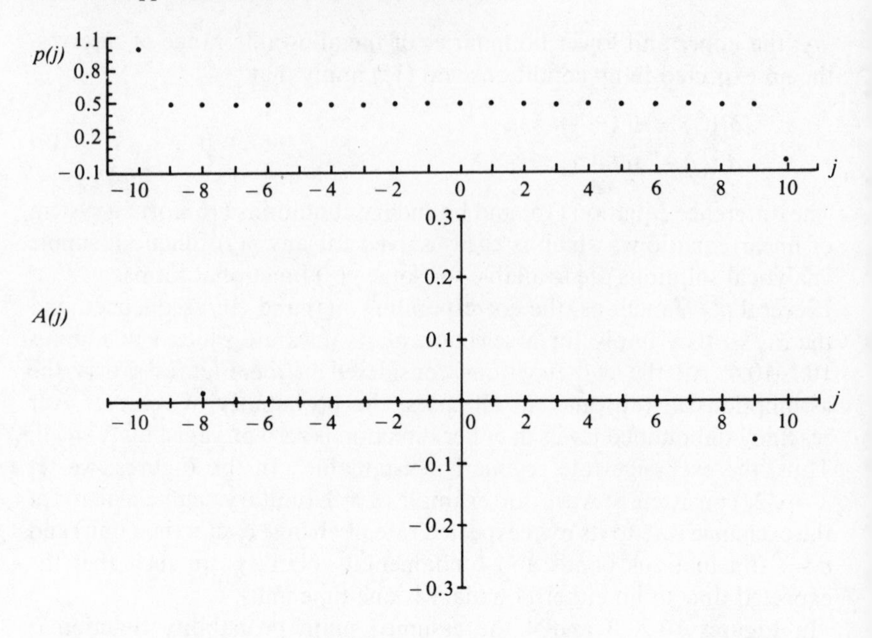

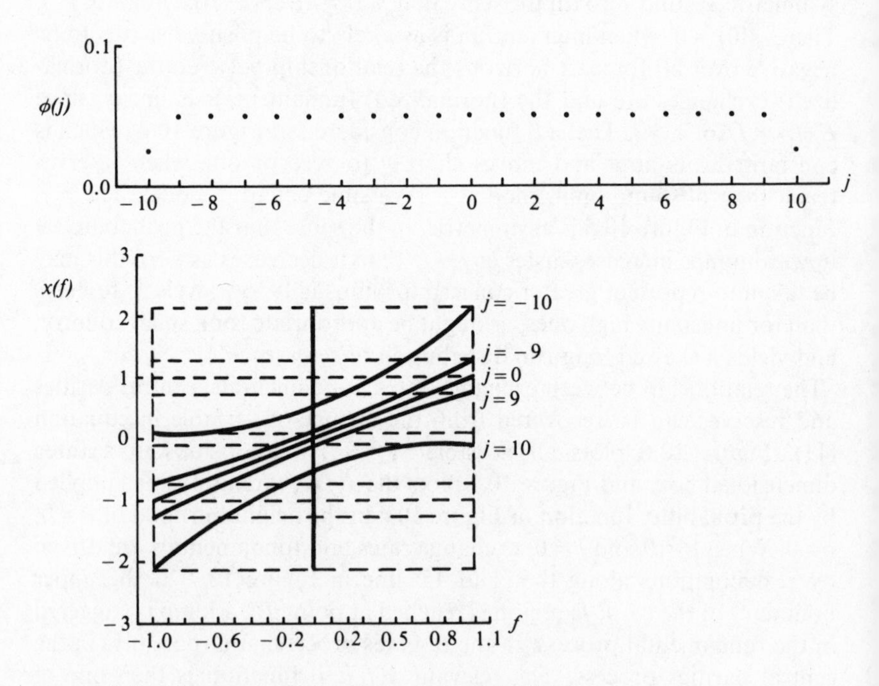

Figure 10.2 (Almost) constant realignment probability

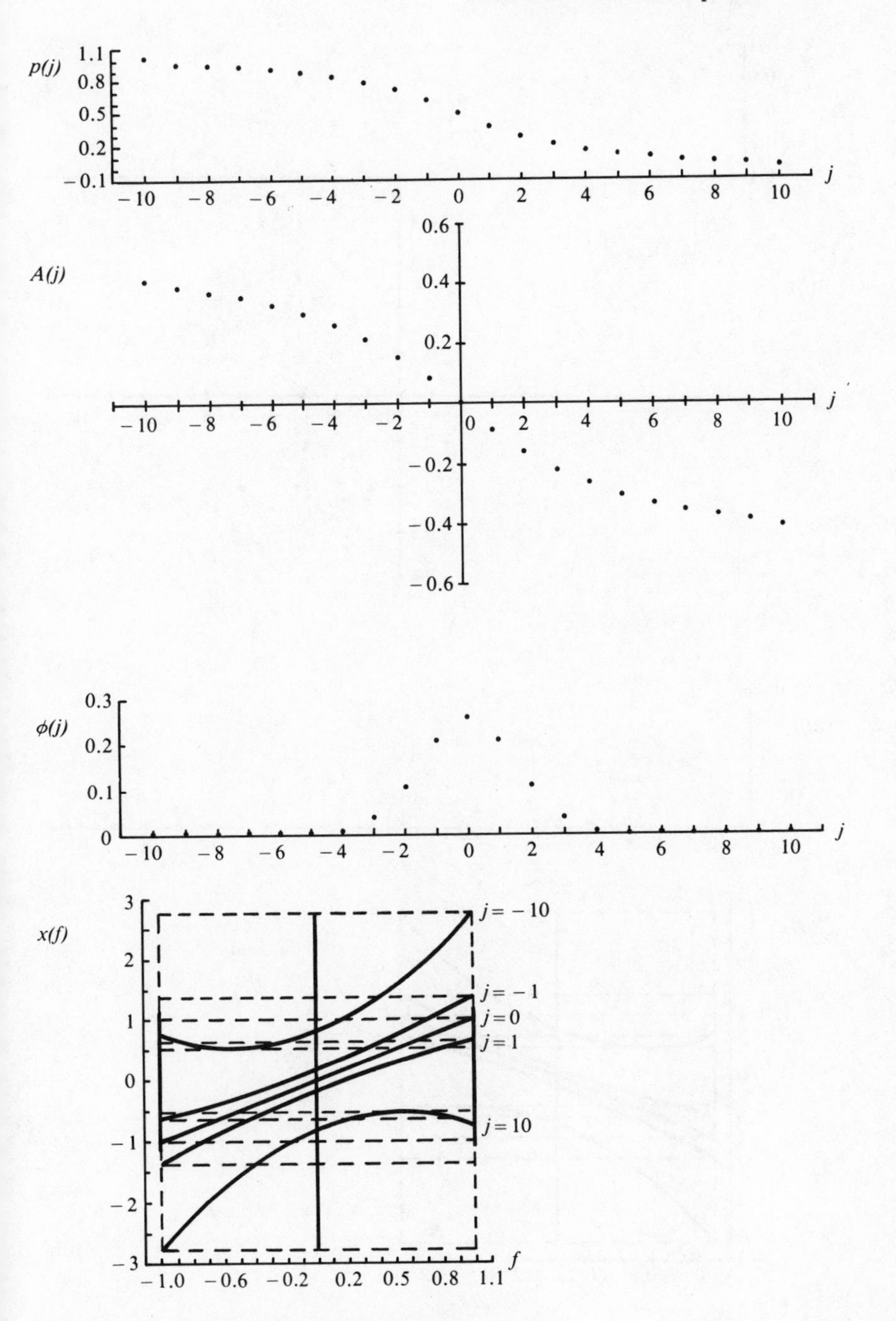

Figure 10.3 Linear realignment probability

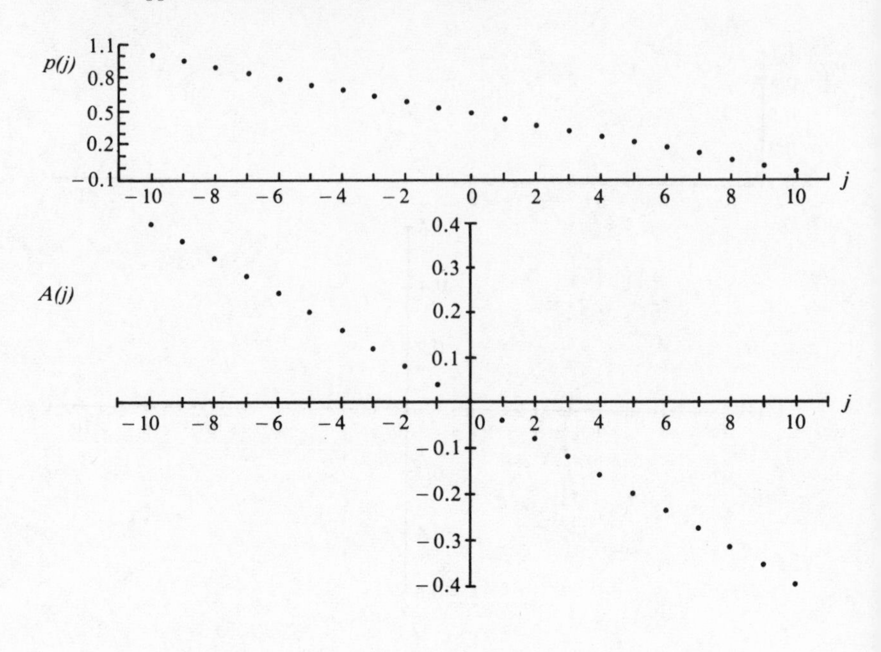

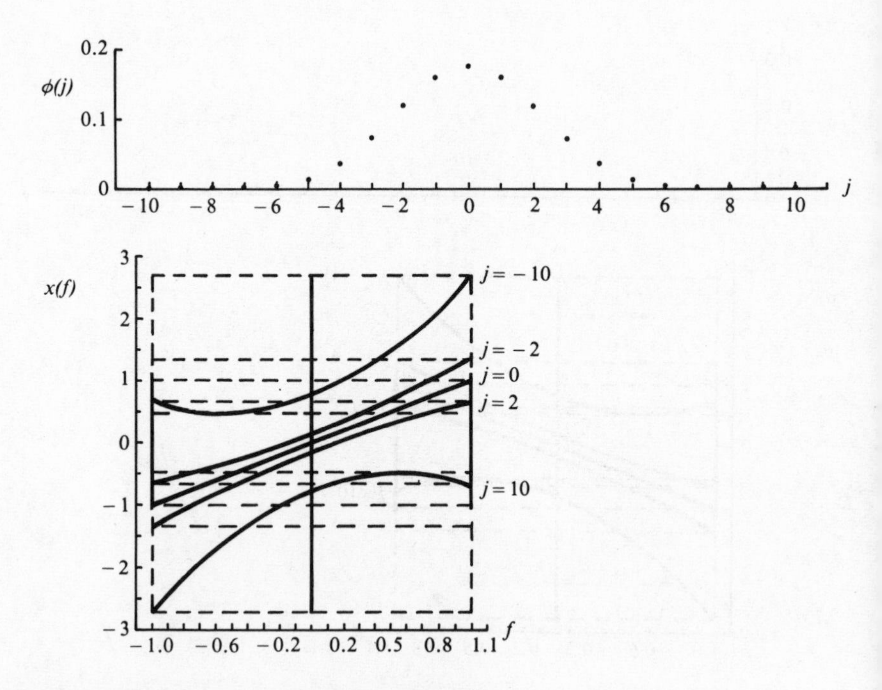

Figure 10.4 Symmetric realignment probability

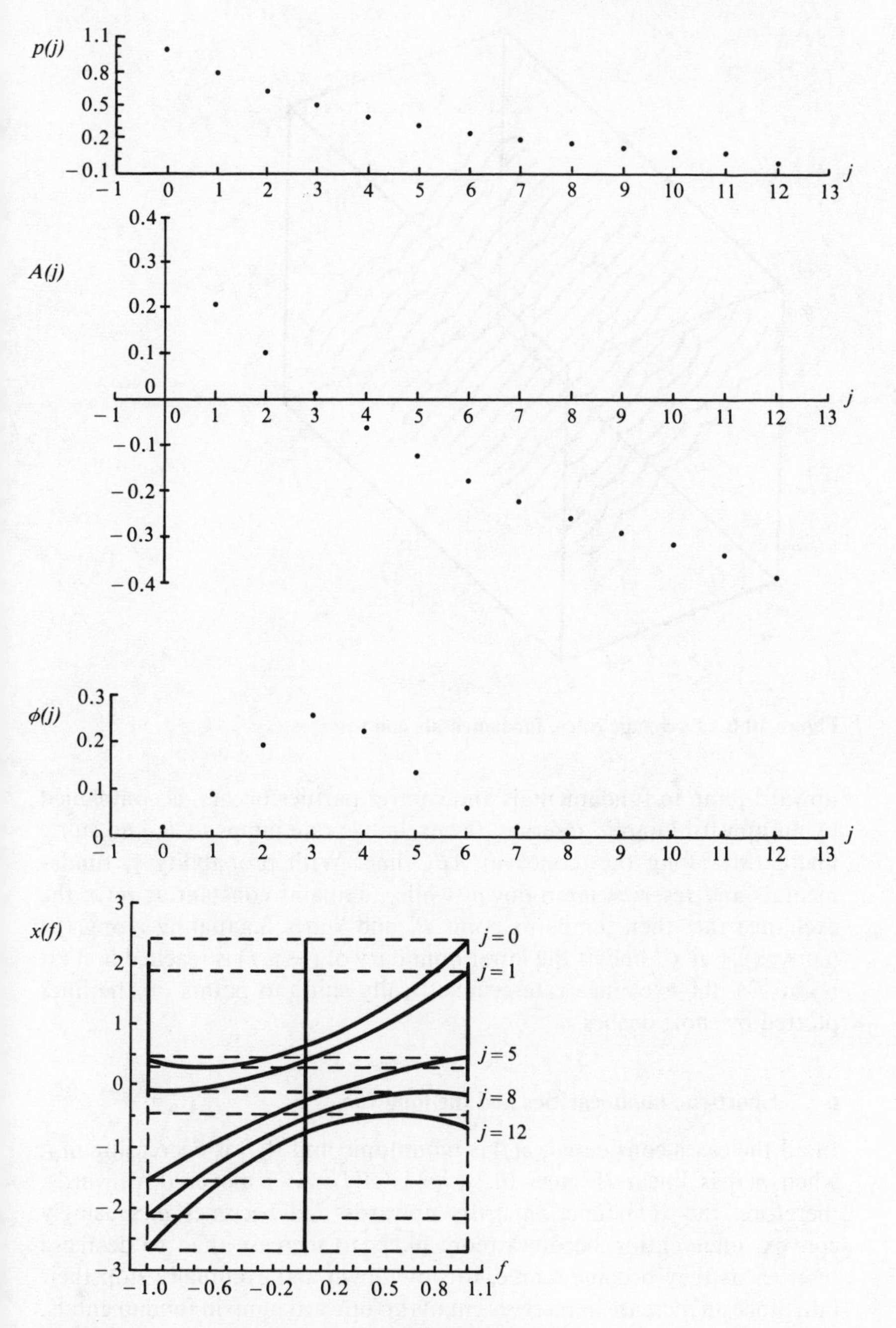

Figure 10.5 Asymmetric realignment probability

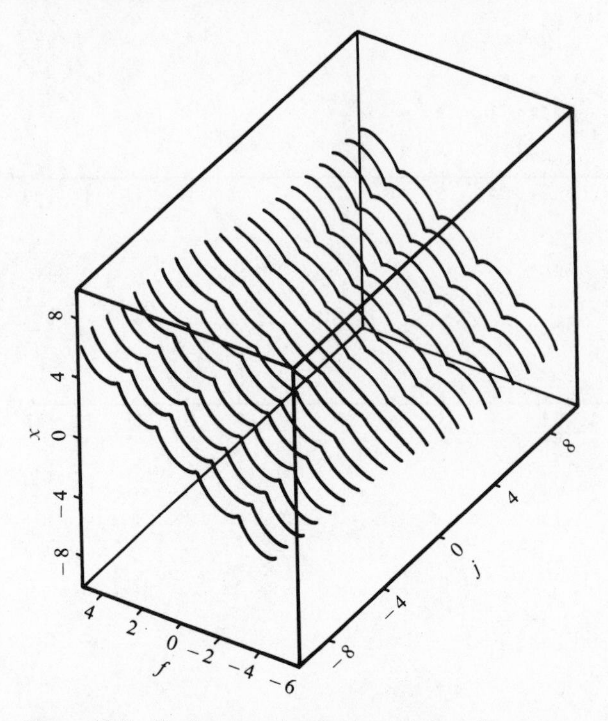

Figure 10.6 Exchange rates, fundamentals and reserves

upward jump in fundamentals and central parities occurs, accompanied by an upward jump in reserves: the exchange rate jumps to B, and starts fluctuating along the (concave) ABC line. With probability $\frac{1}{2}$, fundamentals and reserves jump down, while c remains constant at zero: the exchange rate then jumps to point B' and starts fluctuating along the (convex) $A'\,B'\,C'$ line. If the lower boundary of $(-\bar{f}, \bar{f})$ is reached first (at point T'), the exchange rate symmetrically shifts to points on the lines plotted by short dashes.

6 Short-run nonlinearities and the long run

In all the cases considered, $p(j)$ is monotonic and $A(j)$ is decreasing in j; when $p(j)$ is linear (Figure 10.3), so is $A(j)$. As j moves downwards, therefore, the $\tilde{x}(\tilde{f})$ function drifts upwards and becomes increasingly convex: intervention becomes more likely to increase than to decrease reserves as they become scarce, to slow down and eventually stop their fall. Since an increase in reserves entails an upward jump in fundamentals, the expected level of f_τ at all future time is *higher* than it would be if

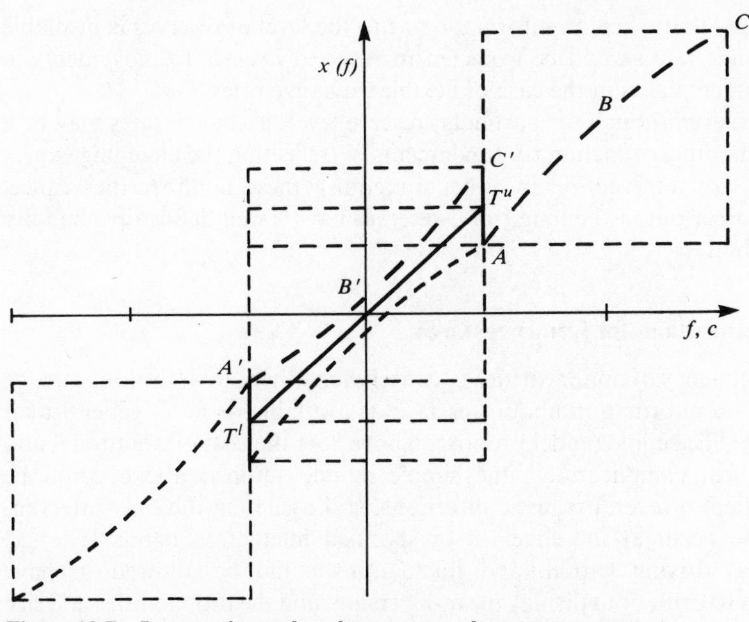

Figure 10.7 Intervention and exchange rates when reserves matter

intervention were never to occur, and the exchange rate is, correspondingly, higher (more depreciated) for every level of fundamentals.

It is apparent from the Figures that the relationship between exchange rates and fundamentals depends on the level of reserves, $j\bar{f}$. Not all values of j are equally likely, of course: in particular, our assumptions in (8b) ensure that very large or very small values of j are seldom or never observed.

Taking an expectation over all possible j values, we then obtain the *unconditional* relationship between exchange rates and fundamentals,

$$E\{\tilde{x}(\tilde{f};j)|\tilde{f}\} = \sum_{j=\underline{j}}^{\bar{j}} \phi(j)\,\tilde{x}(\tilde{f};j)$$

$$= \tilde{f} + (e^{\tilde{\lambda}\tilde{f}} + e^{-\tilde{\lambda}\tilde{f}}) \sum_{j=\underline{j}}^{\bar{j}} \phi(j)\,A(j) \qquad (17)$$

The $\phi(j)$ probability distribution can be computed by (9), and is plotted in the third panel of Figures 10.2–10.4 for the cases we consider.

The Appendix shows that if the $p(j)$ function satisfies the assumptions in (8a), then

$$\sum_{j=\underline{j}}^{\bar{j}} \phi(j)\,A(j) = 0 \qquad (18)$$

to imply that when no information as to the level of reserves is available exchange rate should be expected to respond *linearly* to movements in fundamentals, as in the case of flexible exchange rates.

Thus, even though for particular reserve levels exchange rates may be a very nonlinear function of 'fundamentals' (reflecting the changing expectations of intervention in either direction), these nonlinearities cancel each other out in the long run if reserves have a well-defined probability distribution.

7 Directions for further research

The tendency of nonlinearities to cancel each other out in the long run (or when no information about 'reserves' is available) is more general than the specific simple model proposed above.[6] At the cost of notational and analytical complications, the simple model outlined above could be extended in several realistic directions, still assuming the only intervention to occur at the edges of prespecified fluctuation bands. The $\{z_t\}$ process driving within-band fluctuations could be allowed to have non-zero drift, or to display mean-reversion; and the probabilities and size of jumps in fundamentals and reserves could be modified so as to allow an interpretation of intervention as a 'defence' or 'realignment' of a given target zone.

For 'infrequent' intervention to be sustainable, the probability and size of jumps in either direction should still be allowed to depend on cumulative intervention, so as to obtain stationarity of the reserves process. If exchange rate bands are more likely to be defended than to be realigned, realignments will generally need to be large to keep cumulative intervention bounded; since these two elements interact in determining the shape of the relationship between exchange rates and 'fundamentals' (see our earlier paper), the concavity or convexity effects of infrequent intervention schemes would still be ambiguous in such an extended model, and would still tend to offset each other out as longer and longer periods of time are considered.

It may be more fruitful, however, to relax the assumption that interventions occur only at the boundaries of fluctuation bands. The behaviour of EMS exchange rates suggests that in 1979–87 fundamentals followed within-band processes with small drifts and low variability, and that the probability of large realignments in the direction of a Deutsche Mark appreciation was very close to one at the boundary of the target zone (see our earlier paper). If intervention were indeed occurring only at the boundaries of exchange rate bands, these facts would unrealistically imply a tendency of reserves to *increase* in 'weak' currency countries. In fact, *sustainability* of intervention need not be related to its *infrequency*, a purely technical device. Central banks may well monitor and control exchange rates in the interior of target zones, expending reserves, and reconstitute reserves by infrequent realignments: to model this realistic feature in a probabilistic framework similar to that outlined above, the probability of realignments and interventions should be allowed to depend on $\{z_t\}$ as well as on $\{i_t\}$.

Appendix:[7] The long-run relationship between exchange rates and fundamentals

The recursions in (9a–b) and in (15–16) can be written in matrix form as

$$(I - T)\phi = o \quad \Rightarrow \quad \phi = T\phi$$

$$\phi' l = 1$$

$$(T' - \delta I)A = \tfrac{1}{2}l - p \quad \Rightarrow \quad T'A = \delta A + \tfrac{1}{2}l - p$$

where $\delta = (e^{-\bar{\lambda}} + e^{\bar{\lambda}})/2 > 1$, l is a vector of ones, o is a vector of zeros, I is an identity matrix, and

$$T = \begin{pmatrix} 0 & 1 - p(\underline{j}+1) & 0 & \dots & 0 & 0 \\ 1 & 0 & 1 - p(\underline{j}+2) & \dots & 0 & 0 \\ 0 & p(\underline{j}+1) & 0 & \dots & 0 & 0 \\ \vdots & 0 & \ddots & & \vdots & \vdots \\ 0 & \vdots & \dots & & 1 - p(\bar{j}-1) & 0 \\ 0 & 0 & \dots & & 0 & 1 \\ 0 & 0 & \dots & & p(\bar{j}-1) & 0 \end{pmatrix}$$

$$p = \begin{pmatrix} 1 \\ p(\underline{j}+1) \\ \vdots \\ p(\underline{j}+1) \\ 0 \end{pmatrix} \quad A = \begin{pmatrix} A(\underline{j}) \\ A(\underline{j}+1) \\ \vdots \\ A(\bar{j}-1) \\ A(\bar{j}) \end{pmatrix} \quad \phi = \begin{pmatrix} \phi(\underline{j}) \\ \phi(\underline{j}+1) \\ \vdots \\ \phi(\bar{j}-1) \\ \phi(\bar{j}) \end{pmatrix}$$

Thus

$$\sum_{j=\underline{j}}^{\bar{j}} \phi(j)A(j) = \phi' A = \mathrm{tr}((T\phi)'A) = \mathrm{tr}(\phi'(T'A))$$

$$= \phi'(\delta A + \tfrac{1}{2}l - p) = \delta\phi' A + \phi'(\tfrac{1}{2}l - p)$$

to imply that

$$(1 - \delta)\phi' A = \phi'(\tfrac{1}{2}l - p)$$

Then (noting that $\phi l = 1$)

$$\sum_{j=\underline{j}}^{\bar{j}} \phi(j)\,A(j) = 0 \quad \Leftrightarrow \quad \phi' p = \tfrac{1}{2}$$

We can prove that, in fact, ϕ' p $= \frac{1}{2}$. Rearranging (9a),

$$p(j+1)\,\phi(j+1) + \phi(j) = p(j-1)\,\phi(j-1) + \phi(j+1)$$

Summing the two sides of this relationship up from $j = \underline{j}$, we obtain

$$\sum_{k=\underline{j}}^{j} p(k+1)\,\phi(k+1) + \sum_{k=\underline{j}}^{j} \phi(k) = \sum_{k=\underline{j}}^{j} p(k-1)\,\phi(k-1) + \sum_{k=\underline{j}}^{j} \phi(k+1)$$

or

$$\sum_{k=\underline{j}}^{j} p(k+1)\,\phi(k+1) - \sum_{k=\underline{j}}^{j} p(k-1)\,\phi(k-1) = \sum_{k=\underline{j}}^{j} \phi(k+1) - \sum_{k=\underline{j}}^{j} \phi(k)$$

which simplifies to

$$p(j+1)\,\phi(j+1) + p(j)\,\phi(j) - \phi(\underline{j}) = \phi(j+1) - \phi(\underline{j})$$

Summing over j on each side, and noting that $\phi(j) = 0$ for $j < \underline{j}$ and $j > \bar{j}$, we obtain

$$2\sum_{j=\underline{j}}^{\bar{j}} p(j)\,\phi(j) - \phi(\underline{j}) = \sum_{j=\underline{j}+1}^{\bar{j}} \phi(j) = 1$$

to imply that $\phi' p = \frac{1}{2}$ as was to be shown.

NOTES

A previous draft titled 'Reserves and Realignments in a Target Zone' was presented at the CEPR–NBER Conference on Exchange Rate Targets and Currency Bands (July 10–11, 1990). We thank Lars Svensson for insightful comments, Hyeng Keun Koo for extremely competent research assistance supported by the John M. Olin Program for the Study of Economic Organization and Public Policy, and the National Science Foundation for financial support (grants SES-9010952 and SES-9010443).

1 To see this, consider the simple case of constant, symmetric jump probabilities $p_t^u = p_t^d = p$, for all t. The $\{i_t\}$ process then has no moments unless either p or $\bar{f}$ is infinitesimally small; we consider these two possibilities in turn. If $\bar{f}$ is larger than infinitesimal, let one downwards (or one upwards) jump have probability $p \approx 1 - e^{-\gamma\Delta t}$ over a Δt time increment. In the continuous time limit, $\{i_t\}$ is the sum of two Poisson process with equal probability intensity γ and increments of equal absolute size and opposite sign. Alternatively, we may let the jump probabilities remain finite and normalize the size of jumps. If we let $\bar{f} = \gamma\sqrt{\Delta t}$, as $\Delta t \rightarrow 0$ the $\{i_t\}$ process converges to Brownian motion with variance γ^2 per unit time. In both cases, $E_t\{f_\tau\} = f_t$ for all $\tau \geq t$, and $x_t = f_t$. More general cases can be analysed along similar lines.

2 If its drift were positive, the $\{z_t\}$ process would be more likely to hit $\bar{f}$ first rather than $-\bar{f}$; the probability that a Brownian motion process with drift ϑ and standard deviation σ hits $\bar{f}$ before $-\bar{f}$, starting at zero, is

$$q(\vartheta, \sigma) = (1 - e^{-\frac{2\vartheta\bar{f}}{\sigma^2}})/(e^{\frac{2\vartheta\bar{f}}{\sigma^2}} - e^{-\frac{2\vartheta\bar{f}}{\sigma^2}})$$

if $\vartheta \neq 0$. The $\{i_t\}$ 'reserves' process would then follow a random walk with drift. These and other equally straightforward extensions are omitted for simplicity.

3 The model we propose, although phrased in terms of a single exchange rate and a single set of fundamentals, can easily be interpreted in a two-country framework. If the sum of the two countries' reserves is constant, which might be appropriate in a model of the gold standard, then unboundedly positive levels of j are just as unsustainable as unboundedly negative ones. Even more stringently, reserves should sum up to zero in a model of fiat money creation, where one central bank's assets must be offset by another's liabilities. Delgado and Dumas (1989) somewhat unconvincingly assume instead that reserves consist of assets in infinitely elastic supply.

4 The assumption of hard limits on reserve decumulation is particularly unrealistic in the context of the exchange rate mechanism of the European Monetary System: central banks often intervene to prevent excessive *appreciation* of their currency, thus accumulating reserves, and when intervening to prevent excessive depreciation they have statutory access to – in principle – unbounded credit from the issuer of the appreciating currency.

5 Once again, we might want to allow for a drift in the process driving the within-band fluctuations. The transition probabilities of the $\{j_t\}$ process would then have to be modified by the $q(\vartheta, \sigma)$ function of note 2.

6 Nonlinearities cancel in the long run of collapse models as well: the expectational effects emphasized by these models disappear in the long run if their assumption of reversion to perpetual float is to be taken literally.

7 We are very much indebted to Hyeng Keun Koo for decisive help on this proof.

REFERENCES

Bertola, G. and R.J. Caballero (1990), 'Target zones and realignments', CEPR Discussion Paper No. 398.

Bertola, G. and L.E.O. Svensson (1990), 'Stochastic devaluation risk and the empirical fit of target zone models', Working Paper.

Blanco, H. and P.M. Garber (1986), 'Recurrent devaluations and speculative attacks on the Mexican peso', *Journal of Political Economy* **94**, 148–66.

Delgado, F. and B. Dumas (1989), 'Monetary contracting between central banks and the design of sustainable exchange-rate zones', Working Paper, Wharton School.

Flood, R.P. and P.M. Garber (1984), 'Collapsing exchange rate regimes: some linear examples', *Journal of International Economics* **17**, 194–207.

(1989), 'The linkage between speculative attack and target zone models of exchange rates', Working Paper, NBER, see also this volume.

Froot, K.A. and M. Obstfeld (1989), 'Exchange rate dynamics under stochastic regime shifts: a unified approach', Working Paper, NBER.

Karatzas, I. and S.E. Schreve (1988), *Brownian Motion and Stochastic Calculus*, New York: Springer-Verlag.

Krugman, P. (1979), 'A model of balance-of-payments crises', *Journal of Money, Credit and Banking* **11**, 311–25.
(1991), 'Target zones and exchange rate dynamics', *Quarterly Journal of Economics*, (forthcoming).
Miller, M. and P. Weller (1989), 'Exchange rate bands and realignments in a stationary stochastic setting', in M. Miller, B. Eichengreen and R. Portes (eds.), *Blueprints for Exchange Rate Management*, New York: Academic Press.
Svensson, L.E.O. (1989), 'Target zones and interest rate variability', Seminar paper No. 457, Institute of International Economic Studies, University of Stockholm.

Discussion

LARS E.O. SVENSSON

This is an excellent paper on the short- and long-run dynamics of an exchange rate target zone when the probability and direction of realignments depends on the level of reserves. Different approaches to modeling realignments are clarified in an admirable way, and the paper contains several interesting results. The most striking is that the long-run relation between the exchange rate and fundamentals is linear, in contrast to the short-run nonlinear relation that has received a lot of interest. The long-run relation is similar to the relation between the exchange rate and fundamentals that would occur under a free float: so target zones do not matter in the long run! This is indeed a striking result; but we should realize that an important reason for it is that the parameters of the underlying exogenous fundamentals (denoted z_t in the paper) are assumed to be unaffected by the existence of a target zone (as in most or even all of the recent target zone literature).

Long-run sustainability of the target zone is assured by assuming that the probability of devaluations decreases, and the probability of revaluations increases, with the level of reserves. Hence, if reserves are low, on average they will be increased through devaluations; if they are high, on average they will be reduced through revaluations. We should note, however, that there are situations when the sustainability of the target zone is fairly clear, namely if monetary policy is exclusively focused on maintaining the target zone. Consider, for example, a cooperative bilateral target zone, in which case one can interpret the intervention variable i_t as $i_t = m_t - m_t^*$, the difference between domestic and foreign (log) money supplies m_t and m_t^*. Here there is a trivial mode of cooperation that will sustain the target zone indefinitely: let the domestic central bank carry out all interventions at the strong edge of the exchange rate band, and let the foreign central bank carry out all interventions at the weak edge of the exchange rate band. The reserves of the two central banks will never decrease, only increase, and the target zone can be maintained indefinitely, even without any realignments at all. (Of course, the target zone could be associated with a high rate of inflation in both countries.)

Even a unilateral target zone can be maintained indefinitely, if that is the sole focus of monetary policy. If the central bank is losing reserves, it can always reduce domestic credit so as to stop the capital outflow and even regain the lost reserves. Put differently, there is always a level of domestic interest rates that is sufficient to compensate for any devaluation risk and make investors indifferent between domestic-currency and foreign-currency denominated assets. This way capital flows can be balanced, and realignments are not needed.

Hence, a target zone can always be sustained indefinitely, if that is the sole focus of monetary policy. Sustainability of the target zone becomes a nontrivial issue only in situations when there are constraints on monetary policy that preclude its sole focus on defending the target zone. Such constraints may arise for instance if there is a politically motivated, explicit or implicit, ceiling for domestic interest rates, or if monetary policy is conducted with concern for its short-run effect on employment, or its effect on inflation. In cases when there is a ceiling on domestic interest rates, it appears that reserves are likely to be one of the factors affecting realignments. However, with other constraints and concerns for monetary policy, it is not clear that the level of reserves will be the crucial factor. Instead it may be other macro variables, like relative inflation rates, real exchange rates, current accounts or unemployment that determine the likelihood of realignment. It would indeed be very interesting to see empirical studies of what the principal determinants of realignments actually are; my conjecture is that for industrialized countries it will often be macro variables other than the level of reserves.

Incidentally, Bertola and Svensson (1990) demonstrate a method for extracting the time series of implicit devaluation risk from target zone data on exchange rates and interest rate differentials. In principle the devaluation risk's dependence on reserves and other macro variables can be examined empirically, in order to evaluate the relative importance of reserves in determining realignments.

In the model of Bertola and Caballero, realignments take place only at the edges of the exchange rate band. An alternative approach is to allow realignments to occur with positive probability even when the exchange rate is in the interior of the band. In fact, daily data reveal that few of the realignments in ERM occurred when the exchange rates were exactly at the edge, and sometimes the exchange rates were quite far away. This is also the case for devaluations in the Nordic countries outside the ERM. A concrete alternative is to have the probability intensity of a devaluation to be independent of the exchange rate's position in the band but decreasing in the level of reserves. It seems that the main result of the paper about the long-run linearity between exchange rates and fundamentals would still follow under this alternative specification. In all likelihood, the main result will be rather robust to different specifications of the devaluation risk.

As a final comment, we note that it is easy to derive very specific implications about the interest rate differentials in the Bertola–Caballero model, and in particular how these depend on the parameters of the model and the level of the reserves. The implications for the interest rate differentials could also be very useful in trying to distinguish empirically this particular model of realignments from other models.

REFERENCES

Bertola, G. and L.E.O. Svensson (1990), 'Stochastic devaluation risk and the empirical fit of target zone models', Seminar Paper No. 481, Institute for International Economic Studies, Stockholm University. Also available as CEPR Discussion Paper No. 513.

PART V
ESTIMATION AND TESTING

11 Estimation and testing in models of exchange rate target zones and process switching

GREGOR W. SMITH and MICHAEL G. SPENCER

1 Introduction

Theoretical models of exchange-rate target zones and of process-switching figure prominently in recent research in international finance. They have developed partly due to new theoretical tools (e.g. those in Harrison, 1985, and Krugman, 1991) and partly due to their practical relevance to existing and proposed schemes to manage exchange rate movements (e.g. Williamson, 1985). Empirical research on the appropriateness of the theoretical models has perhaps not kept pace with the theory. In this paper we sketch possible methods for econometric estimation and testing in models of target zones and process-switching.

The methods we propose are applicable to the models of the gold standard in Buiter (1989), the UK return to gold in 1925 in Flood and Garber (1983) and Smith and Smith (1990), target zones in Krugman (1991) and Miller and Weller (1989) and more generally those outlined in Froot and Obstfeld (1989) and Flood and Garber (1989). One reason for a shortage of econometric work based on these models is that they typically make an assumption about the nature of the forcing process followed by some fundamental variable rather than about the identity of the fundamental. This is an advantage in that the results may be consistent with various exchange-rate models but a disadvantage in that traditional econometric tests cannot readily be applied, since it is unclear how to apply regression methods and it may be difficult to calculate theoretical population moments of observable variables.

Section 2 outlines the application of recent developments in method-of-simulated-moments (MSM) estimation and testing to target zone models. Section 3 considers an application to the case of a Wiener process for fundamentals with two reflecting barriers and also presents an example of approximate MSM estimation of a target zone model for the daily Dm/Li spot rate from 1987 to 1989. Section 4 examines a case in which there is a permanent process switch in fundamentals, due to an absorbing barrier (i.e. an exchange-rate peg). In that case the underlying environment is not ergodic and we propose Bayesian methods for estimation and testing.

2 Unobservable forcing processes and simulation estimation

We use the following notation: z is a standard Wiener process, w is an unrestricted Wiener process with instantaneous drift η and variance σ^2, k is a forcing process or fundamental which is a function of w and of an intervention policy, x is the spot exchange rate, and g is the forward exchange rate. We assume that x and g are observable but that k and w are not. Barriers at which intervention occurs may be treated as observable or unobservable; we shall be explicit in the examples below. Time is continuous and observations are point-sampled rather than time-averaged. The symbol p will be used for probability density functions.

The structure consists of mapping from t to w, from w to k, and then from k to x and g. First, consider a model for $w(t)$ which we shall use throughout the chapter. Let w be a scalar, real-valued forcing variable with stochastic law of motion as follows:

$$dw(t) = \eta\, dt + \sigma\, dz(t) \qquad \eta > 0, \quad t \in [0, \infty) \tag{1}$$

a Wiener process with instantaneous mean η and variance σ^2.

This underlying process is used for several reasons. One is that solutions for spot rates as present-value functions of fundamentals are known for this type of underlying process under a variety of barrier policies. Another is that, in the absence of any barriers influencing the Wiener process, some exchange-rate models predict that the spot rate itself should follow a Wiener process; the uncorrelatedness in the increments of such a process seems reasonable empirically for the conditional means of some exchange-rate data.

Next, we need to be precise about how the fundamental or forcing variable k is related to the underlying process w. The variable k is simply a controlled or regulated Brownian motion. If $k = w$ then there is a pure float while target zones involve barriers ($\bar{k}$ and $\underline{k}$) and an intervention policy. In some applications the barriers $\bar{k}$, $\underline{k}$ may be unknown and hence regarded as parameters and estimated. In other applications the values of the barriers may be announced or known so that the mapping from w to k involves no parameters other than those of the intervention strategy. Suppose that the process $\{k(t)\}$ is adapted to an underlying filtration $\mathbb{F} = \{\mathcal{F}_t : t \in [0, \infty)\}$ where $\mathcal{F}_t$ is a sequence of σ-fields on a probability space. The operator E will denote a conditional expectation with respect to this sequence.

Finally, the last set of parameters describes the mapping from fundamentals k to observable prices x. This set includes parameters of central economic interest such as discount rates and perhaps measures of risk aversion. In Sections 3 and 4 we consider a standard exchange-rate model in which the spot exchange rate is determined according to:

$$x(t) = k(t) + aE(dx/dt \mid \mathcal{F}_t) \qquad (2)$$

In the absence of bubbles the solution to (2) is:

$$x(t) = E\int_t^{\infty} \exp\left\{\frac{t-\tau}{a}\right\} k(\tau)/a\, d\tau \qquad a > 0 \qquad (3)$$

The asset's price equals the expected present value of the stream of future fundamentals with discount rate $1/a$. In Flood and Garber (1983) equation (3) arises from a version of the monetary model of the exchange rate in which x is the logarithm of the nominal exchange rate, a is the semi-elasticity of money demand with respect to an interest rate, and k is a linear combination of the logarithms of domestic and foreign money supplies, real incomes, money-demand shocks, and real exchange-rate shocks.

With this background, we now turn to discuss estimation and testing. For the moment, assume that k is a scalar, ergodic process which is a function of w. In turn, a vector of observable variables denoted x (for simplicity; this vector will typically include spot and forward exchange rates) is adapted to an econometrician's information, denoted by $\mathbb{E} = \{\mathscr{E}_t : t = [0, i, 2i, 3i, \ldots, \infty)\}$, which is simply the sequence of σ-fields generated by current and past observations of the vector x.

Estimation and inference are based on a q-vector of sample moments of the observable variables

$$M_\tau = T^{-1} \sum_{t=0}^{T} m(k_t) \qquad (4)$$

where T is a sample size, m is a q-dimensional vector of $\mathscr{E}_t$-measurable, continuous functions which, for example, determine spot rates from fundamentals and parameters, and M is a vector sample moments of the observable variables. For example, M could include the sample means and variances of spot and forward exchange rates. In applications to target zones the existence of all moments is assured by the presence of upper and lower barriers on $\{k(t)\}$.

Next suppose that an economic theory generates a vector $\tilde{m}(k_t, \gamma)$ where γ is a v-vector of parameters, and the model determines the endogenous variables x from the forcing variable and the parameters. Denote the true parameter values γ_0 so that unconditionally $E(m(k_t)) = E(\tilde{m}(k_t, \gamma_0))$. The researcher is interested in the parameters of the economic model (such as a) and perhaps also in those of the controlled forcing process (such as η or $\bar{k}$). These are all included in the vector γ and, if identified, may be consistently estimated if $q \geq v$.

One rationale for simulation estimation is that analytical expressions for moments to be used in estimation may not be known. For example, one may not know the theoretical steady-state probability density of the spot rate in a target zone and hence will not be able to use standard method-of-moments estimation to choose parameters which minimize the discrepancy between the moments of that density and those of the empirical density. Of course this specific matching may not identify all parameters of interest either; for example, the steady-state density with driftless fundamentals is uniform and thus its moments would identify $\bar{k}$ and $\underline{k}$ but not a and σ. In that case one might seek to calculate other moments of the theoretical model by simulation.

Moreover, the unobservability of k precludes direct estimation of a nonlinear regression model linking x to k. In most target zone models the unobservability also precludes maximum likelihood estimation or analytical calculation of the moments of the exchange rate. Given the special form of equation (1) the Kolmogorov equations can be solved, with boundary conditions, to give the transition pdf or likelihood function for a point-sampled sequence of k's. However, it is straightforward to show that the Jacobian in solutions to equation (2) (such as those of Froot and Obstfeld) cannot be inverted and expressed as a function of x (although Bodnar and Leahy, 1990, perform this inversion numerically to allow standard GMM estimation). Thus we cannot write the likelihood function for a point-sampled sequence of x's. This provides a second rationale for basing estimation on the method of simulated moments (MSM). That method requires that the form of the probability law generating k be specified. Then discrete-time simulations are drawn from this probability law and functions $\{\tilde{m}(k_n, \gamma)\}$ (where n indexes simulated observations) are calculated using specific values of γ. Numerical values for all elements in γ are needed to produce simulations but in some cases one might consistently estimate some parameters even if others are assigned incorrect values. Estimation of these parameters involves matching the sample moments M_T with the simulated moments by minimising a loss function of the discrepancy between the two.

Let N be the simulated sample size. Let $L_{TN}: \mathbb{R}^q \rightarrow \mathbb{R}$ be a non-negative discrepancy function which is zero if its argument is zero. Then an MSM estimator is given by:

$$\gamma_{TN} = \underset{\gamma}{\operatorname{argmin}}\, L_{TN}\left[T^{-1}\sum_{t=0}^{T} m(k_t) - N^{-1}\sum_{n=0}^{N} \tilde{m}(k_n, \gamma)\right] \tag{5}$$

Simulation estimation is feasible under time or state-contingent intervention rules provided that the regulated fundamentals process has some ergodicity properties. Under ergodicity the two sample moments which are matched in (5) converge, as T and N approach infinity, to two population moments which are equal at γ_0; this equality forms the basis of estimation. Obviously the parameter estimates will depend upon the loss function and the choice of moments used in matching. Consistency results stem from the matching of time averages such as moments or, alternatively, coefficients of artificial regressions in simulated and historical data. MSM identification and estimation are discussed by McFadden (1989), Pakes and Pollard (1989), Ingram and Lee (1987), Duffie and Singleton (1988), and Gregory and Smith (1990a).

Sampling error in the simulated moments will make the MSM estimators less efficient than comparable GMM estimators. These efficiency losses can be reduced by averaging over independent simulations each of length T or by increasing the length of the simulated time series relative to the observed sample size. With R replications (or $R = N/T$) the asymptotic covariance matrix of the MSM estimator is $(1 + R^{-1})$ times that of the GMM one.

If $q > v$ so that there are more moments available than there are parameters to be estimated, then the estimated model can be tested using the resulting overidentifying restrictions. For example, if L_{TN} is a quadratic function with the appropriate weighting matrix then estimation and testing can be carried out as in Ingram and Lee (1987). Or suppose that the model has been numerically parametrized and that a specific moment, not used in estimation, remains to be matched. The model can be simulated with a large sample size to find the population value for this moment. The distance between that value and the sample moment can be gauged with a J-test just as in Hansen (1982). Without such additional structure on L_{TN} we do not have a distribution theory for γ_{TN}, so we refer in this chapter to tests of model adequacy rather than hypothesis tests on γ. As an alternative to asymptotic tests, we simulate repeatedly with a more realistic sample size and use the proportion of simulated sample moments close to the historical sample value as a test of the model. This simple approach to testing is outlined in Gregory and Smith (1990b) and demonstrated below in Section 3.

While the exchange-rate model we have outlined is standard, this discussion of estimation so far has been rather abstract. With this underlying Wiener process and exchange-rate model, we next consider two examples of barrier policies and hence of specific spot-rate functions. Section 3 provides an example of MSM estimation in a target zone with infinitesimal intervention at the boundaries and no realignments. In this case the fundamental and exchange-rate processes have ergodic properties suitable for MSM estimation. Section 4 turns to an absorbing barrier case and discusses the issues arising with non-ergodic forcing processes.

3 Example 1: two reflecting barriers

The two-reflecting-barrier case is of interest as a characterization of exchange-rate target zones such as the EMS (as in Bertola and Caballero, 1989, and Svensson, 1989) or Williamson's (1985) proposal for exchange rate management (see also Krugman, 1991). Here, the fundamentals driving the exchange rate are assumed to be constrained to lie within a certain band and the authorities are assumed to defend this policy by intervening whenever the fundamentals reach boundary values.

3.1 Spot-rate solution

The saddlepath solution for infinitesimal intervention and irrevocably fixed bands is derived in Froot and Obstfeld (1989) and, for driftless fundamentals, in Krugman (1991) as:

$$x(t) = k(t) + a\eta + A_1 \exp(\lambda_1 k(t)) + A_2 \exp(\lambda_2 k(t)) \tag{6}$$

$$A_1 = \frac{a\sigma^2}{2\Delta}[\exp(\lambda_2 \underline{k}) - \exp(\lambda_2 \bar{k})]\lambda_2 < 0$$

$$A_2 = \frac{a\sigma^2}{2\Delta}[\exp(\lambda_1 \bar{k}) - \exp(\lambda_1 \underline{k})]\lambda_1 > 0$$

$$\Delta = \exp(\lambda_1 \bar{k} + \lambda_2 \underline{k}) - \exp(\lambda_1 \underline{k} + \lambda_2 \bar{k}) > 0$$

$$\lambda_i = -\eta/\sigma^2 \pm (\eta^2/\sigma^4 + 2/a\sigma^2)^{1/2}$$

The properties of this function are well-known. It gives rise to an S-shaped saddlepath relating x to k. The conditional variance of exchange rate changes can be shown to depend on the value of k, being zero at the boundaries and positive everywhere else, but is always less than the conditional variance of purely free-floating exchange rates. This implies a stabilizing property to credible bands even if intervention never occurs.

3.2 Forward (expected future spot) rate solution

In theory observations on forward premia also should provide information useful in testing models of target zones or process switching. The idea is simply to seek overidentification and hence to improve inferences. A test of a numerically parametrized version of the model is whether it can reproduce moments of forward premia, given some theory linking forward rates to spot rates or fundamentals.

Define $g(t, j)$ to be the logarithm of the forward price of the currency at t for delivery at $t + j$ so that $g(t, 1)$, for example, is the one-period forward rate. Throughout the chapter we shall consider only the simplest case in which the forward rate is equal to the expected future spot rate:

$$\begin{aligned} g(t, j) = E(x(t + j) \mid \mathcal{F}(t)) &= a\eta + E(k(t + j) \mid \mathcal{F}(t)) \\ &+ A_1 E(\exp(\lambda_1 k(t + j)) \mid \mathcal{F}(t)) \\ &+ A_2 E(\exp(\lambda_2 k(t + j)) \mid \mathcal{F}(t)) \end{aligned} \tag{7}$$

The integrals on the right-hand side of (7) can be solved using the forward Kolmogorov equation, as outlined in Appendix 11B for the case of an absorbing barrier. Denote the width of the band by $b = \bar{k} - \underline{k}$. The forward rate has been derived by Spencer (1990b):

$$\begin{aligned} g(t, j) = a\eta + &\sum_{h=-\infty}^{\infty} \{(k_t - 2hb + \eta j)\exp(\eta(k_t - 2hb)/\sigma^2)[\Phi_1(\bar{k}) - \Phi_1(\underline{k})] \\ &- (k_t - 2\underline{k} + 2hb - \eta j)\exp(-\eta(k_t - 2k + 2hb)/\sigma^2)[\Phi_2(\bar{k}) - \Phi_2(\underline{k})]\} \\ &- \sigma^2 j[p(\bar{k}, j) - p(\underline{k}, j)] + A_1 \sum_{h=-\infty}^{\infty} \exp(\sigma^2 j\lambda_1^2/2)\{\exp((\eta(k_t - 2hb) \\ &+ \sigma^2\lambda_1(k_t - 2hb + \eta j))/\sigma^2)[\Phi_3(\bar{k}) - \Phi_3(\underline{k})] + \exp((-\eta(k_t - 2\underline{k} + 2hb) \\ &- \sigma^2\lambda_1(k_t - 2k + 2hb - \eta j))/\sigma^2)[\Phi_4(\bar{k}) - \Phi_4(\underline{k})]\} \\ &+ A_2 \sum_{h=-\infty}^{\infty} \exp(\sigma^2 j\lambda_2^2/2)\{\exp((\eta(k_t - 2hb) \\ &+ \sigma^2\lambda_2(k_t - 2hb + \eta j))/\sigma^2)[\Phi_5(\bar{k}) - \Phi_5(\underline{k})] + \exp((-\eta(k_t - 2\underline{k} + 2hb) \\ &- \sigma^2\lambda_2(k_t - 2k + 2hb - \eta j))/\sigma^2)[\Phi_6(\bar{k}) - \Phi_6(\underline{k})]\} \end{aligned} \tag{8}$$

where the Φ_i are various standard normal distribution functions (defined in Appendix 11A) evaluated at the upper and lower boundaries and $p(\bar{k}, j)$ and $p(\underline{k}, j)$ are the transition density function for k evaluated at the same points. In practice, the infinite sums can be approximated very well using $h = -2, -1, 0, -1, 2$ since further terms are extremely small. Svensson (1990a) also provides an analytical (Fourier) series solution for expected future spot rates and checks it numerically. He introduces the solution into a long-maturity uncovered interest parity condition.

3.3 *MSM estimation*

In the notation defined in Section 2 the vector of parameters is $\gamma = (a, \eta, \sigma, \bar{k}, \underline{k})$. If the exchange rate boundaries are observable (as they are for example in the EMS) then these boundary values can be used to calculate $\bar{k}$ and $\underline{k}$ for given values of a, η and σ, leaving only these three parameters to be estimated.

Implementing the MSM procedure requires that we choose a moment-matching loss function and a simulation sample size. The point estimates of the parameters will depend on these choices. In turn, which moments are chosen may depend on the economics involved. For example, some moments obviously are important characteristics of the exchange rate's behaviour (e.g. the rate of change of the exchange rate) and therefore should be included in the loss function while others, such as the kurtosis of exchange rate changes, are perhaps more interestingly used as tests of the model. In this example we have used the sum of squared differences between the actual and simulated variances of x and Δx and the mean of Δx in this function; hence there are $q = 3$ moments and $v = 3$ parameters. For this exactly identified case the moments can be matched exactly by suitable choice of γ, under regularity conditions. Spencer (1990a) finds that while two different loss functions used to estimate the parameters of the Dm/Ffr rate over the same interval as considered below lead to different point estimates, the implied behaviour of exchange rates exhibited by the simulation results is similar. The simulation sample size must be large enough to be realistic and yet small enough to be computationally manageable. In the example the sample size has been set at $N = 2{,}000$. Unfortunately there is no general method for choosing the degree of time aggregation in the simulation.

Our application of MSM is approximate in two senses. First, we have simulated a discrete-time, controlled random walk for k and then calculated the discrete-time exchange rate (by (6)) and its moments. These steps only approximate simulating a stochastic differential equation for k, calculating a continuous record of x, point-sampling, and then calculating moments. Second, we have used a very simple algorithm based on grid search. Although multidimensional grid search requires little knowledge of the function being minimized, it is expensive. For simplicity we have used one-dimensional grid search, and iterated over the v parameters even though this method may not reach a global minimum.

The steps in the algorithm are:

(a) Generate a series of N random elements, $\{\Delta z_n^r\}$, from a standard normal density.

(b) Generate a simulated sample $\{x_n^r\}$ of length N from (6) using the initial condition $k_0 = 0$ and arbitrary parameter values. Generate the fundamentals process $\{k_t^r\}$ according to the approximation:

$$k_n = \begin{cases} \bar{k} & \text{if } \eta + k_{n-1} + \sigma\Delta z_n \geq \bar{k} \\ \underline{k} & \text{if } \eta + k_{n-1} + \sigma\Delta z_n \leq \underline{k} \\ \eta + k_{n-1} + \sigma\Delta z_n & \text{otherwise} \end{cases} \qquad (9)$$

For simplicity we have piled up probability mass at the boundary each time $\bar{k}$ or $\underline{k}$ is reached, rather than using the reflection principle. Spencer (1990a) considers some alternative treatments of reflection, since boundary behaviour is crucial to the calculation of simulated moments and nonlinearities.

(c) Calculate simulation sample moments and evaluate the loss function

$$Lr_j = \sum_{i=1}^{q} (\tilde{M}_{Ni}^{rs}(k_{n,\gamma}) - M_{Ti})^2 \tag{10}$$

where the $\tilde{M}_{Ni}^{rs}$ are the simulated moments from the sth step in a grid in the rth replication and M_{Ti} is the ith observed sample moment. In practice the moments in (10) are scaled arbitrarily since we do not know the orders in probability of the theoretical moments.

(d) Repeat steps (b) and (c) for $S = 10$ different values of parameter υ (where $\upsilon = 1, 2, \ldots v$), holding all other parameter values fixed.

(e) Select $\hat{\gamma}_{r\upsilon}$ the value for the υth parameter which achieves the lowest value for the loss function over the grid.

(f) Repeat steps (a)–(e) for $R = 10$ replications (i.e. R different series $\{\Delta z_n^r\}$).

(g) The υth parameter estimate is then given by

$$\hat{\gamma}_{R\upsilon TN} = (1/R) \sum_{r=1}^{R} \hat{\gamma}_{r\upsilon} \tag{11}$$

(h) Repeat steps (a)–(g) for all υ.

As an example the parameters relevant to the moments of the daily Dm/Li rate over the period 14/01/87 to 20/09/89 were estimated. The point estimates for the three parameters are: $\hat{\alpha} = 1.025$, $\hat{\eta} = -0.00034$, and $\hat{\sigma}^2 = 0.0000106$. As usual, Monte Carlo standard errors could be calculated and variance reduction techniques could be used to improve precision. With these values and an exchange-rate band of ± 6 percent the boundaries on the fundamentals process are: $\underline{k} = -0.062163$ and $\bar{k} = 0.062511$. Implicit bands also could be estimated, or one could test the model against the case with no reflecting barriers.

To evaluate the model, 100 replications were conducted using these parameter values. In each replication the first four sample moments of x and Δx were calculated as were test statistics for normality and autoregressive conditional heteroskedasticity (ARCH). The results are reported in Table 11.1. In the first column the actual moments and test statistics for logarithms of the Dm/Li rate are reported. The second column summarizes the results of the simulations. Each cell contains the average value for that moment or test statistic over 100 replications, with the Monte Carlo standard deviation in parentheses below it. Below these are

Table 11.1. *Actual and simulated moments and test statistics for the daily Dm/Li rate*

	Actual	Band ± 6%	Band ± 2.25%
mean(x)	− 0.01317	− 0.04563	− 0.01238
		(0.00517)	(0.00227)
		[1.00]	
†variance(x)	0.2115E-3	0.0359E-3	0.1216E-3
		(0.222E-3)	(0.360E-4)
		[0.61]	
skewness(x)	0.3115*	1.5209*	1.2126*
		(0.484)	(0.327)
		[1.00]	
		[1.00]	[1.00]
kurtosis(x)	2.0440	5.1561*	3.8476*
		(2.092)	(1.119)
		[1.00]	
		[0.83]	[0.62]
†mean(Δx)	− 0.2658E-4	− 0.2552E-4	− 0.7504E-5
		(0.645E-6)	(0.526E-5)
		[0.56]	
†variance(Δx)	0.7887E-5	0.7479E-5	0.7024E-4
		(0.689E-6)	(0.595E-5)
		[0.27]	
skewness(Δx)	0.0417	0.00295	0.00776
		(0.0676)	(0.0717)
		[0.27]	
		[0.04]	[0.05]
kurtosis(Δx)	7.3022*	3.8034*	3.9336*
		(0.257)	(0.248)
		[0.00]	
		[0.99]	[1.00]
BJ(Δx)	521.53*	60.7456*	79.4259*
		(40.493)	(44.038)
		[0.00]	
		[0.99]	[1.00]
L_{TN}		0.0681	
		(0.177)	
ARCH(1)	116.66*	2.1647	2.4751
		(2.294)	(2.851)
		[0.00]	
		[0.06]	[0.08]
ARCH(2)	122.35*	3.9990	4.6413
		(3.959)	(4.622)
		[0.00]	
		[0.11]	[0.14]

ARCH(3)	127.19*	6.1564 (4.626) [0.00] [0.13]	7.0693 (5.142) [0.16]
ARCH(4)	133.58*	8.0229 (5.634) [0.00] [0.17]	9.2685 (6.241) [0.22]
ARCH(5)	132.72*	9.5394 (6.241) [0.00] [0.17]	11.0598 (6.988) [0.25]
ARCH(8)	136.54*	13.8857 (7.726) [0.00] [0.16]	15.9322 (8.589) [0.28]
ARCH(12)	137.00*	19.2614 (9.258) [0.00] [0.18]	22.0672 (10.204) [0.27]
ARCH(24)	121.09*	32.8964 (11.275) [0.00] [0.20]	37.5488 (12.794) [0.30]
Hits at $\bar{x}$	0	0.19 (1.34)	10.66 10.77)
Hits at $\underline{x}$	0	258.56 (59.83)	283.45 (56.029)

Notes: Actual data: Logarithms of daily deviations of Dm/Li rate from central parity and differences in these logarithms over 14/01/87 to 20/09/89; $T = 676$, $N = 2{,}000$ in simulations. BJ(Δx) Bera-Jarque test statistic for normality in the distribution of Δx; ARCH(m) is the LM test for conditional heteroskedasticity at m lags; * denotes significance at the 1% level; † denotes a moment used in estimation; ( ) denotes a Monte Carlo standard deviation; [ ] denotes a proportion.

frequencies with which to compare the simulations to the actual data. These give the proportion of replications in which the simulated value is greater than the observed value, for positive sample statistics, or is less than the observed value, for negative ones. Thus, 56 of the replications yielded a mean change in the exchange rate lower than was observed. For the test statistics a second bracketed term is reported which gives the proportion of replications in which the simulated value exceeded the 1 percent critical value for that statistic. Thus 6 of the ARCH(1) test statistics exceeded the critical value though none exceeded the observed

Table 11.2. *Actual and simulated moments and test statistics for point-sampled Dm/Li data*

Statistic	Actual	Band ± 6%
mean(x)	− 0.01326	− 0.04574 (0.0519) [1.00]
variance(x)	0.2031E-4	0.3040E-3 (0.224E-3) [0.63]
skewness(x)	0.3761*	1.5047* (0.486) [0.99] [0.99]
kurtosis(x)	2.0542	5.0575* (0.916) [1.00] [0.67]
mean(Δx)	− 0.7338E-4	− 0.2310E-3 (0.898E-4) [0.93]
variance(Δx)	0.1238E-4	0.6508E-4 (0.122E-4) [1.00]
skewness(Δx)	− 0.7830*	− 0.0155 (0.248) [0.01] [0.06]
kurtosis(Δx)	5.9891*	3.9248* (0.541) [0.00] [0.59]
BJ(Δx)	66.425*	11.5809* (11.523) [0.00] [0.47]
L_{TN}		3.6199 (2.196)
ARCH(1)	12.441*	3.5738 (3.624) [0.03] [0.15]
ARCH(2)	12.407*	5.9724 (4.771) [0.09] [0.25]

ARCH(3)	12.437*	8.2205 (5.479) [0.19] [0.24]
ARCH(4)	12.367*	9.8775 (5.717) [0.30] [0.26]
ARCH(5)	13.055*	11.4282 (6.009) [0.30] [0.26]
ARCH(8)	13.395*	16.1807 (6.910) [0.63] [0.28]
ARCH(12)	15.713*	22.0911 (7.875) [0.81] [0.30]
ARCH(24)	20.783*	35.2963 (8.2794) [0.95] [0.18]

Notes: ARCH(*m*) is the LM test for conditional heteroskedasticity at *m* lags; * denotes significance at the 1% level; $T = 140$, $N = 200$; ( ) denotes a Monte Carlo standard deviation; [ ] denotes a proportion.

value. We note that these are marginalized proportions, although joint probabilities (of the parametrized model's ability simultaneously to match several moments) could be calculated in the same way.

Testing the model involves examining its ability to match the observed characteristics of the Dm/Li exchange rate. A statistic is considered to be well-matched if the proportion of replications in which the simulated value exceeds the historical value is, roughly, no less than 0.05 and no greater than 0.95. Those moments not used to estimate the parameters can be used to test the model. Thus the model predicts greater skewness and kurtosis in exchange rate levels and significantly less kurtosis in exchange rate changes than are observed. The model also predicts significantly less conditional heteroskedasticity in exchange rate changes than is observed in the data. In fact none of the replications yielded any value for the ARCH test statistics that exceeded the observed values. While the model (at least with $N = 2{,}000$) can explain only part of the excess kurtosis and conditional heteroskedasticity that are observed in the data, it is consistent with the broad characteristics of exchange rates that have attracted attention, namely the non-normality and non-stationarity in exchange rate changes. For example, 99 of the replications yielded a kurtosis for exchange rate changes that exceeded the 1 percent critical value and in a significant number of replications the ARCH test statistics reject the hypothesis of conditional homoskedasticity. Again, these are not analytical results, despite our knowledge of the controlled forcing process, because of the non-invertibility of the Jacobian in the transformation from k to x.

A similar comparison can be made between the model and the observed characteristics of weekly exchange-rate data. The first column in Table 11.2 presents the moments and test statistics for Wednesday observations of the Dm/Li rate over the same time period ($T = 140$). In comparison with the daily data summarized in Table 11.1 note that the test statistics for conditional heteroskedasticity all have much lower values and the null hypothesis of conditional homoskedasticity is not rejected for lag lengths greater than three. Also, the excess kurtosis in the distribution of exchange-rate changes is less significant. Any model of the EMS must be consistent with this observed decline (with time aggregation) in the significance of the non-normality and non-stationarity in the distribution of exchange-rate changes.

The second column of Table 11.2 reports the same moments and test statistics for skip-sampled simulated data. The calculations are based on every tenth observation in each replication, so that $N = 200$. The format is the same as in Table 11.1. Statistics from the skip-sampled simulated data have virtually the same ability to match those from the observed weekly data as was found in Table 11.1 for daily data with the exception of the variance of exchange-rate changes which is now generally higher in the simulations than in the data. Note that there is no significant difference between the average values of the kurtosis of exchange-rate changes between the two sets of simulated data. Also, both sets of simulations fail to find evidence of excess kurtosis as great as is observed. However, the proportions of replications in which the null hypothesis that the kurtosis is 3.0 is rejected is much lower in the simulations with skip-sampled data (0.59) than in the disaggregated data (0.99). In this sense the model suggests that the kurtosis of exchange-rate changes is less significant in aggregated data.

The skip-sampled model does a much better job of matching the test statistics for conditional heteroskedasticity. The average values for the test statistics in the simulated data are similar to those in Table 11.1, but since the weekly data are less heteroskedastic than the daily data the match between the model and the weekly data is much closer than was obtained with the disaggregated data. One possibility is that day-of-the-week effects in the daily data account for the poorer match there, given their absence from the simulations (though it is not clear how to use dummy variables in this nonlinear model). Moreover, while the average values of these statistics never reject the null of homoskedasticity at the 1 percent level, a significant number of replications results in values for these statistics which did. However, heteroskedasticity does not seem to decline with time aggregation in the simulated data.

Once parametrized by numerical methods, the model can be used to examine a number of economic questions. Consider, for example, the switch to narrower bands undertaken by the Italian authorities on 5 January 1990. The model can be used to predict the effect of this change on the behaviour of spot exchange rates if we assume that the change in the bands was unexpected (or at least expected in the near future with a low probability, as seems reasonable for our sample, which ends in September 1989) and did not affect a, η and σ^2. This predictive test again involves running 100 replications of the model with the point estimates for a, η and σ^2 but with narrower boundaries on the fundamentals due to the narrower band for exchange rates. With a band width of 4.5 percent the new boundary values are: $\underline{k} = 0.024663$ and $\bar{k} = 0.025011$. The results of these simulations are given in the third column of Table 11.1. These suggest that exchange rates will be much less variable (as would be expected) and the mean rate of change also is lower than in the second column. The hypotheses of normality and stationarity are still easily rejected and the average values of the test statistics are higher (although not significantly so). Thus the model would predict that the recent Dm/Li exchange rate data should exhibit slightly greater kurtosis and conditional heteroskedasticity than was observed prior to the move to narrower bands. This hypothesis remains to be examined.

Our final experiment uses the estimated parameter values to simulate the steady-state moments and test statistics. As an example, one replication was conducted with a sample size of $N = 10{,}000$ observations, with both sets of boundaries. The results are reported in Table 11.3. For both target zones the distribution of exchange-rate levels shows significant skewness and kurtosis, while the distribution for exchange-rate changes shows significant kurtosis. The test statistics for conditional heteroskedasticity reject the null of constant conditional variances only for autoregressive lag lengths longer than three. It is interesting to note however, that the reported values for most of these moments and test statistics are within two Monte Carlo standard deviations of their values reported in Table 11.1. This suggests that a simulation sample size of 2,000 observations may be simulating population moments rather than small-sample moments as intended.

Table 11.3. *Simulated steady-state moments and test statistics for the Dm/Li rate ($N = 10{,}000$)*

Statistic	Actual	Band ± 6%
mean(x)	− 0.04728	− 0.01251
variance(x)	0.2584E-3	0.1233E-3
skewness(x)	1.9753*	1.1998*
kurtosis(x)	7.4899*	3.5859*
mean(Δx)	− 0.5576E-5	− 0.1827E-5
variance(Δx)	0.7422E-5	0.7121E-5
skewness(Δx)	0.0176	0.0252
kurtosis(Δx)	3.8621*	3.9431*
BJ(Δx)	310.178*	371.655*
Hits at $\bar{x}$	0	42
Hits at $\underline{x}$	1372	1439
ARCH(1)	0.1777	0.4857
ARCH(2)	2.0438	2.6672
ARCH(3)	5.5900	6.7009
ARCH(4)	20.2957*	23.5263*
ARCH(5)	26.9161*	30.1741*
ARCH(8)	28.8154*	32.4844*
ARCH(12)	36.8860*	43.9063*
ARCH(24)	66.9916*	75.7877*
L_{TN}	0.04847	

Notes: ARCH(m) is the LM test for conditional heteroskedasticity at m lags; * denotes significance at the 1% level.

A third form of test would begin with generation of forward rates from equation (8) and construction of simulated forward premia. These could be used to calculate simulated values of the test statistics obtained from linear regression tests of forward-rate unbiasedness. The comparison with observed moments and test statistics would then provide an interesting test of the model, as there is some evidence that the hypothesis of forward-rate unbiasedness is not rejected for at least some intra-EMS exchange rates.

The overidentifying restrictions arising from the use of forward rates are available because of the auxiliary assumption (in equation (7)) that the forward rate is equal to the expected future spot rate. Further auxiliary assumptions could generate further implications. For example, Svensson (1989, 1990b) and Flood, Rose and Mathieson (1990) use uncovered interest parity to replace the expected discrete-time change in the exchange rate with a short-term interest differential, while Svensson (1990a) derives implications for the entire term structure of interest rates.

Pessach and Razin (1990) posit an observable fundamental in monthly Israeli data in order to test the nonlinearity suggested by a model with one reflecting barrier. They find some support for the one-sided band model. Meese and Rose (1990) consider some candidate observable fundamentals for EMS and Bretton Woods regimes and test for nonlinearities by nonparametric methods. Information on foreign exchange reserves or capital flows also might be incorporated. These extensions allow some tests that do not require simulation. Nothing precludes even simpler tests such as those based on the unconditional density of the spot rate (as in Bertola and Caballero, 1989, or on the domestic currency rate of return of foreign investment, as in Svensson, 1990b).

Most tests along these lines (including the cross-regime evidence of Flood, Rose and Mathieson, 1990) find little support for simple target zone models. However, the same simulation techniques proposed here could be applied to other ergodic regulators including discrete or uncertain interventions as in Bertola and Caballero (1989, 1990), Flood and Garber (1989), Miller and Weller (1989), Svensson (1989), and Lewis (1990). For example, realignment models typically add further unobservable forcing processes (e.g. the time-varying jump frequency, jump size, and central parity of Bertola and Caballero, 1990, or the stochastic devaluations of Bertola and Svensson, 1990) and hence also provide natural settings for simulation estimation. Lewis (1990) models intervention in dollar/DM/yen rates as a probabilistic function of deviations from a target. The various probability laws she suggests could be simulated, along with a fundamentals process, to allow estimation of the parameters of both.

4 Example 2: one absorbing barrier

As a second example, we consider the case of the process-switching model of Flood and Garber (1983). In this example, the forcing process approaches an absorbing barrier so that there is a state-dependent policy rule. Let T be the first-passage time of w to the absorbing barrier at $\bar{k}$:

$$T(\bar{k}) = \inf\{t: w(t) = \bar{k}\} \tag{12}$$

which is well-defined since the sample paths of w are continuous almost surely. Assume that $w(0) < \bar{k}$ so that $T > 0$. The regulator consists of the following policy for k:

$$k(t) = w(\min[T, t]), \qquad t \geq 0 \tag{13}$$

Thus k is fixed at $\bar{k}$ as soon as it reaches that level, an event which will happen almost surely since the drift is towards the barrier. Equation (13) describes a plan to peg the currently floating exchange rate once it reaches $\bar{k}$.

4.1 Spot-rate solution

The closed-form, saddlepath solution for the exchange rate prior to absorption is given by Smith (1990) and Froot and Obstfeld (1991) as:

$$x(t) = k(t) + a\eta - a\eta \cdot \exp[\sigma^{-2}[\eta - (\eta^2 + 2\sigma^2/a)^{1/2}] \cdot (\bar{k} - k(t))] \tag{14}$$

This model might be applied to the process switch in the dollar-sterling exchange rate arising from the return to the gold standard in the UK in 1925. Sterling appreciated from its pegged, wartime level of \$4.76 in March 1919 until it returned to prewar parity at \$4.86 at a realized first passage time of 28 April 1925. Moggridge (1972) discusses this process switch. Before discussing formal estimation and testing of this model, we again derive the implied, observable forward rate.

4.2 Forward (expected future spot) rate solution

In the case of the UK return to gold, weekly data are available for the one- and three-month forward premium on sterling from January 1921 to May 1925. The forward rates and aligned spot rates were recorded by Einzig (1937, Appendix I) and collected weekly in New York on Saturdays. Again if the forward rate is equal to the expected future spot rate, then from equation (14):

$$\begin{aligned} g(t, j) = E(x(t+j) \mid \mathcal{F}_t) &= a\eta + E(k(t+j) \mid \mathcal{F}_t) \\ &\quad - a\eta \exp(\lambda \bar{k}) E(\exp(-\lambda k(t+j)) \mid \mathcal{F}_t) \end{aligned} \tag{15}$$

where $\lambda \equiv \sigma^{-2}[\eta - (\eta^2 + 2\sigma^2/a)^{1/2}]$.

It is clear that the j-period forward premium should decline smoothly (in expectation) over time from ηj to 0. To calculate the expectations in equation (15) we need the conditional density of $k(t+j)$. The forward Kolmogorov equation is:

$$(\sigma^2/2)\partial^2 p/\partial k^2 - \eta \partial p/\partial k = \partial p/\partial t \tag{16}$$

with boundary conditions

$$p(k, t) = \delta(k - k(t)) \tag{17a}$$

$$p(\bar{k}, j) = 0 \qquad j > 0 \tag{17b}$$

The solution to this partial differential equation is given by Cox and Miller (1965, p. 221 eq. (71)):

$$p(k,j)=\frac{1}{\sqrt{2\pi\sigma^2 j}}\exp\left[\frac{-(k(t+j)-k(t)-\eta t)^2}{2\sigma^2 j}\right]$$
$$\cdot[1-\exp(2(\bar{k}-k(t))\cdot(k(t+j)-\bar{k})/\sigma^2 j)] \tag{18}$$

where the last term modifies the unrestricted solution, lim $(j\to\infty)p(k,j)=0$, and $\lim(\bar{k}\to\infty)p(k,j)$ is the normal density. With an absorbing barrier at $\bar{k}$, $k(t+j)$ is not (conditionally) normally distributed due to the possibility of absorption. The solution can be rewritten as:

$$p(k,j)=\frac{1}{\sqrt{2\pi\sigma^2 j}}\left\{\exp\left[\frac{-(k(t+j)-k(t)-\eta j)^2}{2\sigma^2 j}\right]\right.$$
$$\left.-\exp\left[\frac{2\eta a}{\sigma^2}-\frac{(k(t+j)-2a-k(t)-\eta j)^2}{2\sigma^2 j}\right]\right\} \tag{19}$$

where $a(k(t))=\bar{k}-k(t)$. Observe that $p(k,j)$ does not integrate to one since at horizon j the barrier will be expected to have been reached with probability $1-\int_{-\infty}^{\bar{k}}p(k,j)\,dk$. Appendix 11B uses equation (19) to solve for each of the two expectations on the right-hand side of equation (15) in turn.

Again the solution is written in terms of standard normal integrals, defined in Appendix 11B. The solution for the forward rate is

$$\begin{aligned}g(t,j)=\ &\bar{k}\cdot(1-\Phi_7-\exp(2\eta(\bar{k}-k(t))/\sigma^2)\cdot\Phi_8)\\&+k(t)\cdot(\Phi_7+\exp(2\eta(\bar{k}-k(t))/\sigma^2)\cdot\Phi_8)\\&+\eta(a+j)\cdot(\Phi_7-\exp(2\eta(\bar{k}-k(t))/\sigma^2)\cdot\Phi_8)\\&-a\eta\exp(\lambda(\bar{k}-k(t)-\eta j))\exp(\lambda^2\sigma^2 j/2)\\&\quad\cdot(\Phi_7'-\exp(2a(\eta/\sigma^2-\lambda)\cdot\Phi_8'))\end{aligned} \tag{20}$$

As a check on the solution, we observe that at $j=0$, $g(t,j)=x(t)$, that when $k(t)=\bar{k}$ also $g(t,j)=\bar{k}\forall j$, that $g(t,j)=\bar{k}$ when $j=\infty$, and that $g(t,j)=k(t)+a\eta+\eta j=x(t)+\eta j$ when $\bar{k}=\infty$.

4.3 Bayesian estimation and testing

An obvious problem with standard MSM estimation and inference arises in this example because of the non-ergodicity of the controlled fundamentals. For example, establishing asymptotic normality of a simulation estimator requires that the sequences $\{m(k_t,\gamma_0\}$ and $\{\tilde{m}(k_n,\gamma\}$ satisfy a strong law of large numbers, which requires some memory restriction (such as ergodicity) on the $\{k_t\}$ process. This scalar process is ergodic if there exists a probability measure π on the Borel subsets of $\mathbb{R}$ such that for any measurable function m that is integrable with respect to π it is the case that

$$\lim(T \to \infty) T^{-1} \sum_{t=0}^{T} m(k_t) = \int m(k) d\pi(k) a.s. \tag{21}$$

In the absence of such memory restrictions we cannot argue that the observed realization is typical or that time averages allow inference about population measures.

It is straightforward to show that ergodicity does not hold in the case of a plan to peg the exchange rate, with an absorbing state at $\bar{k}$. For example, from the perspective of Markov chain methods notice that the states do not all communicate i.e. once the process reaches $\bar{k}$ it cannot return to a lower value. States below $\bar{k}$ are transient. Thus the limiting time average of the number of times the process is found in the transient states does not exist; the number of observations in such states is finite even as $T \to \infty$. For a demonstration of non-ergodicity see Grimmett and Stirzaker (1982, chapters 6 and 9) and Tweedie (1975). Note that the non-ergodicity does not arise from either the drift η or from the econometrician's simulating with an arbitrary initial value; see Tweedie (1983) and Duffie and Singleton (1988).

Bayesian methods provide a coherent method for estimation and inference in these circumstances. For example, a discrete-time density is given by:

$$\Delta k_t \sim \text{IIN}(\eta, \sigma^2) \tag{22}$$

$$x_t = X(k_t, a, \eta, \sigma^2) \tag{23}$$

with k_0 given, $t = 1, 2, 3, \ldots, T$. Here $\bar{k}$ is known and so suppressed in the notation. Equation (22) arises from the underlying Wiener process in (1). Equation (23) is simply a shorthand for equation (14), the spot-rate solution.

Now a frequentist objection to the use of (22) is that the transition probability density function for the regulated Wiener process is not normal due to the presence of the absorbing barrier (the solution to the Kolmogorov equation is given in (18) or (19)). But while classical interpretations involve consideration of the entire ensemble of possible realizations, Bayesians require only the sample distribution or likelihood of the sample observations. In the frequentist approach one can imagine the likelihood $f(x_1, x_2, x_3, \ldots, x_T|\gamma)$ as having arisen from a single replication in which, in the event, absorption did not occur until time T. In the Bayesian approach one conditions on the observed data and need not study other data sets which did not occur (see Poirier, 1988). Note that equations (12) and (13) can be viewed as a stopping rule for sampling random numbers or collecting data. The stopping rule depends on the sequence of numbers generated or data collected; but since it does not depend on the parameters its presence does not affect Bayesian estimation and inference.

Let x' denote the sample of observations on the observable asset prices. Denote a prior by $p(\gamma)$ and a likelihood by $p(x'|\gamma)$. In example 2 the distribution of the fundamentals, viewed as a function of the parameters and an initial condition, is the normal likelihood:

$$p(k'|\gamma, k_0) = (2\pi\sigma^2)^{-T/2}\exp[-(\Delta k - \eta)'(\Delta k - \eta)/2\sigma^2] \quad (24)$$

From (23) the likelihood of x' is given by:

$$\begin{aligned} p(x'|\gamma, k_0) &= \frac{\partial X}{\partial k}(k', \gamma)^{-1}\cdot p(k'|\gamma, k_0) \quad (25) \\ &= [1 + \lambda a\eta \exp(\lambda\bar{k})\exp(-\lambda k'(x'))]^{-1}(2\pi\sigma^2)^{-T/2} \\ &\quad \exp[-(\Delta k(x') - \eta)'(\Delta k(x') - \eta)/2\sigma^2] \end{aligned}$$

using the inverse of the Jacobian. We require a function of observable data, so that the inverse Jacobian and the likelihood itself must be written as functions of x'. This is not possible analytically in this example, so numerical methods must be used (they will be necessary for integration in any case).

With this change of variables from k to x the problem admits no natural conjugacy but one could examine various priors (including improper ones) for tractability and to provide evidence on the sensitivity of the results. Since there are non-negativity constraints on the parameters, one possibility is that the prior $p(\gamma)$ is an indicator function taking the value 1 when the constraints are satisfied and 0 when they are not.

The posterior density is:

$$p(\gamma, k_0|x') = p(x'|\gamma, k_0)p(\gamma)/\int p(x'|\gamma, k_0)p(\gamma)\,d\gamma \quad (26)$$

by Bayes' Theorem. One could regard k_0 as a nuisance parameter and integrate it out of this joint density function, leaving the marginal posterior of γ. Then the mean

$$E(\gamma) = \int \gamma p(\gamma|x')\,d\gamma \quad (27)$$

would provide point estimates. The results could be used for standard hypothesis tests of a, η, and σ^2 or for the prediction of other observations with the parameters integrated out.

Economic interest might centre on the comparison with the case of a pure float. A conceptually simple way to study this issue would be to treat $\bar{k}$ as an unknown parameter and estimate its posterior density function. Testing the hypothesis that $\bar{k}$ equals the value announced by the authorities is straightforward. Alternatively, one could study a pure float as a different likelihood function or window; the Jacobian in that spot rate model is simply a vector of ones. Since the pure-float model is linear the form of the posterior is known analytically for certain priors.

Geweke's (1986) importance sampling provides a computationally tractable scheme for numerical integration in the problem sketched so far. In future work we hope to use that technique to do estimation and testing in this second example.

5 Conclusion

In this chapter we have outlined methods for estimation and testing in standard models of exchange-rate target zones or process switching. Both examples studied in the chapter involve numerical methods. The first example (in section 3) adopts the method of simulated moments where forcing variables are unobservable or analytical expressions for population moments of exchange rates cannot be found. That method does not require numerical integration. We estimate the parameters a, η, and σ^2 in a standard target zone model of the Dm/Li spot exchange rate. We also test the model by simulation, finding that it can account for significant predictable conditional heteroskedasticity and fat tails in exchange-rate changes. The second example (in section 4) suggests the use of Monte Carlo integration to calculate the posterior density function of the parameters in the case of a non-ergodic fundamentals process. Since we have only sketched the two methods much empirical work remains to be done even in these specific models and historical applications. Unresolved issues include the effect of formally incorporating data on forward rates.

The methods outlined here may be applied to other behavioural models (such as those with sticky prices) or to other interventions in standard target zone models. One objection to standard models based on time-homogeneous Wiener processes is that they imply that exchange-rate changes should be iid and normal under pure floats since in a pure float the nominal exchange rate is a linear function of the fundamental. Thus a very large body of evidence inconsistent (at high frequencies) with that iid property could be used to suggest fundamental processes which (unlike equation (1)) allow for heterogeneity in that distribution. Melino (1990) outlines some more general continuous-time stochastic processes which might be used to describe fundamentals. Their adoption might require numerical methods to solve for the exchange rate.

Appendix 11A: Definitions used in the forward rate for two reflecting barriers

In the characterization of the forward exchange rate with two reflecting barriers given in equation (8) the Φ_i functions are standard normal distribution functions defined as follows:

$$\Phi_1(\bar{k}) = \Phi((\bar{k} - k_t + 2hb - \eta j)/\sigma\sqrt{j})$$

$$\Phi_1(\underline{k}) = \Phi((\underline{k} - k_t + 2hb - \eta j)/\sigma\sqrt{j})$$

$$\Phi_2(\bar{k}) = \Phi((\bar{k} + k_t - 2\underline{k} + 2hb - \eta j)/\sigma\sqrt{j})$$

$$\Phi_2(\underline{k}) = \Phi((k_t - \underline{k} + 2hb - \eta j)/\sigma\sqrt{j})$$

$$\Phi_3(\bar{k}) = \Phi((\bar{k} - k_t + 2hb - \eta j - \sigma^2\lambda_1 j)/\sigma\sqrt{j})$$

$$\Phi_3(\underline{k}) = \Phi((\underline{k} - k_t + 2hb - \eta j - \sigma^2\lambda_1 j)/\sigma\sqrt{j})$$

$$\Phi_4(\bar{k}) = \Phi((\bar{k} + k_t - 2\underline{k} + 2hb - \eta j - \sigma^2\lambda_1 j)/\sigma\sqrt{j})$$

$$\Phi_4(\underline{k}) = \Phi((k_t - \underline{k} + 2hb - \eta j - \sigma^2\lambda_1 j)/\sigma\sqrt{j})$$

$$\Phi_5(\bar{k}) = \Phi((\bar{k} - k_t + 2hb - \eta j - \sigma^2\lambda_2 j)/\sigma\sqrt{j})$$

$$\Phi_5(\underline{k}) = \Phi((\underline{k} - k_t + 2hb - \eta j - \sigma^2\lambda_2 j)/\sigma\sqrt{j})$$

$$\Phi_6(\bar{k}) = \Phi((\bar{k} + k_t - 2\underline{k} + 2hb - \eta j - \sigma^2\lambda_2 j)/\sigma\sqrt{j})$$

$$\Phi_6(\underline{k}) = \Phi((k_t - \underline{k} + 2hb - \eta j - \sigma^2\lambda_2 j)/\sigma\sqrt{j})$$

Appendix 11B: Expected future spot rates with one absorbing barrier

In this appendix we derive an expression for the forward (expected future spot) exchange rate in example 2 (Section 4). The first term in equation (15) is

$$E[k(t+j)\,|\,\mathcal{F}_t] = \int_{-\infty}^{\bar{k}} k(t+j)\,dP(k,j)$$

where the notation allows for the atom at $\bar{k}$. Let T be the period in which first passage of k to $\bar{k}$ occurs. Then

$$\begin{aligned} E[k(t+j)\,|\,\mathcal{F}_t] &= \bar{k}\cdot\text{Prob}(T < t+j) + E[k(t+j)\,|\,\mathcal{F}_t, T > t+j] \\ &= \bar{k}\cdot\text{Prob}(k(t+i) \geq \bar{k} \quad \text{for some } i \in (0,j)) \\ &\quad + E[k(t+j)\,|\,\mathcal{F}_t, k(t+i) < \bar{k}\,\forall i \in (0,j)] \\ &= \bar{k}\cdot[1 - \text{Prob}(k(t+i) < \bar{k}\,\forall i \in (0,j))] \\ &\quad + E[k(t+j)\,|\,\mathcal{F}_t, k(t+i) < \bar{k}\,\forall i \in (0,j)] \\ &= A + B \end{aligned}$$

The third equality reflects the duality between the transition and first-passage-time densities. Denote the first term A and the second by B. This expression simply says that the expected value of the fundamental in some future period $(t+j)$ is equal to $\bar{k}$ with the probability that in the interval

$(t, t+j)$ the process reaches $\bar{k}$ plus the expected value of the process conditional on its not having reached the boundary by time $t+j$.

Consider the first term, A:

$$A = \bar{k}\cdot\left[1 - \int_{-\infty}^{\bar{k}} p(k, j)\, dk(t+j)\right]$$

$$= \bar{k}\cdot\left[1 - \int_{-\infty}^{\bar{k}} \frac{1}{\sqrt{2\pi\sigma^2 j}} \exp\left(\frac{-1}{2\sigma^2 j}(k(t+j) - k(t) - \eta j)^2\right) dk(t+j)\right.$$

$$\left. + \int_{-\infty}^{\bar{k}} \frac{1}{\sqrt{2\pi\sigma^2 j}} \exp\left(\frac{2\eta a}{\sigma^2} - \frac{(k(t+j) - 2a - k(t) - \eta j)^2}{2\sigma^2 j}\right) dk(t+j)\right]$$

The first integral is the distribution function for the standard normal variable $(k(t+j) - k(t) - \eta j)/\sigma\sqrt{j}$. By separating the two terms in the exponent of the second integral we can see that what is left is also a standard normal distribution function, evaluated at a different point:

$$A = \bar{k}\cdot\left[1 - \Phi((\bar{k} - k(t) - \eta j)/\sigma\sqrt{j})\right.$$

$$+ \exp(2\eta a/\sigma^2) \int_{-\infty}^{\bar{k}} \frac{1}{\sqrt{2\pi\sigma^2 j}}$$

$$\left. \exp\left(\frac{-(k(t+j) - 2a - k(t) - \eta j)^2}{2\sigma^2 j}\right) dk(t+j)\right]$$

$$A = \bar{k}[1 - \Phi((\bar{k} - k(t) - \eta j)/\sigma\sqrt{j})$$
$$+ \exp(2\eta a/\sigma^2)\Phi((\bar{k} - 2a - k(t) - \eta j)/\sigma\sqrt{j})]$$

The second term is

$$B = \int_{-\infty}^{\bar{k}} p(k, j) k(t+j)\, dk(t+j)$$

$$= \int_{-\infty}^{\bar{k}} \frac{1}{\sqrt{2\pi\sigma^2 j}} \exp\left(\frac{-1}{2\sigma^2 j}(k(t+j) - k(t) - \eta j)^2\right) k(t+j)\, dk(t+j)$$

$$- \exp(2\eta a/\sigma^2) \int_{-\infty}^{\bar{k}} \frac{1}{\sqrt{2\pi\sigma^2 j}}$$

$$\exp\left(\frac{-1}{2\sigma^2 j}(k(t+j) - (2a + k(t) + \eta j))^2\right) k(t+j)\, dk(t+j)$$

Calling the first integral C and the second D we begin by solving C. Let

$$\beta(k(t+k)) \equiv \exp\left(\frac{-1}{2\sigma^2 j}(k(t+j) - k(t) - \eta j)^2\right)$$

Therefore

$$\beta'(k(t+k)) = \frac{-(k(t+j) - k(t) - \eta j)}{\sigma^2 j}\beta(k(t+j))$$

$$\int_{-\infty}^{\bar{k}} k(t+j)\beta(k(t+j)dk(t+j) = (k(t)+\eta j)\int_{-\infty}^{\bar{k}} \beta(k(t+j))dk(t+j)$$

$$-\sigma^2 j\int_{-\infty}^{\bar{k}} \beta'(k(t+j))dk(t+j)$$

Multiplying by $(2\pi\sigma^2 j)^{-1/2}$ gives us C. Therefore,

$$C = (k(t)+\eta j)\int_{-\infty}^{\bar{k}} \frac{1}{\sqrt{2\pi\sigma^2 j}} \exp\left(\frac{-(k(t+j) - k(t) - \eta j)^2}{2\sigma^2 j}\right) dk(t+j)$$

$$-\frac{\sigma^2 j}{\sqrt{2\pi\sigma^2 j}} \exp\left(\frac{-(\bar{k} - k(t) - \eta j)^2}{2\sigma^2 j}\right)$$

Again the first integral is a standard normal distribution function, so the solution for term C is

$$C = (k(t)+\eta j)\Phi((\bar{k} - k(t) - \eta j)/\sigma\sqrt{j})$$
$$-\frac{\sigma^2 j}{\sqrt{2\pi\sigma^2 j}} \exp\left(\frac{-(\bar{k} - k(t) - \eta j)^2}{2\sigma^2 j}\right)$$

The term labelled D is solved in a similar way. Now let

$$\delta(k(t+j)) \equiv \exp\left(\frac{-(k(t+j) - 2a - k(t) - \eta j)^2}{2\sigma^2 j}\right)$$

Therefore

$$\sigma^2 j\delta'(k(t+j)) = -k(t+j)\delta(k(t+j)) + (2a + k(t) + \eta j)\delta'(k(t+j))$$

Thus

$$\int_{-\infty}^{\bar{k}} \frac{\exp(2\eta a/\sigma^2)}{\sqrt{2\pi\sigma^2 j}} \exp\left(\frac{-(k(t+j)-(2a+k(t)+\eta j))^2}{2\sigma^2 j}\right) k(t+j)\, dk(t+j)$$

$$= (2a+k(t)+\eta j)\exp(2\eta a/\sigma^2) \int_{-\infty}^{\bar{k}} \frac{1}{\sqrt{2\pi\sigma^2 j}}$$

$$\exp\left(\frac{-(k(t+j)-(2a+k(t)+\eta j))^2}{2\sigma^2 j}\right) dk(t+j)$$

$$-\exp(2\eta a/\sigma^2)\sigma^2 j \int_{-\infty}^{\bar{k}} \frac{1}{\sqrt{2\pi\sigma^2 j}} \delta'(k(t+j)\, dk(t+j)$$

and the result is

$$D = (2a+k(t)+\eta j)\exp(2\eta a/\sigma^2)\Phi((\bar{k}-2a-k(t)-\eta j)/\sigma\sqrt{j})$$
$$-\frac{\sigma^2 j}{\sqrt{2\pi\sigma^2 j}}\exp(2\eta a/\sigma^2)\exp\left(\frac{-(\bar{k}-2a-k(t)-\eta j)^2}{2\sigma^2 j}\right)$$

Equations A, C and D give the solution for $E[k(t+j)|\mathcal{F}_t]$, which after combining common terms is

$$\begin{aligned} E[k(t+j)|\mathcal{F}_t] = \bar{k} &+ (k(t)+\eta j-\bar{k})\cdot\Phi((\bar{k}-k(t)-\eta j)/\sigma\sqrt{j}) \\ &- (2a+k(t)+\eta j-\bar{k}) \\ &\exp(2\eta a/\sigma^2)\Phi((\bar{k}-2a-k(t)-\eta j)/\sigma\sqrt{j}) \\ &-\frac{\sigma^2 j}{\sqrt{2\pi\sigma^2 j}}\left[\exp\left(\frac{-(\bar{k}-k(t)-\eta j)^2}{2\sigma^2 j}\right)\right. \\ &\left.-\exp\left(\frac{2\eta a}{\sigma^2}-\frac{(\bar{k}-2a-k(t)-\eta j)^2}{2\sigma^2 j}\right)\right] \end{aligned}$$

The last term is simply $p(\bar{k}, j)$ which is equal to zero by the boundary condition for the absorbing barrier. Therefore this term drops out of the solution, and

$$\begin{aligned} E[k(t+j)|\mathcal{F}_t] = \bar{k} &+ (k(t)+\eta j-\bar{k})\cdot\Phi((\bar{k}-k(t)-\eta j)/\sigma\sqrt{j}) \\ &+ (k(t)-\eta j-\bar{k})\cdot\exp(2\eta(\bar{k}-k(t))/\sigma^2) \\ &\cdot\Phi((\bar{k}-2a-k(t)-\eta j)/\sigma\sqrt{j}) \end{aligned}$$

To solve the last term in equation (15) define $y = \exp(-\lambda k)$. Then

$$\begin{aligned}E[y(t+j)|\mathcal{F}_t] &= \bar{y}\cdot\text{Prob}(T < t+j) + E[y(t+j)|\mathcal{F}_t, T > t+j] \\ &= \bar{y}\cdot\text{Prob}(y(t+i) \geq \bar{y} \quad \text{for some } i \in (0,j)) \\ &\quad + E[y(t+j)|\mathcal{F}_t, y(t+i) < \bar{y}\forall i \in (0,j)] \\ &= \bar{y}\cdot[1 - \text{Prob}(y(t+i) < \bar{y}\forall i \in (0,j))] \\ &\quad + E[y(t+j)|\mathcal{F}_t, y(t+i) < \bar{y}\forall i \in (0,j)] \\ &= F + G\end{aligned}$$

where $\bar{y} \equiv \exp(-\lambda\bar{k})$. To simplify notation, let

$$\Phi_7[k(t)] = \Phi((\bar{k} - k(t) - \eta j)/\sigma\sqrt{j})$$

$$\Phi_8[k(t)] = \Phi((\bar{k} - 2a - k(t) - \eta j)/\sigma\sqrt{j})$$

$$\Phi_7'[k(t)] = \Phi((\bar{k} - k(t) - \eta j - \sigma^2\lambda j)/\sigma\sqrt{j})$$

$$\Phi_8'[k(t)] = \Phi((\bar{k} - 2a(t) - k(t) - \eta j - \sigma^2\lambda j)/\sigma\sqrt{j})$$

Then the first term is simply

$$F = \bar{y}\cdot[1 - \Phi_7 + \exp(2\eta a/\sigma^2)\Phi_8]$$

The second term is

$$\begin{aligned}G &= \int_{-\infty}^{\bar{k}} p(k,j)\cdot\exp(-\lambda k)\,dk \\ &= \exp(-\lambda(k(t)+\eta j))\cdot\exp(\lambda^2\sigma^2 j/2) \\ &\quad \cdot[\Phi_7' - \exp(2\eta a/\sigma^2)\Phi_8'\cdot\exp(-2\lambda a)]\end{aligned}$$

which is found by completing the square in the exponents in $p(k, j)$.

Combining $A + B + F + G$ gives the solution for the forward rate:

$$\begin{aligned}g(t,j) = \bar{k}&\cdot(1 - \Phi_7 - \exp(2\eta(\bar{k} - k(t))/\sigma^2)\cdot\Phi_8) \\ &+ k(t)\cdot(\Phi_7 + \exp(2\eta(\bar{k} - k(t))/\sigma^2)\cdot\Phi_8) \\ &+ \eta(a+j)\cdot(\Phi_7 - \exp(2\eta(\bar{k} - k(t))/\sigma^2)\cdot\Phi_8) \\ &- a\eta\exp(\lambda(\bar{k} - k(t) - \eta j)\exp(\lambda^2\sigma^2 j/2) \\ &\quad \cdot(\Phi_7' - \exp(2\eta a/\sigma^2)\Phi_8'\cdot\exp(-2\lambda a))\end{aligned}$$

which is equation (20) in the text.

NOTES

We thank Giuseppe Bertola, Bernard Dumas, Allan Gregory, Vittorio Grilli, Francesco Papadia, Hossein Samiei, Anthony Smith, Lars Svensson and Michael Wickens for helpful comments and criticism. Lars Hansen, Steve Heston and Stan Zin advised us on Section 4 but are not responsible for our errors. We gratefully acknowledge the support of the Social Sciences and Humanities Research Council of Canada. The views expressed are those of the authors and do not necessarily represent those of the International Monetary Fund.

REFERENCES

Bertola, G. and R.J. Caballero (1989), 'Target zones and realignments', Columbia University Working Paper.

(1990), 'Reserves and realignments in a target zone', mimeo.

Bertola, G. and L.E.O. Svensson (1990), 'Stochastic devaluation risk and the empirical fit of Target Zone Models', mimeo.

Bodnar, G. and J. Leahy (1990), 'Are target zone models relevant?', mimeo, University of Rochester.

Buiter, W. (1989), 'A viable gold standard requires flexible monetary and fiscal policy', *Review of Economic Studies* **50**, 101–17.

Cox, D.R. and H.D. Miller (1965), *The Theory of Stochastic Processes*. Methuen: London.

Duffie, D. and K.J. Singleton (1988), 'Simulated moments estimation of diffusion models of asset prices', mimeo, Stanford University.

Einzig, P. (1937), *The Theory of Forward Exchange*, London: Macmillan.

Flood, R.P. and P.M. Garber (1983), 'A model of stochastic process switching', *Econometrica* **51**, 537–51.

(1989), 'The linkage between speculative attack and target zone models of exchange rates', Working Paper No. 2918, National Bureau of Economic Research and see this volume.

Flood, R.P., A.K. Rose and D.J. Mathieson (1990), 'Is the EMS the perfect fix? An Empirical Exploration of Exchange Rate Target Zones', IMF mimeo.

Froot, K.A. and M. Obstfeld (1989), 'Exchange rate dynamics under stochastic regime shifts: a unified approach', Working Paper No. 2835, National Bureau of Economic Research.

(1991), 'Stochastic process switching: some simple solutions', This volume, and *Econometrica* **58**, forthcoming.

Geweke, J. (1986), 'Exact inference in the inequality constrained normal linear regression model', *Journal of Applied Econometrics* **1**, 127–41.

Gregory, A.W. and G.W. Smith (1990a), 'Calibration as estimation', *Econometric Reviews* **9**, 57–89.

(1990b), 'Calibration as testing: inference in simulated macroeconomic models', mimeo, Queen's University.

Grimmett, G.R. and D.R. Stirzaker (1982), *Probability and Random Processes*, Oxford University Press.

Hansen, L.P. (1982), 'Large sample properties of generalized methods of moments estimators', *Econometrica* **50**, 1029–54.

Harrison, J.M. (1985), *Brownian Motion and Stochastic Flow Systems*, New York: John Wiley and Sons.

Ingram, B.F. and B.-S. Lee (1987), 'Estimation by simulation', mimeo, Cornell University.

Krugman, P. (1991), 'Target zones and exchange rate dynamics', forthcoming in the *Quarterly Journal of Economics*, forthcoming.

Lewis, K.K. (1990), 'Can managed float intervention make exchange rate behavior resemble a target zone?', mimeo, NBER and New York University.

McFadden, D. (1989), 'A method of simulated methods for estimation of discrete response models without numerical integration', *Econometrica* **57**, 995–1026.

Meese, R.A. and A.K. Rose (1990), 'Non-linear, non-parametric, non-essential exchange rate estimation', *American Economic Review (P)* **80**, 192–96.

Melino, A. (1990), 'Estimation of continuous-time models in finance', mimeo, Department of Economics, University of Toronto.

Miller, M. and P. Weller (1989), 'Exchange rate bands and realignments in a stationary stochastic setting', in M. Miller, B. Eichengreen and R. Portes, eds. *Blueprints for Exchange Rate Management*. New York: Academic Press.
Moggridge, D.E. (1972), *British Monetary Policy 1924–1931*. London: Cambridge University Press.
Pakes, A. and D. Pollard (1989), 'Simulation and the asymptotics of optimization estimators', *Econometrica* **57**, 1027–57.
Pessach, S. and A. Razin (1990), 'Targeting the exchange rate: an empirical investigation', IMF Working Paper No. 90/61.
Poirier, D. (1988), 'Frequentist and subjectivist perspectives on the problems of model building in economics', *Journal of Economic Perspectives* **2**, 121–44.
Smith, G.W. (1990), 'Solution to a problem of stochastic process switching', *Econometrica* **58**, forthcoming.
Smith, G.W. and R.T. Smith (1990), 'Stochastic process switching and the return to gold, 1925', *Economic Journal* **100**, 164–75.
Spencer, M.G. (1990a), 'Nominal exchange rate dynamics in the European Monetary System', Working Paper No. 779, Queen's University.
(1990b), 'Forward exchange rate dynamics in the EMS', mimeo.
Svensson, L.E.O. (1989), 'Target zones and interest rate variability', Seminar Paper No. 457, Institute for International Economics.
(1990), 'The term structure of interest rate differentials in a target zone: theory and Swedish data', Seminar Paper No. 466, Institute for International Economics.
(1990b), 'The simplest test of target zone credibility', Seminar Paper No. 469, Institute for International Economics.
Tweedie, R.L. (1975), 'Sufficient conditions for ergodicity and recurrence of Markov chains on a general state space', *Stochastic Processes and their Applications* **3**, 385–403.
(1983), 'Criteria for rates of convergence of Markov chains, with applications to queuing and storage theory', in J.F.C. Kingman and G.E.H. Reuter (eds.) *Probability, Statistics, and Analysis*, Cambridge University Press.
Williamson, J. (1985), *The Exchange Rate System*, 2nd ed., Washington: Institute for International Economics.

Discussion

HOSSEIN SAMIEI

The innovative paper by Smith and Spencer should be welcomed as a serious attempt to analyse exchange rate determination under a target zone empirically. Recent theoretical development in this area has benefitted from linking the problem with that of the pricing of derivative assets such as options. While the ability to theorise more freely has opened new and interesting possibilities in exchange rate modelling, the necessary empirical work has been lagging behind. This is important because the issues involved are very immediately policy-oriented. For example the basic target zone model predicts that credible currency bands, via expectations, tend to generate a bias towards the centre, so that exchange rate stability increases even in the absence of interventions. If this is true then for a government that values exchange rate stability, *ceteris paribus*, joining a target-zone system would be preferred to a policy of pure reliance on direct interventions, when the latter are costly and perhaps non-credible. To test this hypothesis, one would want to separate empirically the direct influence of the band on the exchange rate from that via expectations. I shall discuss the implication of this for econometric investigation later.

The paper by Smith and Spencer attempts to test whether the statistical properties of the observed spot rates are broadly compatible with those implied by the theory. To this end it employs the Method of Simulated Moments (MSM). The authors' justification for the use of this method is that due to the apparent unobservability of fundamentals and the analytical complications involved in obtaining the steady-state density function of the exchange rate under a target zone, measuring the theoretical moments of the dependent variable may not be feasible. I will come back to these points later. The study, therefore, aims at estimating the parameters of the model by matching historical moments with those obtained by generating alternative series for the fundamentals $k(t)$ and the exchange rate. The paper also discusses how on the assumption that conditional on the model the forward rate is an unbiased predictor of the future spot rate, the implied over-identifying restrictions may be used to provide further tests of the model.

Turning to the estimation results on the target zone model, as the authors note, some of the historical moments are very different from the simulated ones. This is not surprising given that one is dealing with the properties of a variable that has traditionally been difficult to explain, with the added complications that arise from the presence of a target zone. The results, however, show that the non-normality and conditional heteroskedasticity present in the historical data on the spot rate are also observed in the simulated series. It may be worth noting, of course, that this in fact should be expected as an analytical property of the model. Using Kolmogorov forward equations, it is easy to show that the density function of the fundamental $k(t)$, with two reflecting barriers, is non-normal and does not have a constant conditional variance (see for example Cox and Miller, 1965, page 224 for one reflecting barrier). By implication the exchange rate, under a target zone, cannot be expected to be normal with a constant conditional variance, even if its density function cannot be derived. It is nevertheless comforting that the simulation results confirm this conjecture. The first part of the paper is concluded by presenting various sets of results including estimations based on daily as well as weekly exchange rate data and the implications of narrowing the band given the estimated model. In the second part of the paper the authors suggest a Bayesian strategy for estimating a model with an exchange rate peg. This is due to the fact that in this case the underlying fundamentals do not have ergodic properties, given that an absorbing state does not interconnect with other states in the system. It would be interesting to see the sort of empirical results that one might obtain following this methodology.

The exercise performed in the paper clearly is a worthwhile one. The authors handle a complicated problem in an interesting and innovative manner. In what follows I shall concentrate on the target zone part of their paper and also explore alternative possibilities. To begin with I find the assumption of the unobservability of the fundamentals a little too strong and unnecessary. It implies that one is essentially only using past values of the exchange rate to obtain parameter estimates. I also disagree with the authors that this is one reason for the shortage of econometric work in this area. The fact that the target zone literature does not discuss the identity of the fundamentals simply reflects the focus of the analysis. Indeed I believe that one may fruitfully utilise the extensive literature on empirical exchange rate modelling by estimating and comparing some standard models, after appropriately modifying them to take account of the presence of the zone. Admittedly this will further complicate the analysis and will also substantially increase the number of parameters to be estimated. But this can be tackled within the methodology proposed in the paper. One may, for example, estimate the auxiliary equations on the fundamentals by standard techniques at the first stage, and then using the estimated equations simulate different scenarios for the fundamentals and the spot rate and finally, as in the paper, estimate the parameters of the spot rate by matching moments. Separating the two stages of estimations, substantially reduces the number of parameters that need to be estimated by MSM. Furthermore, as in the paper, despite using historical data on fundamentals, one still would not require the derivation of the theoretical steady-state probability density function of the exchange rate.

The above procedure would make the analysis richer by taking account of the possible determinants of the exchange rate. However, estimation would still lack precision due to reliance on simulating moments. According to the authors the theoretical density function of the spot rate cannot be obtained. Of course the availability of this function would not guarantee that its theoretical moments could be derived analytically and numerical integration may still be required. Alternatively one may search for other ways of modelling the problem. Meese and Rose (1990) consider equations such as (6) and argue that the test of the target zone hypothesis can be carried out by testing for the presence of non-linearities in the exchange rate as implied by the exponential terms in equations like (6). Without specifying the functional form of the non-linear part, they employ non-parametric methods to test the hypothesis. This methodology is not entirely compatible with the theoretical model in the way that it treats the stochastic components in the system. But the exercise may still be rewarding in identifying patterns in the data. My own preferred methodology, however, would be to model the problem from the start in a more conventional and structural econometric manner and then derive an appropriate estimation method. In particular the continuous time framework and the treatment of the stochastic terms in the model may have to be modified. To illustrate such an approach note that within a target-zone, the exchange rate is a limited-dependent variable and a two-limit tobit model is appropriate. Given any particular exchange rate model without expectations, and given the bounds, this model may be estimated by standard maximum likelihood or two-stage techniques. The present case, however, is complicated because of the presence of expectations in the model. Under rational expectations the agents will take account of the bounds in forming expectations. The econometric modelling then has to combine limited-dependence with rational expectations. There is very little work done in estimating such models (see Shonkwiler and Maddala, 1985 for an application to the corn market in the US). One of the difficulties that arises is that closed-form solutions for the expectational variable will not in general exist for such models. However, appropriate estimation procedures may still be obtained (see Pesaran and Samiei, 1990). In such a framework testing for the importance of the indirect effect of the band via expectations would amount to comparing the significance of the expectational variable as an explanatory variable, with and without including the information on the band in the agents' information set.

My final point is in relation to the determination of exchange rate bands. Smith and Spencer in analysing the ERM concentrate on the period 14th January 1987 to 20th September 1989, i.e. a period without any realignments, thus apparently overcoming the problem rising from changing bands or realignments. The problem, however, is clearly not whether realignments take place or not but rather whether the information with regard to the future movements of the band is contained in the information set of the agents. Solutions of the type discussed in the paper (based on the early target zone literature) assume that such information is available to the agents. The validity of this assumption clearly depends on the degree of uncertainty with regard to future events as perceived by governments and agents as well as credibility of government's announcements. The absence of such information will naturally weaken the 'bias due to the band' effect. For empirical purposes one would ideally want to model the determination of the band and thus the expectations of it by the agents. Some papers in this conference have addressed this issue at the theoretical level. Empirical estimation of an exchange rate model with expectations and an endogenously determined target zone will be even more complicated since expectation formation will have to take account not only of the possibility of the exchange rate being on the boundary but also that of realignments. Such an analysis, however, is essential if one is interested in the crucial issue of evaluating the extent to which bands follow the exchange rates and not vice versa.

REFERENCES

Cox, D.R. and H.D. Miller (1965), *The Theory of Stochastic Processes*. Methuen: London.

Meese, R.A. and A.K. Rose (1990), 'Non-linear, non-parametric, non-essential exchange rate estimation', *American Economic Review* **80**, 192–96.

Pesaran, M.H. and S.H. Samiei (1990), 'Estimating limited-dependent rational expectations models', Department of Applied Economics, University of Cambridge, Working Paper No. 9017.

Shonkwiler, J.S. and G.S. Maddala (1985), 'Modelling expectations of bounded prices: an application to the market for corn', *Review of Economics and Statistics* **67**, 697–702.

Index